100 Days

of Actions & Intentions

To Create the Life

You Wish For

★ Also By Susan Balogh ★

BOOKS
Dear Wellbeing: 100 Days on My Path to More Joy. A Self-Discovery Workbook
http://amzn.com/B08PCGR4JD

There's MAGIC in this MANIFESTING JOURNAL: It's Your Imagination
http://amzn.com/B0967TRMSF

FREE MINI-WORKSHOP
3 Steps to Wellbeing & Achieving Your Dreams
https://courses.wishmorewellness.com/courses/Mini-Workshop-3-Steps

AUDIO-VIDEO COURSE
Create the Life You Wish For: A 100-Day Course
Sign up here [https://courses.wishmorewellness.com/] to be notified when it's available

ONLINE SERVICES
1:1 Coaching for Mindset/Happiness/Manifesting
Positive EFT Coaching (Meridian Tapping)
Energy Healing, Guided Meditation
Reiki I & II and Master/Teacher Certification
All or part available by video conference
Set Yourself Free & Be Happy!

★★★

All of the above are available at
http://wishmorewellness.com/services/
Find us on Instagram @Wishmore_Wellness
https://www.instagram.com/wishmore_wellness/
Please join the Wishmore Wellness Facebook Group
https://www.facebook.com/groups/2061444523962316

100 Days

of Actions & Intentions

To Create the Life

You Wish For

Guide Yourself
to a Place Where You're
Happy & Free and
Achieving Your Dreams.
All Day, Every Day.

Susan Balogh

Cover design: Angie Alaya
Interior design: Rachael Cox
Illustrations: Streamline Designs

ISBN eBook: 978-1-7361677-4-8
ISBN Paperback: 978-1-7361677-5-5

Published by Wishmore Wellness
Buffalo, New York
WishmoreWellness.com
Second edition, June 2021.
Printed in the United States of America

This

book is

dedicated to

the free spirit in

you. The one you may

be hiding that's just waiting

to shine through the many layers

of life's little (or big) struggles. It's time

for you to feel the way you're meant

to feel. And that is happy and

free and in charge of your

own destiny. And if you

found yourself

here, you're

ready!

Take 100 Days to Guide Yourself There.
I know you can do it. And you're worth it!

Contents

Step 1: I Am Now Achieving a State of Blissful Wellbeing

Step 2: I Choose to Feel Happy & Free

Step 3: I Am Creating the Life I Wish For

3 Steps in Review: I Bring Harmony to My Mind, Body, and Spirit

Wish*More Wellness' mission is to help as many people as possible reconnect with their true nature and powerful ability to heal, to love, and create the life they wish for.

The name <u>WISH*More Wellness</u> is all about how our **W**ords **I**nspire **S**piritual **H**armony & <u>More Wellness</u>...for ourselves and others.

When we take charge of our thoughts in a more positive and purposeful way, we can think and feel our way into any reality we wish to exist in. Living a life with more wellbeing, joy, and abundance is a choice.

Harmony of your mind, body, and spirit is the direct route to healing and happiness.

Let each kind word, thought, and action begin with you and create a better life for you and those around you, one moment at a time. Your positive energy will spread beyond boundaries.

Hello & Welcome to Your 100-Day Journey!

It's time for you to feel deeply satisfied with every area of your life. Nothing is in the way. It's all available to you, and there's no limit to the amount of wellbeing, happiness, and abundance you can achieve.

Imagine if you used words of joy and abundance to explain who you are and what you want. And you didn't believe anything else but your own words based on faith and trust in your total wellbeing, personal freedom and joy, and your natural attraction of abundance. There would be no such thing as stress or struggle in your life. And this can be the way things are for you.

So imagine there's a new voice in your head...that is *you*, being your own best friend, and it's fully supportive, adores you, and is ready to create everything you've ever desired and knows you deserve it.

The following is instilled in your mind and you believe it and feel it with *all* your heart:

> *By nature...you are in a state of blissful wellbeing.*
> *By nature...you feel happy and free.*
> *By nature...you are abundant and unlimited.*

And by nature, you have the ability to be and have and do *all* that you desire.

As you are *true* to your nature, you're feeling the way you're meant to feel. You're *in love* with life. You are feeling *confident* and at ease with all that life brings you. You're aligning with a state of *blissful* wellbeing. You're feeling *happy* and free. And you are *limitless*.

You're feeling focused and unstoppable in your spirit of joy. And now that you're feeling this way more consistently, you're attracting more good things into your life and having *way* more fun!

You smile your way through your day and see your desires coming to life *right* before your very eyes.

You always practice feeling this way and create the joyful and abundant life you were born to live. You can't imagine there being anything you can't have, and you're easily aligning with your infinite potential.

If you're not feeling this way already, you can be. It's your birthright, and it's natural to you.

You may just need to peel away the layers of life experiences that have either knocked you down, stifled you, or kept you from connecting to your true self, and embrace the wellbeing and abundance that's continually flowing and available to you. Or maybe you just want help feeling that way more often.

This will naturally occur as you practice being in the qualities and energy of anything you wish to be or have or do. And that's what this book is meant to do for you. I wish for it to be your constant friend that coaches you and inspires you to guide your *own* thoughts and energy until your desires feel like a part of you. As you align your energy with them, they are yours to have.

And what is it that I'm supposed to say now? Oh, yeah...*if I can do it, you can do it.*

This is a way of life. It's not just taking a half-hour break or yoga class at the end of the day to destress. It's a choice to feel as amazing as you can feel all day, from morning to night. Living abundantly is a choice and it puts you in the best position to attract what you truly want into your life. The best part is, you're feeling really happy where you are and excited for what's to come.

This book is written from your point of view, with you being the first person. It's intended to help you believe in yourself and believe in your desires as well as believe in your ability to achieve them. It's meant to get you thinking and feeling how you want to feel until it becomes natural for you.

There are three steps that are thirty days each, and the last ten days is a review that offers a quick glance or tool kit to help you maintain continued success in achieving the mindset you've accomplished. Each "day" has many intentions and questions and a few affirmations, as well as some form of action to take.

The intention is to get you thinking about what is possible for you and practice how it feels to be aligned with whatever the topic is for that day. It's written in a particular order to help you gradually build up your positive momentum until you're attracting all your desires. It's all meant to be easy and enjoyable for you.

I expect it to further instill what you already know or help you achieve a wonderfully positive transformation for a life full of more joy, love, laughter, and blissful wellbeing! And it's all you. You're doing the work. Only it doesn't feel like work. Self-discovery is so much fun!

You are meant to be living in the joy of who you are and thriving with energy—free of worry, stress, or pain. I struggled with this for more than twenty years and finally "set myself free" by learning simple yet powerful ways to keep myself in what feels like a very blissful state of wellbeing. The surgeries and countless diagnostic medical procedures came to an end.

I found myself wishing that I could help others feel better, and that led me to use the training I had received to teach and later become a holistic healing and happiness coach.

Eventually I got around to putting this book together, and I made a point to make it all-inclusive of what I've learned, so it holds the potential for the personal transformation that I believe is possible for anyone to achieve.

I learned all of it piece by piece over a period of twenty years, and I wanted it to be available to help others get to live a more joyful life, but much faster than I did.

Putting yourself in charge of your own wellbeing empowers you and sets you free! You are invincible in your new mindset and become a magnet for all your life's wishes!

The only way to believe in the power of your thoughts, intentions, and energy is to experience it firsthand.

When following the steps offered in this book, you will see and feel results. How much and for how long is up to you. It is my wish that you allow yourself to be in the joy of who you are more consistently so that you can live a life that's struggle-free and achieve all your goals and desires.

And no matter how big or small your desires are, you might be surprised at how easily they manifest when you set your mind to it. I have a feeling you'll begin to create bigger desires and get so much more than you ever thought possible. But it's time for you to know just how possible it is. You absolutely deserve to be living a life you love. Are you ready?

That is, are you ready to start being in charge of your own destiny and take the next step to your greatest joy and wellbeing?

When you've brought your mind and body into harmony with the natural free spirit within you, you allow the wellbeing to flow, and when it flows, all good things come your way with effortless ease. The possibilities are limitless. This is only the beginning, and you're moving forward and upward on your journey of life!

Once you experience how much better you can help yourself feel, you won't have any reason to doubt yourself **EVER** again.

In your natural state you are well, your energy is light, and you feel joyful! Life becomes effortless. And when you remain in this state of mind, *everything* seems to look, sound, smell, taste, and feel better.

I believe...

- ★ You were born to be free and live for the purpose of experiencing joy
- ★ You deserve to be deeply satisfied and feel like celebrating your life *every single day*
- ★ You have the ability to purposely design the life of your dreams
- ★ You are now becoming energetically aligned with all of it and it will surely be yours

So, let's begin, shall we?

100 days may seem like a long time to dedicate your time, but you're so worth it! And you can take it at your own pace. So if you're ready, it's time to give yourself the attention you deserve and make your life the way you want it to be.

Congratulations for choosing to do something different! Your life is about to change for the better. I believe it and I wish for you to see it come true for you. And when it does, I truly hope you decide to share your story with me!

My Promise to Myself
(Feel free to change the wording to fit your desires)

This book is all about me guiding myself to align with all my desires. My thoughts, intentions, energy, and actions are creating my life, and I intend to use them to the best of my ability to live a life I love more every day.

As I practice guiding my thoughts to a better-feeling state, I am becoming energetically aligned with all my wishes and dreams.

As I hold a vision of myself as I wish to be, and feel it's a part of me, I am aligning my energy with the greatest version of myself. I wish it. I dream of it. I believe it's who I am. I have faith and trust in it. And I expect it to come. It's all I know. And it must become who I am.

And I am perfect right where I am. I am exactly where I'm meant to be at this time in my life, and I'm always moving toward a better place. I am in a constant state of change and becoming better every day in every way.

I am doing whatever it takes to feel as good as I can feel. I am practicing the feeling state of wellbeing, joy, and abundance until it becomes a part of who I am. I am now aligning with my highest level of wellbeing and prosperity.

The more positive my thoughts and emotions, the better I feel and the higher my vibration. The higher my vibration, the closer I am to achieving all my desires.

I intend to use this book to practice guiding myself to a good-feeling place from morning to night until I'm struggle-free and living the joyful life I'm meant to be living.

I choose to align with my natural state of blissful wellbeing, where I feel happy and free, and aligned with all my desires.

I am now on my path to more joy. And I am limitless.

I will do my best to trust in the power of my thoughts, intentions, and energy.

I am committed to allowing myself to begin a life-changing positive transformation in the weeks ahead.

I am focusing on solutions from this point on.

I have all the answers within me and will be more intuitively guided as I connect with myself on a deeper level.

I will do my best to believe that the words I'm hearing in this book are true for me. I will know that I am free to change the process or wording of the action or intention to align with my desire or preference.

For the next 100 days and beyond, I am doing my best to practice powerful actions and intentions until I feel that blissful wellbeing and limitless abundance are a part of who I am and must become the only way I know how to be.

What other intentions would you like to add?

____

____

____

____

____

____

____

____

____

____

____

____

____

Are you ready to set yourself free and be as happy as you were born to be? Yay! Let's begin by diving into Step 1. You can do it!

How to Get the Most Out of This Book

Whatever you *believe you* can be, you can achieve.

Based on the universal law of attraction, our thoughts have varying frequencies, and we can purposely choose thoughts and intentions that align with the same energy or frequency of our desires.

It's also known that our brain doesn't know the difference between what is real and what is imagined, and this gives us the ability to create anything we wish to achieve.

Perhaps you have heard about these concepts before and you're unsure about it. There's no need to believe what you hear. All you need to do is practice applying it in your life and see the proof in the results you're getting.

For best results, do your best to:

Believe the words you hear in this book are true for you, and feel free to change them to fit your desires and preference.

Choose the same time and place to read your day's actions and intentions, somewhere quiet and comfortable. Allow yourself the time to let the words sink in and feel how your body responds. Each "Day" chapter may take anywhere from 5-20 minutes, and there's a few longer chapters.

Have a notebook or journal on hand every time you read it in case you would like to write out longer answers.

Complete the 100 days in as few days as possible, ideally reading a "Day" chapter every day, or every second or third day. This is to keep your positive momentum going.

Read it in the order it's been written to get the most out of it. The steps are specifically designed in the order they're written for best results.

If you decide to skip ahead, consider alternating every other day with going back to where you left off initially. Make it work the way that's best for you.

The many questions you will be asked as you read this book are to get you thinking about all your potential and possibilities...

Some questions are meant to be answered, but most are not. Some are just meant to be heard and get you thinking.

Your subconscious naturally wants to answer the questions, and your mind and body respond to the suggestions.

They're meant to prompt emotions and get you thinking about all the possibilities that are available to you. Give yourself time to allow your mind and body to respond.

You may feel the proposed buildup of anticipation and possibility, and with some practice you can feel your energy or mindset shifting to another level.

They're also intended to guide your thoughts, and it may work better for you than "I am" affirmations. We're not always ready to say "I am ____."

It's a great way to transform emotions that are more set-in from old thought patterns.

If an answer is being requested, there will be a line or space for it. Do your best to answer it to get the most benefit from the exercise.

Even if you're not prompted to answer a question, follow your intuition if you feel an impulse to write an answer down. There's a great benefit in writing out your thoughts.

There's no need to write the questions down in your journal, as you may never look back on it. The benefit of writing it out is just to practice guiding your thoughts.

The reason it's 100 days long:

It gives you enough time to form new beliefs or thought patterns, if desired. Or let's say that it's long enough to practice guiding your thoughts to an even better-feeling state, until you're so good at it that you keep it going for the rest of your life. That's the goal. It just takes practice.

And finally, please buy two notebooks or journals that you will be using along with this book at some point.

Be sure to be gentle with yourself as you work through this book, and never feel pressured to do any more than you feel the desire to.

Most importantly, have fun!

I wish you magnificent success in achieving all your goals, wishes, and dreams. I'm so excited for you!

Step 1

I Am Now Achieving a State of Blissful Wellbeing

The purpose of this step is to learn how to practice guiding yourself into a state of complete wellbeing until:

> It's a part of who you are.
> You're feeling more ease in your body and throughout your day.
> Your mind is clearer and you feel more present and joyful.
> You're full of energy and feel resilient to any negative energy around you.
> You're feeling blissfully aligned with your highest level of wellbeing.

If desired, set this intention for the next thirty days, or create your own:

> I intend to use my powerful thoughts and intentions to achieve my desired results.
> I intend to practice feeling my way into a state of blissful wellbeing until it's who I am.

Making thoughts of total wellbeing a part of your daily life can help you create or maintain your wellbeing.

All you really need to do is allow yourself to be at ease more often and focus on anything that brings you joy in your life.

It's the best way to get to where you *want* to be. And it's easy. But it takes practice. And now is a great time to start! You can do it! And if you're already there, even better!

Day 1

I Choose Wellbeing

I wish to achieve my highest level of wellbeing. Wellbeing is natural to me and my body has the ability to heal anything that needs to be healed. All I need to do is practice the feeling of wellbeing until it feels like a part of me and it's who I am.

My body responds to my consistent thoughts of wellbeing, and when I notice how much better I'm feeling, my belief gets stronger. I feel empowered in my ability to feel any way I wish to feel.

I begin to feel invincible. As I practice my alignment with wellbeing, there's no other way for me to be. Nothing but the thought of wellbeing will ever come to mind. I'm feeling well and feel certain that I always will. With my unwavering faith, I think it, feel it, and believe in it, and make it mine. It must become my reality.

This is how powerful my thoughts and intentions are. I can create anything I wish to be or have or do. I am meant to feel good all day, every day. And that is what I intend to do.

I Am Setting Powerful Intentions for My Blissful Wellbeing and Desired Outcomes

Here's what I promise to do in order to align with my highest level of wellbeing. I will do my best to:

Practice a state of blissful wellbeing
Acknowledge and release any worries, fears, or limiting beliefs
Connect with my body and my breath
Find ease and feel as good as I can feel
Be my best supporter
Nurture my body
Create space for inner peace and positive change
Be open to trying simple, yet powerful, self-healing techniques
Increase, maintain, and protect my energy
Improve my focus and gain clarity and insight
Continually guide my thoughts to a good-feeling place
Take responsibility for my wellbeing
Follow my path to more joy
Remember to have fun along the way!

During the next 100 days, I intend to practice being in the physical and mental state I wish to be in to align with all my desires. Do I know all of what that is right now? Possibly, but I may surprise myself as I discover more about myself and my wishes and dreams.

So how do I want my life to go? Where am I now, and where do I want to be? Do I wish to make any changes?

I'm going to write a wish list in a moment, but here are some things to consider, first.

In what ways do I wish to feel better than I do right now?
Do I want more energy to do the things I love to do?
Do I want to feel happier throughout my day?
Do I want to feel more ease in my body?
Do I want a clearer mind or to feel more peaceful?
Do I want to make any changes in my body or health?
Do I want to improve my relationships, and if so, in what way?
Do I want to make changes in my work or social life?
How would I feel after the changes?

If any changes are desired, I want it because I know how wonderful it will feel.

And now I'm ready to write my wish list.

Action: Take a moment and close your eyes and think of the things that you want for your overall wellbeing. Take yourself there and feel how it would feel to be living it. And now grab a notebook or journal and write out a wish list with the following categories or make up your own.

A Wish List for Improving My Overall Wellbeing

Write the desired result you want for the following areas:

My Health is:

My Body looks and feels:

My Mind is:

My Home and Family are:

My Relationship is:

In My Personal Time I:

My Career is:

My Social Life is:

My Activities or Hobbies are:

My Dreams and plans are:

My Lifestyle is:

We will revisit this list in more detail during Step 3. It's going to be so much fun!

After you're done, circle the desires that feel really good when you think about them. See the end result in your mind and how you would look and feel when you've achieved them. Think of it often. Put your list in a safe place or keep it on you to be reminded of your goals.

Now, silently ask yourself these questions and take a moment to contemplate them:

When I've achieved my desire for blissful wellbeing, how does it feel?
What does my life look like when I've achieved everything on my wish list?
How does it feel to be living it?
What qualities and characteristics am I in?
How does it feel to have more energy?
How does it feel to give myself permission to feel good all the time?
How does it feel when I allow myself to feel blissful?

Close your eyes and ask that last question again. Give your body and energy time to respond. Relax and breathe. Repeat the question a few more times, and say it very slowly.

Now say "My body, thank you so much for transforming to accommodate me now and in the days and months ahead!"

If not now, with a little practice you will begin to feel the effects of guiding your thoughts and be able to feel any way you wish to feel.

Here are some last thoughts and intentions for you today:

My desires will continue to change as I evolve. As I evolve, my life keeps getting better and better. I'll always be moving forward and upward. Even when my life's pretty great, there's always a way to make it even better.

And from now on I focus on solutions. As I practice guiding my thoughts in the weeks or months ahead, anything that was once considered a problem will no longer feel that way to me. I'm looking forward to an amazing, life-changing transformation! This is my powerful intention.

I Am Clearing My Path & Moving Forward

Everything in life can be easy. It's not meant to be hard. And I like knowing that *my* life can be easy if I let it be.

In order to move forward in my life, I want to acknowledge and release some unwanted thoughts or beliefs and anything else that no longer serves me. Thankfully, that doesn't mean I have to dig up old wounds.

My positive emotions have a higher energy and they will naturally override any hindering beliefs or lower energies. They will naturally transform or dissolve on their own. In other words, I only need to focus on my positive thoughts and intentions to clear my path.

The moment I let go of negative emotion is the moment I begin to align more fully with all my desires. My mind becomes clear. My body heals and reaches its highest level of wellbeing. I'm able to reach my potential in all areas of my life. My wishes begin to manifest.

Even though I would love to jump right in and start practicing more positive thoughts like that, I know how beneficial it can be to acknowledge and intend to release any old thoughts or beliefs that no longer serve me.

In a way it's like saying goodbye to them. And when I do this process, I'm able to release the energy of it just by deciding to do so.

Let's just say I'm in charge of how my life goes. If I know my thoughts create my reality, what thoughts do I want to clear and which thoughts do I want to keep?

Slowly read through these questions and feel the effects of these potential changes in my life and what's available to me:

How does it feel to give myself permission to feel good?
How does it feel to make peace with what has been?
How does it feel to truly appreciate where I am?
How does it feel to be free of any constraints or struggle?
How does it feel to have more energy to do what I love to do?
How does it feel to free up my mind to create more blissful thoughts?
How does it feel to allow myself to focus on the joy in my life and let go of anything else?
How does it feel to position myself for better things to come?

When I'm ready, I am making peace with myself and what was. For anything that's been before, it brought me to where I am now. And I feel *so* very fortunate to be who I am.

If I'm experiencing any health concerns or physical pain, I intend to clear it away and think of it like this:

> Pain or illness is just a temporary change in my energy.
> If there are others who've cleared years of chronic pain by guiding their thoughts, why can't I?
> Perhaps my body's flow of energy was blocked or became stagnant.
> Sometimes it shows up when I'm resisting something.
> Quite often it's simply from frequent stress.
> It's just getting me to pay attention.
> An unwanted experience or condition has the potential to bring me to a better-feeling place if I allow it to.
> It's so healthy for me to see it this way.
> It will leave my energy when I allow myself to relax and feel better.
> And it may even leave as soon as I take my attention away from it and focus on how I *want* to feel.
> It's safe to let it all go when I'm ready.
> I am now clearing any and all lower energies from my mind and body.
> My intention alone has the power to get things moving in that direction.
> I'm clearing space for positive energy to flow more easily to me now.

How does it feel when I've turned my focus away from any stress or previous concern for my health?

What's it like when I'm free and clear of any distraction from how I truly want to feel?

What do I think about when my mind is completely free to focus on what's important to me?

What would I be daydreaming about?

Action: If you're comfortable with it, on a blank piece of paper, write down anything you wish to release or let go of. Don't hold back; you're going to rip it up and throw it away afterward.

First consider how it feels to give yourself permission to let go of anything that's been weighing on your mind. What if you could wipe the slate clean and start over? You can. Really!

Grab your pen and paper and make your list; include anything you can think of that you wish to let go of. Be specific, or feel free to use general terms like: I intend to release worries, fears, self-doubt, guilt, resentment, and habits I no longer enjoy.

Then state your intention to release and let go of it. Here's an example but feel free to make up your own:

> I am deciding right now to acknowledge and release any thoughts, beliefs, or lower energy that no longer serve me.
> I'm making peace with myself and my past, and it's clearing my mind.
> In this moment or in the days or weeks ahead, any concerns or negative emotions about this will leave me and any issues associated with them are being resolved.
> I give myself permission to let go of it as I become ready, and know that it's safe to do so.
> My positive thoughts will transform these old beliefs without any further effort on my part.
> I release all of this, and I am free.

Review your list one more time if you'd like. And then draw a big smiley face over it and rip it up to bits. Intend to call back all of your energy now.

This is only meant to be done once as a way to say goodbye to your unwanted thoughts, and it's not necessary to do this to align with your desires. Focusing on what makes you happy is the key. But know that if you were to try and write another list six months or a year from now, you may find that there's nothing left to write. Well done!

One last intention for you today: *As I release these unwanted thoughts, I'm raising my vibrational energy and will align more easily with my highest level of wellbeing. I'll look back one day and realize that I stopped thinking about that thing that seemed to linger on my mind for so long.*

And then I'll realize I'm also not continuing old patterns or situations that seemed to repeat themselves before. They only came up because I gave them my attention. It feels so good to notice when these positive changes occur!

★ Your path is clear and you're on your way to more joy!

I Honor My Body's Wishes

When my body's energy is in balance, I feel good and I am well. When anything is *off*-balance, my body eventually lets me know with signs and symptoms. My wish is to know my body's needs before it gets to that point.

To stay aligned with a higher level of wellbeing, my body needs me to:

Pay attention to its signals. My body is always telling me what it needs with little nudges or impulses to get up, stretch, drink some water, or rest.

Be at ease as often as I can, if not always. The more ease I feel, the more I allow my body the calm environment it needs to activate its natural healing response. My entire body and cells are able to replenish and repair and maintain wellbeing.

Breathe deeply as often as I can, if not always. The deeper and slower my breath, the more energy I will have, and the more my body detoxifies. The lungs are said to be responsible for about 70 percent of the body's detoxification process.

Move as often as I can and want to, doing something I enjoy. The more I move, the more I thrive. Strenuous workouts are not required!

Honor and genuinely appreciate my body. Loving my whole self will energetically align me with a higher level of wellbeing.

Feel as good as I can feel. This is truly the most wonderful gift I can give myself. And I deserve it!

I am already more aware and sensitive to what my body needs. And I intend to notice what it's telling me. And I love the idea of spending more time nurturing myself! I so deserve it, and so does my body.

If there's anything else my body needs, I trust my emotional guidance system will let me know. When I cherish and respect my body, I care enough to do whatever it takes to feel good. I like to tell myself often, "I love my body, and my body loves me! Thank you for the wellbeing!"

Why is it so easy for me to do this now? How does it feel to cherish and respect my body? What would I say to the following?

When I cherish myself, I know I deserve to ___________________________?

I have a perfectly functioning body, and it's about time I appreciate ___________ about myself.

I want to thank my body for _________, __________, and __________.

How does it feel to honor my body? How does it feel to be so tuned into my body that I know what it needs?

What are the signs that my body has given me recently? Can I think of one or more right now? What are they?

I intend to honor my body's requests to ___________________________________.

If I wanted to offer words that would honor my body, what would I say? What are three or more things that I appreciate about my body?

    1. _______________________________
    2. _______________________________
    3. _______________________________

I allow myself to feel good about my favorite things about me, and know that I am now becoming more accepting of *every* part of me.

If my body could speak to me, what do I think it would be telling me? I can close my eyes right now and tune in to my body and feel anywhere that may be asking for attention. Take a moment to do this now.

If I'm not feeling connected to myself in the way that allows me to sense what my body needs, all I really need to do is practice. Ideally, I want to make a habit of tuning into myself as part of my daily routine. It's a great step toward any self-healing that's needed.

Most importantly, I intend to stay focused on the feeling of total wellbeing to improve or maintain my good health. I can be my own cheerleader! It just takes practice.

Action: Paying attention to yourself and loving yourself nurtures your body and promotes healing. And loving your life and all it brings is healing for you. And your body always responds to your thoughts.

Whether or not you have any specific desire for healing, consider this next action to be healing you from the inside out. If it feels good, practice it as often as you'd like. It's a wonderful way to fall asleep, and truly has the potential to heal anything that needs to be healed with regular practice. You may feel its effects immediately.

So get comfortable now or when you're going to sleep tonight. Once you close your eyes, bring your attention to the top of your head, and in your mind's eye see the words "thank you" or just think of them. Slowly repeat "thank you" as you very slowly work your way down to your toes. You're thanking your body and appreciating it for keeping you strong and well.

Be sure to include your eyes, ears, nose, and mouth, throat, heart, lungs, kidneys, liver on the right, and spleen on the left. Or you can do a general thank you to all your organs, glands, cells, and all body systems for its perfect functioning. Try it both ways and see which feels better.

Now visualize or feel the meaning of the words over your entire body, front and back.

Try it once again, as though you're seeing yourself standing in front of you. See the words written over you from head to toe, or just over your head and heart center. Or again, just think of the words as you put your attention on each part of you.

This is a great way to feel tuned in and connected to yourself on a deeper level. You can always shorten it if it feels better to keep it simple; just thank your whole body and cells for the wellbeing. Find what works for you. Sweet dreams, Lovely!

I Am in Charge of How I Feel

I like where I am right now, but I also love knowing that I am now and will always be in a state of becoming who I am. And it just keeps getting better.

The more I practice thoughts, actions, and intentions that align with my true nature, the better I feel. And the better I feel, the more I attract more love, joy, wellbeing, and abundance into my life. I am so excited for what's to come.

I'm in charge. I make the rules. I get to choose. I get to decide how I feel and how I react to things. And I practice it *so* masterfully that I end up being able to feel good no matter what is happening around me.

How does it feel to know that I can take charge of my life and feel any way I wish to feel?

This is how it can be for me. And it's easy. It's kind of like giving myself a pep talk that I repeat over and over again until I believe it. Until I believe in me. Until I believe in my ability to be and have and do anything I wish. My thoughts, intentions, and energy are that powerful!

So how do I get there?

> I guide my thoughts to a good-feeling place.
> I catch myself when I'm not going there and redirect myself.
> I focus on what I want and what I like about things
> and take my attention off of anything else.
> And I have fun in the process!
> I build a super-positive momentum that leads to the best outcomes.
> And what I want or desire becomes a part of who I am.
> I see it, feel it, and make it a part of me.

What's one answer I put on my wish list on Day 1 for how I want to feel? How does it feel to allow myself to feel that way right now?

What are the many words that would describe the feeling? By the time I'm done thinking of the many words that could describe that feeling, I begin to feel it. This is how I guide myself to a better-feeling state.

With more practice, I love knowing I can feel however I want to feel.

What if all I needed to do was feel really good about myself and what's happening around me to start attracting more of what I want into my life?

Isn't it nice to know that I don't have to try believing any of this? I'm going to experience the positive changes and outcomes for myself as I practice the feeling state I want to be in.

Anything that I consistently think of will attract its vibrational match. And that means I can be or have or do anything I wish. Yay! I love it.

Action: To practice any feeling you wish to feel more often, begin asking yourself how you want to feel each day. You can also set intentions for the day ahead or week or year and actually create a better day for yourself.

So, how do you want your day to go? Close your eyes and think of anything you can think of in one- to three-word answers or phrases that describe how you want to feel today (or tomorrow if it's late).

One word at a time, think of how it would feel, and allow your body to respond. Do your best to feel the emotion associated with each word. Some examples might be: energetic, fun, ease. Imagine you're breathing it in, and let a smile form on your face. And then say that it's your intention to feel this way today and every day.

This is a nice thing to do for yourself any time, but also a great help if you're feeling indecisive or stressed. If it helps, see yourself in your favorite place to be while you're trying to guide yourself to that feeling place.

Journal Exercise: As of today, there will be additional questions or intentions about your day at the end of each "day" chapter. This will only be during Step 1, which is enough time to get you in the habit of making it a part of your daily routine.

Write your answers in a notebook or journal that you can call your "Appreciation Journal." Feel free to write as much as you want to.

Today's exercise is a longer version to give you more ideas of what you can write about. The purpose of doing daily thoughts of appreciation is to feel good about your day as well as build a positive momentum that brings more of what you like into your life.

Enjoy creating more of everything you want to experience in your day-to-day life!

Your Daily Thoughts and Intentions

Write your answers to the questions below in your "Appreciation Journal." Do this before you go to sleep so it's the last thought on your mind to ensure better sleep, better dreams, and better outcomes. Writing out the answers can be more effective, but if time doesn't allow, just think of the answers. Repetition will instill the habit.

What was my favorite part about today?
What are three or more things I felt appreciation for?
What was the best conversation I had?
Did anything make me laugh? Or did I learn anything new?
What is one thing that happened or one thing I did today that made me feel really good?

Intentions for Tomorrow

What is my intention for tomorrow? How do I expect my day to go from morning to night? Name all the things you want to experience:
     I will feel ______. I will be ______. I will have ______. I will do ______.
What's inspiring me to accomplish what I set out to do?
What will my focused attention be on?
What am I choosing to be my defining qualities tomorrow?
What's inspiring me to feel good all day?
How do I feel at the end of the day?

Why is it so easy for me to allow myself to feel good now?

I am practicing the state I wish to be in to attract what I desire most. I am now accomplishing any short- or long-term goal I set out to do.

Now, read over your intentions for tomorrow (aloud if possible). Then close your eyes and take about thirty seconds to visualize your day going the way you want it to, from morning to night. Imagine yourself waking up feeling blissful.

Then see a smile on your face at the end of the day, knowing that you accomplished what you set out to do and felt great all day. Do your best to feel the certainty that it will happen as you expect it to be, or better.

★ *First thing in the morning, before you get out of bed or when you first look in the mirror, ask yourself: "How do I wish to feel today? I choose to feel ______." Think of two or three answers.*

I Can Feel My Way into a State of Total Wellbeing

How does it feel to allow myself to feel blissful? This is something I ask myself every day to remind me of what is possible, and it immediately shifts my energy. I start to feel better, and it seems to give me a clearer perspective throughout my day.

This may sound silly, but I think my body actually likes it when I intentionally decide to let myself feel better. But sometimes I don't even realize that I'm holding any tension in my body until I ask the question.

When I'm able to release tension that I didn't even know I had, it clearly shows me what I can do with my powerful thoughts and intentions. Just imagine what else will improve in my body when I simply give myself permission to relax.

What if making time to find more ease allows my body's energy, oxygen, and blood to flow more freely? And allows my entire body to function better?

How does it feel to have more energy and vitality?

How much better do I feel when I have total clarity?

What if it makes me feel like being more active?

How does it feel to align with my highest level of wellbeing?

I can see how the ability to guide my thoughts is empowering me to create more of what I want in my life.

I intend to practice blissful wellbeing until it's a part of who I am. At that time all my thoughts, subconscious or otherwise, will naturally come from a good-feeling place.

What does blissful wellbeing mean to me? How do I look and feel when I'm in that energy all day, every day?

When I want to feel this way, what kinds of words will guide me there?

Right now I can close my eyes, focus my attention on the center of my mind, and think of any words that describe the feeling I have when I'm in a state of blissful wellbeing. See or think of each word, one at a time. I soon find that I'm feeling the true meaning of the words. I can even feel my body's response. I'm going to practice this more in the days ahead.

I decided to align with blissful wellbeing, and *every* little feeling I can feel in a blissful state is finding its way to me now. When I say "I decided" something, that means to me that in that moment I know it's going to happen. And my body is going to work with me. And it's coming to be, in the most effortless way imaginable.

Action: Keep doing whatever it takes to feel as good as you can feel. And if you're not already doing so, do your best to redirect any negative thoughts that come up throughout your day.

Rather than denying or stifling it, think of it as transforming or replacing that thought with a more positive thought. The more aware you are when you're having those thoughts, if any, the more quickly you can redirect them so they don't affect your day.

So when you catch yourself thinking a negative thought about a person or situation, you can immediately redirect it by thinking something like this:

> Every day I am better at letting this go.
> Every day I find something to appreciate about this.
> I choose wellbeing.
> I choose to feel good.

If you can remember the phrase "I choose" or "Every day I," you can always redirect a thought. Just finish the sentence with whatever you're *wanting* to feel at the time.

What are five or more things I felt appreciation for today?
What was the best conversation I had or something that surprised me in a good way?
Every day I get better at ________.
How do I expect tomorrow to go?
Imagine your day going as you want it to. How big is that smile on your face at the end of the day?

If I'm wanting to feel my way into a state of wellbeing, I'm going to find the feeling of ease, and I'm going to create peace wherever I go. It will happen as I expect it to, or better.

Day 6

I Allow Myself to Be at Ease

I decided that everything I do can be done in an easier way so that it's more enjoyable for me. I am meant to be living in a state of ease and joy, and I wish to feel that way *all* the time. No matter what I need to get done on any given day, I always have time to find ease.

The more I enjoy a state of ease, the more I notice when I'm not feeling it. When that happens, how I feel becomes more important than anything else.

So how can I guide myself to a place of ease?

What kinds of words can I say that will guide me there?

How does it feel when I slow my breath, and as I slow my breath, I slow my mind and my thoughts?

I start by slowing my breath, breathing in and out through my nose. And while putting my focused attention on slowing my breath, I notice immediately how easily and quickly my thoughts are clearing. Try this now.

I take a couple of cleansing breaths by exhaling through my nose, and when I think I've exhaled all the way, I gently push the last bit out through my mouth. This allows my abdomen to naturally fill back up. This is a great way to get started when I want to take deeper abdominal breaths.

And then I ask myself, "How does it feel when I *allow* myself to be at ease?"

Doing my best to hear the question without trying to answer it, I close my eyes and ask it again nice and slow.

Then I relax and notice if my body responds. I may feel my muscles soften or my body's energy get lighter, now or in the minutes to follow. Or I might just feel like smiling.

As long as I'm comfortable, I repeat the question slowly again and again until I feel a response.

When I'm needing additional comfort for any overwhelm or pain, I ask more specific questions or direct them to specific parts of my body.

I go from head to toe and ask things like this:

How does it feel when I *allow* my body to be free of tension?

How does it feel to soften my eyelids and the area around my eyebrows?

How does it feel when I *allow* my shoulders and neck to relax?

How does it feel when I *allow* my back to be at ease?

When I'm working or busy and don't have time to do this longer process, I just slow my breath, take a cleansing breath, and ask myself how it feels to allow myself to feel at ease. And that's all it takes.

The more I practice a state of ease, the easier it gets for me to instantly take myself there no matter how busy my schedule is. I can do this anytime, anywhere.

Sometimes it even feels good to write it down. I start writing a long list of words or one- to three-word phrases that describe the feeling I want to have. As I'm writing it out, I begin to feel the way I believe it would feel. I can do this to feel better about anything. Try it now.

Just thinking about how I want to feel gets my mind off of unwanted thoughts or feelings. And it doesn't have to be about that. Sometimes I guide my thoughts to a better-feeling state when I'm already feeling pretty great. And it often surprises me that I can feel even better. There's no limit to how good I can feel.

Action: From now on, do your best to pay attention to signs of tension or stress in your body. When you catch yourself taking shallow breaths, do a cleansing breath and begin to breathe more deeply.

When you notice that you're tightening up any muscles in your body or even your face or jaw, soften them. Guide yourself there with this process of finding ease or find a way that works for you.

Sometimes all it takes is asking the question: "How does it feel when I *allow* myself to be at ease?" You're deciding to release the discomfort and allow yourself to let it go, and your body will respond to your intention.

What are five or more things I felt appreciation for today?
What was the best conversation I had or something that surprised me in a good way?
How do I expect tomorrow to go?
What's inspiring me to feel more at ease tomorrow?
Now, close your eyes and imagine your day going as you want it to.

Why is it now so easy for me to allow myself to feel relaxed? My life is becoming more and more effortless.
From this point forward, do your best to remember to ask yourself every morning: "How do I wish to feel today? I choose to feel ______."

I Create Space for Inner Peace & Positive Change

I'm determined to have a clearer mind and a body that always feels comfortable. Essentially, I want to feel so good that I easily align with a state of blissful wellbeing. I know it's available to me.

So I want to do what I can to create the best environment for that to happen, mentally *and* physically. But let's start with clearing my mind first.

How does it feel to go from a cluttered mind to inner peace?

Let's clear the internal struggle and find out, shall we?

You know the one. Where there's two or more opinions going back and forth inside your head and you're not quite sure which direction to take? Or it may be that your mind is so busy that you just can't think clearly. And feeling this way can take its toll on the body.

For some of us, this is a frequent issue, and not so much for the lucky ones. But when help is needed or I'd like to feel a whole lot better, there's one amazing thing I can do to let go of any of life's little struggles I may have. And I decided to start doing it on a regular basis. It's meditation.

What?! *Me*, meditate? Yep! Just keep reading and consider this...

Until I give it a good try, I won't know what it's all about. Once I get into it, I'll wonder why there isn't a bigger deal made of it. I'll wonder why people didn't stop me in the street and insist that I try it.

There are some (life-changing!) benefits that are not often talked about, but this is how I could be feeling when practicing meditation regularly:

> There's an end to road rage (not that *I* ever experience that).
> Stress is nonexistent because I'm so good at coping with it.
> I am naturally patient and tolerant.
> My relationships are so much better.
> I'm sleeping better.
> Any headaches or pain have subsided.
> I'm clear-minded, decisive, and confident.
> I'm more aware of my vibrational energy.
> I'm expanding my conscious awareness.

I'm more connected to my intuitive guidance and know which direction to turn.
Amazing ideas are flowing on how to follow my dreams.
I've let go of all hindering beliefs.
I release resistance and allow my body to regain or maintain its balance.
My wishes and dreams are manifesting more quickly.

You can also think of it like having the mind filled to the brim with thoughts, like a glass full of water. There's no room left for clear thinking. We wake up and go to sleep with all kinds of thoughts swarming around in our head.

Introduce the regular practice of meditation, and it clears space in the mind to allow positive energy and new ideas to flow. It's fantastic!

And of course there are other incredible health benefits that *are* talked about more often. If I haven't given it a good go before, can I make time for it now?

What if meditation dramatically improves my life and helps me create more joy, love, and abundance?

What's it like to live a life that's struggle-free?

How do I feel when I've released all resistance?

How does it feel to have a peaceful mind?

How does it feel to easily focus on any task?

How does it feel to be more joyful and present in my life?

How does it feel to connect to the deepest part of my soul, which is all love?

How does it feel to allow my mind and body to reach a state of blissful wellbeing?

How does it feel to be in harmony with my true self?

What's my life like when I've opened myself up to reach my highest potential?

I love knowing I can do all of this in just a few minutes a day!

Action: So let's begin. There are many different ways to meditate, but if it's new to you, we'll start with something simple. Stay open to finding your own way so that you'll enjoy it and stick to it.

You may hear otherwise, but there's no wrong way to meditate. Let the experience be what you want it to be. Just let the goal be to focus on something; whether it's your breath, a sound, word or mantra, or an image of candlelight or a tree, it's up to you.

Choose a time and place to meditate daily and set a reminder. Doing it in the morning is a great way to start your day, but midday can also be a nice break. Choose a favorite spot where you won't be disturbed.

Set an alarm before you begin. Just start with 5 minutes. Increase it to 10 minutes in a few days or so, and work your way up to 15 minutes or longer as desired.

Fifteen minutes is enough to see the benefits, but some people will practice it morning and evening or more if they're wanting to clear up any health conditions. But enjoying it is the key.

So, let's try it now. Get yourself comfortable. As long as your back is straight and your neck is aligned, sit in whatever position is comfortable. Even lying back in an upright position works well.

Read through what's written below and then start your alarm and begin meditating.

Begin by closing your eyes, slowing your breath, and thinking, "Mind and body, it's time to relax." Then close your eyes and slow your breath, with a very slight pause between breaths.

Lightly focus your attention on the space in front of your eyes as though you're looking at the horizon, while sensing the rise and fall of your abdomen.

Don't try to stop your thoughts; just keep guiding yourself back to your breath. Be patient with yourself.

If you find it hard to stay focused on your breath, you can try using a mantra that you can silently sing or say. As you breathe in and out, think of the words "in, out" or "so, hum," which is a Hindu mantra meaning "I Am." Or choose any two words that have no meaning to you.

So you're thinking "Sooooo" for as long as you inhale, and "Hummm" for as long as you exhale. The purpose of the mantra at this time is only to replace your thoughts. The mantra will fade out as you connect with your energy.

If you find it helpful, you can also practice using a hand mudra, where you bring together two or more fingers. There are many forms, and they're felt to promote balance or even healing of various health conditions by bringing together different elements of the body that are represented by each of the fingers.

For the purpose of increasing focus during meditation or any time, set an intention that the moment you bring together your thumb and index finger on one or both hands, you will achieve instant clarity.

At the same time that you bring your fingers together, close your eyes and take a nice, slow breath. Feel how your body feels. Continue focusing on your breath until the alarm goes off.

Alternatively, just consider this to be a breathing exercise. There's no pressure to clear your mind; just focus on your breath. The idea is to be in quiet stillness and enjoy tuning in to your energy. In a very short time, you will feel the harmony of your mind, body, and spirit and never turn back!

You might notice you're feeling better early on, but give it a good few weeks or so to see more results. You'll start to enjoy it more when you reach that gap of time during meditation that feels like time has stopped and you're completely in the zone of your internal mind.

And then an amazing peaceful feeling will wash over you. And you'll never want to stop meditating!

★ Meditation also allows us to tap into the unified field of energy or consciousness that connects us to all that is. You may, in time, notice that you can see the movement of energy or images during your meditation and receive insights on ways to achieve your goals.

What was my favorite part about today?
What are five or more things I felt appreciation for?
What was the best conversation I had or something that surprised me in a good way?
How do I expect tomorrow to go?
        I will feel ______. I will be ______. I will have ______. I will do ______.
What's inspiring me to feel more present tomorrow?

If I'm looking for clarity tomorrow, I'm going to create more and more ease in my mind. I'm going to be in the joy of the moment. *It will happen as I expect it to, or better.*

Why is it so easy for me to allow my mind to feel a little freer now?

Day 8

I Am Cultivating My Energy

(This day will take longer than most. Feel free to split it up over two days.)

If you're open to it; as you slowly read the following intentions and questions, gently tap on the K-27 acupressure points. These points are on the kidney meridian (a pathway of energy) and tapping here can increase energy and relieve stress, among other benefits. Locate it by placing finger tips on each side of the notch between the clavicle bones (collarbone), and go an inch to the side, then down an inch where it feels soft. Cross your hands, place them on your chest and gently tap fingertips near each point or use one hand to tap with thumb on one point and two fingers on the other point.

It's time to allow myself to have as much energy as I desire. Even when I'm feeling my best, I know there's an abundant supply of energy that I have access to. It's all around me and within me. All I need to do is tap into it.

So I intend to use my thoughts, intentions, and actions to revitalize and maintain my body's energy. And I *love* the idea of building my resilience to any negative energy in my environment!

My goal is to have the kind of energy that feels boundless, where there's always more than enough to do everything I wish to do. I'm able to feel my way there, and with that belief and expectation, it will come. I'm truly in charge of how I feel.

How does it feel to have *inexhaustible* energy?
When I want to feel this way, what can I say or do that will guide me there?
How does it feel when I believe in the energy I have available to me?
How does it feel to allow myself to receive it?
And why am I *so* glad to know that major workouts aren't required?
What if I started breathing slowly and deeply often enough to maintain my highest energy?
What if I believed that the deeper my breath, the more pure positive life-force energy I would take in?
How does it feel to breathe in energy to *every* cell in my body?
What if I knew that I was increasing the energy of each and *every* one of my trillions of cells?
And what if a taller posture with an expanded chest allowed for more oxygen and blood circulation to energize my *entire* body?
How does it feel to have energy *all* day long?

How does it feel to have enough energy to fill a room?
What am I expecting when I think of feeling more energetic?
What if I were to go to sleep each night expecting to wake up with *abundant* energy?
And what if I were to wake up every day expecting to have that energy stay with me *all* day?
How much better would my day go with that expectation?
Better yet, how much better would my day go with all of that energy?
What if I practiced that thought long enough for it to be my belief?
Isn't it great to know that my beliefs are making things happen for me?
And how would my life change if I just started noticing all the abundant energy around me?
I like knowing that I can find it wherever I go if I'm looking for it.
Isn't it great to know that my attention to it will call more of it to me?
What forms of energy have I been noticing around me?
What if I became more aware of the strengthening energy of the earth?
And the magnificent energy I get from nature?
Or from food that's infused with the energy of the sun?
What about the vast and limitless energy of the universe?
Or the reservoir of energy within me?
An energy that I can build on and call upon.
How does it feel to intentionally connect with this energy and actually feel it uplifting me?
What's it like to feel it physically raising my vibrational energy?
And to be so aware of it that I can sometimes feel the pulsation of the energy in my body?
Isn't this the way it was felt thousands of years ago before traffic or loud noises existed?

Feel free to stop tapping.

How good does it feel to have more than enough energy, as well as clarity, to do everything I set out to do?

What would I be doing if I had twice as much energy as I have now?
In what way would it change my life?

Action: There are so many ways to tap into your natural-born energy. Here's a bunch you can try now, or feel free to come back to the list and try one a week. And if you're already full of vitality and feeling great, see if there's one that appeals to you for the sake of connecting with yourself on a deeper level.

So, are you ready for some work? Just kidding. Or am I?

To feel more connected to your energy and the energy that's available to you, let's practice connecting to the three life forces that are continuously providing us with energy: the earth, the universe, and nature. Intentionally tuning in to this unlimited supply of energy as needed or on a daily basis can help you feel more balanced and energized.

Connect to the three forces:

- ★ It's best to stand for this practice, but it can easily be done sitting or lying down. And outside in bare feet is great too!
- ★ Place your hands with your palms facedown toward the earth.
  - o With your attention on your palms, breathe in with the intent of drawing in the earth's magnetic energy. Feel the energy come up to meet you.
  - o Allow your whole body to breathe it in. Allow it to soothe and strengthen you.
  - o Try it again with your eyes closed; breathe in to the count of 2 or 3 and out for 4 or 5 with your attention on the palms.
- ★ Then face your palms upward and take a moment to connect with the universe's revitalizing energy.
  - o Breathe in with the intent of taking in the pure positive life-force energy that's all around you and always flowing to you and through you. Allow it to breathe new life into you.
  - o Try it again with your eyes closed and breathe in to the count of 2 or 3 and out for 4 or 5 with your attention on the palms.
- ★ Lastly, hold your hands up in front of your chest and face the palms outward and intend to breathe in the energy of nature or all plant life.
- ★ Then place one hand over the other on your chest and state an intention like this or in your own words: "I am now refreshed and energized by my natural energy and intend to keep myself centered and guarded in this golden light."
- ★ If desired, send out wishes for wellbeing to all. It's a great time to do this if you're feeling more connected to your positive energy.

Next, let's try one of the best ways known to cultivate your energy...

There are meridians or pathways of energy that run through your body and branch off to every part of you. These are the same energy pathways treated in acupuncture. And you have the ability to guide your energy for the purpose of clearing, balancing, and increasing your energy.

You can do this with your thoughts and intentions, as well as some ancient practices such as Qi Gong (pronounced "chi-gung") or Tai Chi. Both have amazing health benefits. Practicing it daily keeps the doctor away, I say.

There is a wonderful Qi Gong practice that you can do in the morning to get your body moving, and another for the evening to help you relax before sleep. There are many different teaching styles in Qi Gong, but try to find the ones that keep you moving and shaking. Literally.

The Qi Gong style that's suggested here coordinates the breath with soft, flowing movements and includes what is known as "qi massage" and "knocking" on key pressure points. Some guided imagery is also used. It feels as though you're doing nothing, and before you know it, your energy's moving, and you're heating up and clearing toxins or blocked energy. You end up feeling relaxed and energized at the same time.

The more you practice, the more connected you become to your body, your breath, and your core energy. You begin to feel the pulsation of this subtle life-force energy that's always flowing and available to you. Although it can be called upon with your intention, there will be no need as you become more aware of it.

****Please note:** Check with your physician before trying the following suggestions if you have any back, neck, or health issues; also stop doing it if you experience any discomfort whatsoever. Other than "the fountain," pregnant women should avoid them as well.

Qi Gong: try these now or tomorrow morning, and if it feels good, consider doing it every morning:

- ★ Knocking on the Door of Life:
    - o Stand in an upright posture with your feet shoulder-width apart; keeping your shoulders soft, arms loose, and knees slightly bent, you're going to move from your core.
    - o Begin to slowly and gently turn from side to side, allowing your arms to swing as they will.
    - o Slowly gain enough momentum for your arms to knock on your waist and back. Your forearm or hand should be knocking on your back right around your kidney area, and your abdomen or rib area on the front and sides.
    - o Do this for a couple minutes or as long as you're comfortable. This is a great way to enliven your body's organs and energy and has many health benefits.
    - o If desired and comfortable, deepen your turn to look over your shoulder slightly. You can also switch to tapping your chest or shoulder with an open hand, while allowing the back hand to stay at waist level.

- ★ Qi massage: Knocking in the same direction that energy flows along the meridian gets the energy moving while breathing in and out:

- o Gently knock with a closed fist on your chest just inside your shoulder a few times, and continue knocking all the way down the *inside* of your arm about every inch until you get to your wrist.
- o Go back up the outside of your arm and knock all the way up to the top of the shoulder, and repeat 2 more times, starting just inside the shoulder again.
- o Then switch to the other arm.
- o So, you're knocking about 8 times or so down the inside of your arms, then back up the outside of the arms for a total of 3 times on each side, as long as it feels good. And breathe evenly throughout.
- o Now do the same thing but on your legs; begin knocking on your low back, then hips, and down the side of the legs to the ankles, and come back up the inside of the legs.
- o Be very gentle on the inside of the legs; the acupressure points along the spleen meridian that runs along here can be very tender, especially around the ankle.

★ Breathing exercise: Put your attention on what is known as the dan tian in Qi Gong, just under the navel. It's said to hold a reservoir of energy that can be cultivated and drawn from as the body's need arises.
- o Breathe in to the dan tian, and as you slowly exhale imagine golden light spiraling there in a clockwise motion.
- o Repeat several times or more and allow it to energize you.
- o You can also gently tap on this area to stimulate your energy.
- o Many Qi Gong practitioners can feel a strong pulsation of energy in their dan tian during or after their Qi Gong practice or at will.

★ Ear massage: now take a few seconds to massage your ears from top to bottom and repeat a few times. There are dozens of acupoints here that coincide with the body. In Qi Gong we massage the ears with the intention of stimulating energy, as the ears are associated with the kidneys, which are said to be the "batteries of the body." And it's interesting how they're shaped similarly!

★ Feel your energy; place your hands close together with palms facing each other. With fingertips close together but not touching and your hands relaxed, slowly breathe in and out. See if your hands begin to move with your breath. As you breathe in, they should come together and move apart as you exhale. Try it again with a few quick breaths, and again with your hands farther apart. If you don't notice anything today, try it another day.

Qi Gong exercise for before bed:

- ★ The Fountain: Try this now or this evening before bed, and if it feels good, consider doing it every night.
  - o Stand with your feet a little more than shoulder-width apart and knees slightly bent, and always move with ease and from your core to stay balanced. During this exercise, keep your hands, elbows, shoulders, and spine soft.
  - o Bring the *backs* of your hands close together (just the fingers) in front of your legs.
  - o As you breathe in, slowly float your hands up the center of the body, keeping the fingers close but not touching.
  - o As you reach the front of your face, turn your palms outward and open or push them out to the side, slowly floating your arms down as you exhale, bringing the hands back in front of the abdomen and repeat several times.
  - o Allow your body and spine to move freely like a soft wave that flows as your hands go up and down.
  - o Repeat the movement for a couple minutes or more, always slowly breathing *in* as your arms float up, breathing *out* as your hands come down. Allow for a slight pause between wave-like breaths.

This is a great way to bring energy to your spine and balance to your body before bed so you can wake up feeling refreshed and energized.

Enough cannot be said for the health benefits of practicing Qi Gong. It has even brought some people back from some life-threatening conditions.

Here are some other suggestions for increasing your energy, but always stay open to your intuitive guidance for ways that feel right to you or may work best for you.

- ★ Drink plenty of water.
- ★ Consider having more fresh or whole foods that can offer a higher quality of energy than processed foods.
- ★ Spend more time in nature and walk barefoot in the grass.
- ★ Take an occasional sipping breath where you breathe in naturally, and sip in a quick breath or two before exhaling.
- ★ Visualize yourself doing the activities you'd like to do more of. Feel how you would feel when performing at your highest potential. If athletes can improve their results, so can you! Remember that what you imagine is what your mind sees as real and that brings it into your reality.
- ★ Last but not least, ask yourself daily, in conjunction with putting on your shoes or coat or some other action that reminds you to ask: "How does it feel

when I allow myself to have twice as much energy right now? I am going to have energy all day long!"

Here's your new mantra: I look and feel younger every day!

★ *Feeling your way into anything you wish to experience in life is all about the quality of your intention.*

What are five or more things I felt appreciation for today?
What's my intention for tomorrow? How do I expect my day to go?
What's inspiring me to feel energetic all day tomorrow?
Close your eyes and see a smile on your face at the end of the day, knowing that you accomplished what you set out to do and felt energized all day.

I Gain More Clarity

The more mindful I become, the more I notice my environment and how it affects me. What if I decided I only want to surround myself with things that bring me joy for the sake of inspiring more clarity? *And more* joy, of course.

It's often said that our external environment reflects what we've got going on inside. But if that's the case, why do I feel so much better as soon as I spruce things up?

I generally feel pretty great either way, but there's something to be said for taking the time to create a space I find uplifting, even if it's just my work space or that one special room in the house that I spend a lot of time in. Until I change something, how will I know what I'm missing?

When I close my eyes and picture this place, I imagine filling it with anything that would brighten my day. Some examples would be quotes, affirmations, photographs, colorful paintings or pictures, crystals, a cozy cushion, more color, or aromatherapy.

> What would spark ideas in me?
> What would energize me?
> What soothes me?
> What kinds of things would make me smile or laugh?
> What have I seen before in someone's house or business that inspired me and made me wish I had one?
> Would I consider trying aromatherapy? Like frankincense that can improve focus or lemongrass to increase energy?

If or when I'm inspired to, I can collect a few things to add to my home or work space. If I see even one picture or painting that makes me feel really good when I look at it, I must have it!

Another way to stay more focused and gain clarity, and likely make me feel all kinds of better, is to organize or clear any unnecessary clutter. Yeah, I said it. I know it's not the most fun idea, but there's always an easier way to do everything.

Firstly, I remind myself how good it's going to feel when it's done. It's going to create more space to put things I *do* want around me, and it's a great way to gain more clarity, among other things. Is that enough? Well let's see how easy we can make it.

Unless there's no clutter to be found, I'm going to add a 10-minute appointment in my calendar right now with a reminder to do it every 2–4 weeks, whichever one feels doable for me.

When I get the "appointment" reminder, or the next chance I get that day, I'm going to set a timer for 10 minutes and go right to it. I will pick one drawer, one corner, one closet, or one *something.*

I will clean or organize it until the timer goes off. I easily let go of things by asking "Will this bring me joy?" If not, I can discard it. I have two bags or boxes, one to keep, one to discard or give away. If it's feeling good, I'll keep going. But all of it will get done in time. And it will feel so good.

How does it feel to have done something I've wanted to do for the longest time? And if I'm a super clean king or queen, good for me. I'm way ahead of it. I can always use the time to get other things done that are always on my mind like phone calls and such.

All that said, I do my best to never look at anything that I have as a mess. It could be organized chaos. Whether it's mine or someone else's, I think of it as having a much more interesting life. I see it as having more character and creativity. And if I see a messy desk, then more ideas must be flowing.

When I get to be in an environment that's more my style or feels aligned with my true nature, I gain a piece of clarity I didn't know was missing. It's evident to me when my creative side starts to come out.

This is the ultimate good-feeling place to be.

> Isn't it great to know I can create more clarity in my mind?
> How does it feel to have more clarity?
> How does it feel to be so clear on who I am and what I want, that I know what my next step is?
> My next step is always going to be following my joy. I take the direction that feels good to me. This will always be my path of least resistance.
> Why is this getting so easy for me now?
> When did my path become so clear to me?
> How does it feel to allow good things into my life?
> What's feeling right to me? What's not feeling right to me?
> Are there any choices I need to make right now that will lead me on a path to more joy?
> I know that what I pay attention to or what I focus on is what I'm going to experience in my life. What things am I paying attention to now?

From now on I'm going to do my best to focus on what I want. I'm going to speak of what I want, think of what I want, and choose what I want.

I will ask myself each morning before I start my day: "How do I want to feel today? What feeling do I want to focus on? Joy? Fun? Clarity?" I pick one or more and let that intention carry me through my day!

I am practicing until it's natural to me and the clarity keeps flowing. My mind is free and clear.

Action: Sit comfortably with one or both hands resting on your lap with the index finger and thumb together. Keep your fingers together while *very slowly* and silently reading these intentions, with a slight pause after each question. Feel as though the words are resonating in the center of your mind:

> I can guide my mind and body to align with my desires.
> Mind, it's time to focus.
> It's time to set aside my repetitive thoughts.
> Show me how it feels to have clarity.
> How does it *feel* when I allow clarity to flow?
> Are my eyes and forehead feeling more at ease? Can it feel even softer?
> How does it feel when I *allow* my mind to clear?
> Can I feel my mind creating space?
> How spacious is it?
> Do I notice my head space feeling lighter?
> How much lighter can it be?
> Could it be as light as a feather?
> Is it clearing now or more so in the minutes to follow?
> Is this what it feels like to have an illuminated mind?
> When I look up, do I suddenly feel as though my vision is clearer?
> Is my breath slowing down and becoming deeper?
> Can I feel my vibration rising as I do this?
> Does this make me feel like smiling?
> How will it feel when I allow myself to have clarity all day?
> I have the feeling that my day's going to go easier.
> I am going to be sharper.
> I am at an all-new level of clarity.
> Any time I wish to call this feeling back to me, I only need to bring these two fingers together. I will gain instant clarity and feel a heightened focus in my mind the moment they come together.

You can pull your fingers apart now.

Let your intention be: I am now able to call this back to me any time I wish, by simply bringing these two fingers together.

Now close your eyes and breathe in as you bring your fingers together once more and feel as though you're breathing in that clarity. Allow it to resonate with you. Give yourself time to feel an increase in your focus. And open your eyes when you're ready.

You can pull your fingers apart now.

If not now, with practice you will be able to intend this and feel an immediate shift of your energy and clarity will come instantly. After that you can use the process to clear your mind as needed, to help you make a decision or clear overwhelming thoughts or just to feel good.

If coaxing is ever needed, close your eyes, and think of as many words as you can think of that describe how clarity feels to you, pausing between each word or phrase. For example:

> *ease, clear mind, focus, clarity, spacious, ideas flowing, light as a feather, illuminated, clearing now, eyes soften, face softens, smile, raising my vibration, clarity is flowing, feeling sharper, instant clarity, breathing in ease, energy, clarity, and harmony.*

On another note, consider getting a few things to "spruce" up your favorite room or a personal space you like to be in. Something new might inspire you all over again! And consider taking some time to clear away anything that doesn't bring you joy!

Interestingly, some feng shui experts believe that excessive floor-level clutter is associated with holding on to the past, waist-level clutter shows an imbalance or struggle in the present, and clutter above our head on shelves or in closets is associated with a fear of the future or reluctance to move forward.

Of course this is subconscious, and seems that it would be an internal job for us to clear. However, once the physical clutter has been cleared, many issues have been resolved for people. It opens the doors for better health, happiness, and success.

There are even some big companies that seek their counsel and experience an influx of productivity and lucrative projects, simply by clearing out old files.

At the end of the day, it's all about what inspires you and what *you* believe. So no matter what you see in your environment, let it inspire you in whatever way that works for you! Perhaps you see a gray wall and get clarity, or see a gray cloud and expect the sun to come out.

And maybe having more clutter around you means you're a more interesting person! Isn't it true, though? With your powerful mind, you can choose to see everything in a way that will benefit you.

Just for fun, and hopefully a little inspiration, pick a day this week to pop into a store that carries paintings or prints. Take a few minutes or so to walk around and look at each one that catches your eye. Spend time gazing at it with a soft focus. See if it evokes a sense of exhilaration or a soothing feeling in you. Intend to hold on to that feeling the rest of the day. Consider setting a reminder now.

Imagine if you could look at it every day and get that feeling and how much better your day would feel. Pick your favorite one or two, hold the image of it in your mind and think of it any time you wish to feel soothed or inspired. And if the desire strikes, consider buying it. Maybe it will fit in your meditation corner?

What are five or more things I felt appreciation for today?
How do I expect tomorrow to go?
Now, close your eyes and imagine your day going as you want it to.

I Am Resilient

My emotions and how I'm feeling are the result of what I'm focusing on. And I like knowing that my choice in where I put my attention gives me control of what happens in my personal experience. But sometimes I really wish I could control what's happening around me as well.

When it comes to negative energy that randomly or routinely shows up in the environment, it's not always easy to ignore. This is especially true for anyone who tends to be highly sensitive or empathic. In its essence, our body is a biomagnetic energy field and can be affected by the lower energies around us.

And if it *has* affected me, I may not even realize the reason I was feeling tired for *hours* or sometimes *days* was because I was in a stressful encounter or environment. And sometimes it has nothing to do with me, but I felt its effects.

It could be negativity in a person or conversation or situation, or even from an overall vibe in my surroundings. And it can leave some people feeling overstimulated or exhausted. Fortunately, if need be, there are ways to strengthen my resilience and feel less affected by it or eliminate its effects altogether.

And isn't it great to know that the more I practice positive thinking, the more I energetically align with positive energies and circumstances? And none of this other stuff shows up. Or at least I won't notice when it does. Perhaps I'm there already.

But in case it's helpful, here's what I can do to prevent any ill effects or guard myself in preparation for them. With my intentions and some actions, I can:

> Build resilience.
> Guard and protect my energy.
> Have confidence, faith, and trust in my resilience.
> Focus on how beneficial these actions are for my wellbeing.
> And I can choose to go with the flow of my natural-born energy.

In order to harness this energy and build my resilience, I need to build confidence in my mental and physical capabilities. I want to fully believe in the power of my thoughts and intentions. And I want to know the power of my energy and what it can do. I want to allow it to enhance my life in every way that it can. I want to know its strength.

My ultimate goal is to fully believe in my ability to protect my positive energy and keep it from being altered in any way. In other words, I'm in a good-feeling place no matter what's happening around me. And if I'm not already there and I would like to be, I can do this with a little belief, ritual, and intention.

With my intention and beliefs, along with energy work like Qi Gong, I am cultivating a higher frequency of energy. I am rock solid and unstoppable.

Having faith and trust that I am invincibly strong and stable in this energy is now creating a belief that my positive energy is stronger than *any* lower energy out there. I am armed and protected.

But what if I feel extra-sensitive to lower energies or just know that I'm drained a *lot* of the time, and can't quite imagine being able to change that?

What if it was just a choice? What if it was a decision that I could make to replace my belief about that with something else?

Every part of my reality is primarily based on my thoughts and beliefs. So if I can practice a new thought and make it my belief, I can also replace the old beliefs with new ones, no matter what they are.

What if I decided to stop labeling or calling myself highly sensitive or an empath?

What if my attention to it is what's making it seem unchangeable?

What if I decided that I would no longer be sensitive to negativity or lower energies? What if I set an intention that the next time I encounter it, I'm not fazed by it? Or that it will instantly raise my energy way above that of the others involved? Or maybe there's a tune playing in my head and I don't even notice it.

What if I could visualize this and practice the feeling of it until it became my new way of being? My intention before my day starts each day can help make this happen.

And it doesn't mean I don't love or accept myself as I am or that I need to stifle my feelings. It means that I care enough about myself to make feeling good more important than anything else. And to know that I deserve to feel good. And it's a choice.

Isn't it nice to know that I can choose to practice a new thought until it's a belief and change any circumstance I wish to?

I can think of it like this...

I was saying or thinking about how sensitive I was for so long that it was the practiced belief I gave my energy to.

And now I'm giving my energy to the belief of my wellbeing, my resilience, and my happiness. I'm aligning with my true nature. The strong and confident, easy-going, fun-loving, happy me!

As for my gift of sensitivity to my own emotions, I accept and embrace it. I appreciate my emotional guidance system and love using it to create a more harmonious place for me to hang around in.

And when I want to practice the feeling of being resilient to outside energies...

What if I've already become more resilient to any other energy by resonating at a higher energy? And already have the mindset that keeps me there?

That is, a mindset of joy that holds me in a good-feeling place that's stronger than anything I could *possibly* encounter? And as I become more resilient, I'm able to control how much energy I take in from those around me as well.

Why is it now so easy for me to go from feeling *less* of the negative energy effects to none at all?

How does it feel to be so resilient that I'm able to go through my day and handle any potentially stressful situation that comes my way with absolute ease?

How does it feel to know that I'm becoming stronger in every way? All of my intentions and desires are making it so.

How does it feel to know that my mind is stronger? And my body is stronger? And getting stronger every day?

Can I imagine or feel how much stronger my energy is? Or my resilience?

Can I imagine or feel how much stronger my self-worth is? And how much it's changing my life?

I love the harmony of it all. Just the sound of it feels incredibly empowering.

I am strong. And I am stronger every day, in every way.

I am in charge of how I feel. I'm in charge of how I react to things. I'm in charge of my wellbeing. I'm completely in charge of myself, and I'm loving it.

I'm so happy to say that I am now becoming a part of the energy without allowing it to affect my positive energy. Without resistance, the energy can roll off of me rather than stay with me, as it does when I resist it.

This is not about stifling emotions or feelings. This is about transformation. This is about change. This is about me evolving. This is about my expansion. This is about my belief in the power of my thoughts, intentions, and energy.

This is about me taking charge. This is about me taking control of my life and my outcomes and how the rest of my life goes. And most of all, this is about my freedom. To live my life the way I want to live. And feel the way I want to feel. And love the way I want to love.

I decide. I get to choose. I make the rules. And I'm happy to say that I am now becoming more resilient and able to keep my energy up no matter what's happening around me. Life is becoming struggle-free!

The stronger my belief in my ability to do this, the more effective it is and the stronger I feel. It's something that I'm deciding. It's something that I'm choosing. It's something that I have the ability to change.

The more I practice these empowering thoughts, the higher my vibration, and the easier it becomes to go with the flow and allow my ideal life to unfold easily and effortlessly. And perfectly so.

I accept that I am a unique and powerful individual and can practice myself into any reality I wish to be in. So I choose to start thinking of myself as a strong and resilient person who can stay in a good-feeling place no matter where I am, who I'm with, or what I'm doing. The more I say it, the more I believe it, and the sooner it becomes true.

Action: Here are some suggestions for becoming more resilient or preventing depleted energy:

Do your best to guide yourself to feel more ease at the first sign of any stress. Intend to let go of any energy that is not your own and call light to yourself.

Continue daily deep breathing exercises or meditation, walking, Qi Gong, qi massage, or meridian tapping.

Send positive energy ahead of you before leaving the house. For anyone you will see, wish them joy and wellbeing. Imagine you're with them and there's good conversation, teamwork, kindness, or laughter. Wish the same for anyone you'll come across. Intend to arrive safely and on time wherever you go.

If you need to soothe your energy (and you're not pregnant): very gently squeeze your arm about two inches above the wrist or massage the palm of your hand with your thumb.

Or try folding your arms with the palm of your right hand on the side of your ribs about midway, and left palm over the side of your arm near your elbow. There are pressure points here on the spleen meridian and triple warmer and placing your hands here can have a very calming effect. And all of these practices can be easily used while you're in conversation with someone.

Consider trying this visualization exercise for intending to balance your energy:

> Any time you wish to feel better or clear away unwanted energies, imagine seeing or feeling universal light that comes in as a violet light or waterfall that pours over you.

> When it reaches you, it begins to spiral around you from head to toe, cleansing and clearing away any unwanted energy.

> See it settling into a spiral at your heart center.

> You can stop there or intend to connect to the earth's core, pulling in a golden liquid light through the feet or base of the spine.

> See or feel it flowing up into the heart center and connecting with the universal light.

> Imagine the two colors blending together in a spiral and bringing your body's energy into balance.

There may come a time when you feel your body begin to gently move in a spiral motion as you call this light to you. Always stand to do this when possible, and let your body be soft and receptive to this, if desired. Have the intention to allow it to balance all the energy centers in your body. Try it now if you'd like.

This one is a visualization exercise for intending to protect your energy. It may be helpful for anyone who frequently feels zapped of their energy by day's end.

> When you get up or before leaving the house each day, set a powerful intention to guard and protect your energy.

> Briefly intend to connect with the three forces: earth, universe, and nature.

> See or feel a ball of light in the center of your chest at your heart center. It can be pink or green like the heart chakra or any color you wish.

> Each time you breathe in, imagine it increasing in size until it surrounds you in a transparent sphere of energy.

Then imagine a beam of light connecting the base of it to the earth's core, intending for it to keep you balanced and centered.

Intend to seal the energy by bringing your hand all the way up the front of you, with palm facing in, from the base of the torso to your chin. In energy work this is known to strengthen our energy and can be shown by testing arm strength before and after.

Then do a clockwise spiral motion at your solar plexus just beneath the rib cage.

You are guarded, safe, and protected in this energy.

Intend to have this shield of protection wherever you go throughout your day.

Your aura is like a force field of energy around you that's always there. Being aware of it and consciously intending to have it protect you and your positive energy is very effective.

Consider doing this daily before you leave the house and again right before any meetings or outings that you typically find overwhelming, if any.

With practice, you'll be able to easily and quickly visualize this. Minimally, you can just do the last step and seal your energy and think or say "I am guarded throughout my day."

Just keep in mind how powerful your intentions are, as well as your belief. It takes seconds to do and in time you'll feel stronger and free yourself of any sensitivity to anything in your environment.

And always stay open to finding your own way to do any of these processes. Your intuitive guidance might show you a different way or color or intention. Always trust it!

What are five or more things I felt appreciation for today?
How do I expect tomorrow to go?
What's inspiring me to feel good no matter what's happening around me?
Now, close your eyes and imagine your day going as easily as you'd like it to.

I'm peeling away all the layers one by one and healing from the inside out.

I Am in the Power of This Present Moment

What if I could be more present in my life just by reminding myself that right now is all that matters? Right now is the moment that counts. It's always the moment that I can find myself in.

Right now is where I set my intentions. And how I'm feeling right now is setting the tone for what happens next. I want to feel good so the moments to follow are as good as the last. This is where my power lies.

What I'm thinking about today at any given moment is what's creating all my tomorrows. The better I feel now, the more positive momentum I build for all the days to come. This is how I build the momentum that builds my ideal future.

What if I knew that focusing too much on the past or the future was giving up much of the power I have to create my best possible life? And that it was making me miss the joy of the moment? Perhaps it even feels like time passes more quickly than I want it to.

Can I say it in another way? I can't say it enough, can I? Yikes! But when I know all of this, what could possibly keep me from being here in this present moment? Or keep me from enjoying it?

There may be things that busy my mind and make me think that I can't have things any differently, but I have the power to change anything. It's time to let myself be more present, if it is indeed something I need or wish to improve upon. I am now creating a life I love more every day.

I believe I always have access to a solution for any changes I wish to make. I'll start by acknowledging what might be distracting me from being present in my now moments.

Why is it that I sometimes feel as though I don't have time to do the things I'd really prefer to be doing? Or what's keeping me from enjoying the moment?

Am I preoccupied with what happened yesterday or what's going to happen later on? Do I busy myself to keep my mind off of something, or perhaps do this subconsciously? Do I feel overwhelmed by all that I have to get done in a day?

How important are my tasks and projects? In a month, a year, or three years from now, will I be glad I spent time on them? Is there anything that doesn't necessarily *have* to get done but I make it more important than it really is?

Am I thinking of all the options I have? Is there anything I can do to simplify the process to free up more of my time? Can I do routine tasks or errands at the same day and time each week or write a checklist to get them off my mind?

If I want to have more time for myself to feel present more often, and enjoy doing more of what I love and deserve, what am I going to do about it?

If I can believe and expect that time will be freed up for me *somehow, someway*, I can create that for myself. I'm creating it right now.

If I want to practice a belief that I have enough time to do anything I desire, how can I guide myself there?

Well, all I have is time. Really!

So what do I have time for?

I'm stepping into a place where I *do* have a ton of available time. I don't need to know how I got there. I've just been given an endless slot of time where I can do whatever I want.

What have I been wanting to have time for? What will I do with my free time?

Practice it now by completing this sentence with a written or spoken list of dozens of things I would be doing with this free time. Do this before moving ahead.

★ I have time for __________.

And *now* write, think, or say the words that describe how it feels to be doing these things, and how it feels to have all this free time. How has it changed my life?

———————————————————————————————

When I can see myself having more time for things and be in the energy of a life with plenty of spare time, I can change my circumstances.

I now have more free time to do what I want and time that allows me to be more present on a daily basis. This is my powerful intention. I can make it so by believing it so.

My desire for it has set things in motion, and circumstances are now being shifted around for it to come about. My expectation of it is creating an unexpected amount of extra time for me to enjoy.

And now that I have time to be more present, how does it feel to allow myself to be in the joy of this present moment *right now*?

How will being more present improve my life?

What's it like to feel very content with where I am? I am patient and at ease. I'm happy, and I'm always pleasantly aware of what's going on around me.

How does it feel when I'm free of distraction and focused on what's happening right now?

And how does it feel to be so present or in touch with my inner self that I'm in a state of inner peace and joy no matter where I am?

When I want to feel this way, what kinds of things can I say to get myself there?

I can practice how it feels to be joyfully present throughout my day in my mind's eye, and easily recall the feeling place of it. I am now forming the habit of being more present wherever I go.

I can close my eyes and imagine I'm in my favorite park or place to be. How does it feel to be completely present and have so much appreciation for what I see and hear and feel? Imagine this now, and feel how it would feel.

Am I present where I am right now? What's in front of me? What do I see, smell, hear, or feel? Are there any noises I didn't notice before I asked this? Is there anything here that brings a smile to my face?

When I'm here, or being present in a park or elsewhere, what do I love about the moment?

Sometimes being present is about being mindful in the stillness of the moment. Where I'm fully aware of the sights and sounds around me. Or tuned into myself and more aware of my body or breath or deepest desires.

Sometimes it's about being present when I'm focused on a task at home or work or in a conversation. Either way, I intend to be more present in the days ahead. I am practicing it until it's become a part of who I am and how I live.

I am now consistently in the joy of this powerful, present moment. I've turned all of my attention to the present moment and seek joy in everything I do. With practice it's becoming my only way of thinking. I can see how I'm naturally letting go of anything that hinders my purpose for living blissfully.

When I'm focused in my now moment, any clutter in my mind has cleared, and I trust that anything else I've been thinking about can wait.

I cherish my life and believe in giving myself the life I deserve. A life where I have time to do what's important to me. To do what feels good to me. And to know that when I look back one day I'll be so pleased that I followed a path that resulted in achieving my life's goals and dreams. My alignment with all of it is now certain.

What lights me up, makes me happy, makes me laugh, and makes me appreciate the life I have? That's what I'm going to do from now on. Yes, yes, yes! I am.

Action: Start trying to be more present, no matter where you are. Try to notice when you're preoccupied with something else while you're speaking to someone or doing something that you want to focus on.

Catch yourself, and say something to yourself like "I choose to love the present moment." If possible, stop what you're doing, breathe, and look around you.

Allow yourself to feel good about taking some time to nurture yourself! Being more present does wonders for you and your body.

When you're outside in nature or driving, or anywhere, do your best to notice the sun, sky, birds, trees, flowers, colors, or anything you see. Admire the houses and people or anything you pass by and start naming your favorite thing about them.

Also, try to ask yourself daily, as often as you can: "What do I love about this moment?"

As you become more mindful and connected to the present moment, you create a stronger connection and relationship with yourself. You're starting to make yourself and how you feel more important than anything else. Enjoy it! You deserve it!

What was my favorite moment about this day? What did I love about it?
What are five or more things I felt appreciation for?
How do I expect tomorrow to go? Imagine it now.

I Am Inspired to Move My Body

I love the feeling I have when my life is in balance. My body feels good and I'm full of energy. I feel centered, and I have so much clarity.

I've come to realize that in order to maintain that balance, I need to keep my body moving in some way or another, and to do so every day if at all possible. Getting my circulation going not only energizes my body, but keeps my brain stimulated as well.

The best part is that the more physical I am, the more energy I have, the more clarity I have, and the more inspired I feel. I feel happier and more inspired to have a healthier body and live a healthier life.

I've always wanted to exercise more, but I didn't always like the idea of doing another strenuous workout. I like knowing that my body requires movement to maintain balance, but it never requires doing something difficult.

And if I'm going to exercise, I always choose exercise that's fun for me. It's the only reason I stick with it. If I choose an exercise that I dread doing, I would be going against my heart's desire, and that wouldn't necessarily be good for me *or* my energy.

On the other hand, if I push myself to do something I'm not sure I'm crazy about, but love how I feel afterward, I might find myself craving more of it. And things like this can lead to finding a similar exercise routine I like even more. I'm always finding what works for me!

But what if I decided to call it something other than "exercise"? What if I just added another fun activity to my routine? I never do a day of exercise when I'm doing what I love!

When I need inspiration to get moving, what if I kept in mind that I'd be increasing blood flow, qi flow, moving lymph, synovial fluid, stimulating my organs, and more? And that results in more clarity, energy, better digestion, and a stronger immune system, among other things.

It can even affect my success in life because any kind of movement increases my energy, builds positive momentum, and that energy plants the seeds for my desires to grow. Are we stretching it a bit? Maybe. Maybe not. What do *I* believe? Either way, maybe it's just better to focus on doing what I do for the sake of fun and not caring about *any* other reason. I say yes to this!

So if I'm not already doing so, how does it feel to be inspired to move my body more often? Can I imagine what it would be like to have more energy, confidence, and magnetism and attract more of what I want, solely because I've got more oomph in my step?

If being more sedentary creates *low* energy, can I imagine the opposite happening for me? What if I knew it would release any tension in my body? What if I could completely release any physical conditions? What if my mental state became ten times more clear and focused and joyful?

What if I didn't even know that I could feel happier by doing more physical activity, until I got started? Ok, so at times we're into our routine, and feel like there's no time. But there's always time. I'm deciding right now that I have ten minutes or more a day to do wonderful things for my body and mind. And I'll let my spirit soar high as I do so!

Am I ready and willing to do what it takes to feel more vibrant energy flowing through me? If I felt the desire to do so, in what ways would I choose to move my body more frequently?

What if I tried "rebounding" on a mini trampoline, which is an exercise known to move lymph and improve health? If astronauts have used it to restore muscle tone and stamina following one of their long excursions, I wonder what it could do for me. Or I could jump on a full sized trampoline, if I really want to go crazy.

What do I consider fun that gets my body moving? Can I see myself taking an adult tap or jazz class? They do exist, and for all levels! Or what if I just find a beautiful path or quaint village to walk through?

What is one thing that comes to mind that I'd love to try for fun?

When I think of it, how does it feel to imagine myself doing it? Right now I can take a moment to play it out in my mind's eye, and feel how it feels.

How do I feel afterward? And how does it feel to have more energy and better focus to get things done the rest of my day?

What if these activities turn out to be even more fun than I imagined? And wouldn't it be great to meet someone new and engaging that is out there doing the same thing?

When I think about it, have I had any repetitive thoughts that came up in the past for ideas to join an activity or try something new? Have I had inspiration to do something in particular? It could be my intuition directing me toward a life-changing experience for me. Can I think of one or more things? What are they?

From now on, I intend to pay attention to those impulses. I care enough about myself to be mindful of what I may need to further my personal growth, as well as help my physical body function better. And I like treating myself well. I deserve it, and so does my body!

Action: Choose one fun activity that involves moving your body to add to your daily routine, and do it the easiest way possible.

I suggest doing this before breakfast, lunch, or dinner. Turn on your favorite upbeat music, set a timer for ten minutes, and move however you choose to.

Here are some ideas to set yourself up for success:

Promise yourself that you'll do it before a meal at the same time every day.

Choose a day to start doing it daily, and stick with it. Put it in your calendar or on a sticky to remind yourself in the beginning. Decide this now if you're all in.

Don't allow yourself to skip it unless you did another form of movement that day.

Consider choosing a different style of music than you're used to: zydeco, disco, techno, or rap or any fast tempo style. Drumming and violins can also make you feel like moving!

Set your timer, and then dance, sway, or move whatever way you're inspired to. You might start with dancing and end up throwing some punches or kicks. Let it flow whatever way it comes to you.

Or put your earbuds on and take a walk. If it appeals to you, make it your goal to increase your speed each time you walk, as though you're late for an appointment.

Or leave the music behind and let the sounds and sights of nature inspire you!

Do whatever it takes to inspire yourself to continue a regular practice and always make it fun.

You know what you prefer and what will feel best to you. But staying open to trying something new can lead to great things, such as a soul-searching experience or meeting a new friend that leads to more life-changing experiences.

You will benefit from just ten minutes of exercise a day, but you'll very likely go beyond that. And the greatest part is, the more you do this, the better you'll feel. And that makes you want to move even more. It also naturally inspires cravings for healthier food like fresh fruits and vegetables. Really!

I challenge you to challenge yourself right now. Decide now. Don't put this off. Pick something, or you can decide when your timer starts. You'll never look back.

And if you're already very active, obviously there's no need for you to do more unless you'd like to. Doing a little freestyle dancing is good for anyone. Allow yourself to get lost in the moment. You might surprise yourself with the moves you come up with!

What are five or more things I felt appreciation for today?
What's inspiring me to walk or dance or do some fun kind of exercise tomorrow?
Imagine feeling refreshed and energized all day! If you're not already there, play the role and feel your way there. You can talk yourself into anything!

I Eat What I Love & Love What I Eat

I've always felt that eating is one of the most enjoyable experiences in life. And it's always best for my body to eat what I truly enjoy. As I put my focus on what I'm eating and feeling genuine appreciation for it, that positive energy goes into my food, and that food goes into my body.

So there's an energetic exchange happening here. I love knowing this infuses my food and my body with positive energy. When I eat, I'll be thinking that I'm happy to eat what I love and love what I eat. I want to practice making it one of the most blissful experiences of my day.

But how can I enjoy what I eat even more than I do now?

How does it feel to willingly and enthusiastically embrace the plate that sits before me?

What if I give it my full attention so that I notice the color, the aroma, and how flavorful it is?

What if I felt so much appreciation for what I was eating that my entire body resonated with the harmony of blissful wellbeing and the feeling stayed with me throughout the day? What kind of amazing day do you think I'd have?

What else can I appreciate about this food? Can I appreciate the caring hands that were involved in growing it, packaging it, and getting it to the grocery store? Anything else?

And what about eating healthy? I like trying to eat healthier to help my body thrive. But what's healthy? Who decides what's healthy for me?

I do, that's who. Remember, it's what I believe that matters. It's what feels right to me that's important. So, that means I'll eat something if I can enjoy it. And I won't eat something I don't like just because it's supposed to be good for me.

That is, unless I feel so good about eating something because I believe it's good for my body and that makes me feel appreciation as I'm eating it. And I'm finding that the better I feel, the more inspired I am to eat healthier.

And even when I'm not feeling that way, I think about my body and how much it deserves to feel good. I always get a new perspective when I think of making positive changes for my body's sake. That's why I like staying open to trying new things.

The best part is that the more I eat of any kind of food, the more I crave it. So where I once had to be in the mood for something, now I'm loving it.

It's easy. It's effortless. And I like it that way!

It's time to close my eyes now and imagine my idea of three perfect meals: breakfast, lunch, and dinner. I see all the yummy details. I include anything I've been wanting to try or eat more of. Think of this now and visualize one at a time. See it, taste it, touch it, and feel the appreciation for it.

I am now creating a blissful occasion every time I dine. And I love knowing that the more I align with the high vibration of blissful wellbeing, the better everything tastes! And the more I appreciate it, the better my experience will be when dining in *or* out.

If I want to free myself and my dining experience of restrictions:

How would I feel about taking the word "diet" out of my vocabulary?

What if I stopped counting calories or believing I should weigh a certain amount?

I could decide that my only rule is that I eat whatever feels right to me and trust that I have an amazing inner guidance system that is helping me make good choices.

When it's nudging me to stop eating something or try something new, I will know it. And I'll feel good about the idea when it comes.

I can also choose to trust that my body keeps itself in balance no matter what I'm eating.

Allowing myself to feel more at ease about what I eat is great for my body!

When it comes to concerns about food that may or may not be good for my longevity, I can try to think about it like this:

What I believe is what I make real to me. What if I never read or heard anything about what is good or bad for me to eat?

What if I believed that every bite I eat is nourishing for me? And the enjoyment of eating it is nourishing my soul and raising my vibration. Hooray!

I choose to believe that when I eat something I fully enjoy, and it feels good to me, it *is* good for me.

Whenever I feel even a hint of guilt over something I want to eat, or what it will "do" to my body, I can redirect it with this thought: "I love my body and my body loves me. I love this food and it loves me."

There are people living to be over 80, 90, or 100 eating the things that are now said to be bad for you. How do you think they lived that long?

I would imagine they loved their life. They enjoyed their food. They did what they wanted to do without fear or worry about what it would "do" to them. This is the ideal way to live. The way I'm meant to be living. And I intend to feel that free.

What can I do to start trusting that I'm as healthy as I believe I am? My body, my bones, my organs, my cells; every part of me will respond to my belief in my wellbeing and begin to assemble itself to accommodate my desire. It has already begun.

Action: All that being said, you may receive guidance or insights that are prodding you to try something new or eat something that's helping others get healthier. If the idea feels good to you, there's a great benefit in trying it.

There are some foods or natural methods that are worth mentioning that are found to heal or aid in digestion, weight loss, inflammation, or strengthen the immune system and provide other benefits.

You can do your own research and decide if it feels right for you. Always check with your physician before trying something that may affect a medication or condition, including pregnancy.

Some examples are apple cider vinegar, lemon water, turmeric (which can interfere with some medications), triphala, castor oil packs, green juice, juicing, cottage cheese and flax oil, baking soda and lemon juice, elderberry, essential oils, or eating more whole foods and less processed foods. And, oh there's so much more! The more you try, the more you'll discover.

On the other hand, as previously mentioned, what you believe is all that matters. So if you decided that everything you're eating is the equivalent of a whole slew of superfoods (because you said so!) and you believed it so, your body would respond as such.

Don't let any decision on your eating habits be a struggle. There's no need to seek high and low for information on the best food choices, but do whatever gives you peace of mind. You can choose to simply follow your instincts and trust your inner guidance.

If you desire a healthier body, your intuition will take you right to the place you need to be in to hear the next step in achieving it. It's also great to know that as you raise your vibration, your desire for higher vibrational foods will come naturally. In general, the fresher the food, the higher the vibration of the food.

On a personal note: Whenever I start to worry that something I'm eating has the potential to harm me or my body, I always think of my *now* 88-year-old mother. She has lived this long and consumed a lifetime of bacon, eggs, sausage, white pasta and bread, and *tons* of sugary pastries, among other things. She never liked plain water, so she drank a lot of lemonade, juice, tea, or coffee, and a beer or a glass of wine on some days.

With all of this, she never had any troubling issues that required medicine, procedures, or surgery until she fell and hurt her back at 83. Before that she bowled, golfed, and played indoor and outdoor tennis all year round.

To me, the key to her good health all of those years prior to the injury was that she always did what pleased her. She stayed active and was still driving. She always took time for herself to play her sports, make her clothes, and did dozens of paintings.

Later in life she even took an acting class. And she kept herself sharp by doing her daily crossword puzzle and reading the entire newspaper, as well as mastering several versions of Trivial Pursuit.

Best of all, there were countless times when she told me that she felt as though she was 18 years old in her mind.

And she always enjoyed what she ate without qualms or guilt or a thought about it. She liked eating smaller meals because she didn't like being uncomfortably full, and she always ate slowly.

And even though she ate a lot of food that is often considered unhealthy, I also notice that anything that's coming out these days as a healthy habit or food is something she had plenty of. She ate a lot of fruit and vegetables like broccoli, cauliflower, and sauerkraut and always had homemade salad dressing with apple cider vinegar on hand.

As you can see, I admire my mother and how she always lived her life. Mostly what I'd like you to take away from that rather long story is how important it is to live your life to the fullest. And how nothing we ever do has to take its toll on us unless we let it. In other words: unless we believe it will.

So believe in your total wellbeing. And believe in your freedom to enjoy your life *your* way! And design it as you go along, whatever way you wish it to be.

Even when we think we're at our best, there's always more growth and more bliss to be had. Isn't it great to know that? And remember, you are you, and not a statistic. You can be as healthy as you believe you can be.

And the less you think about the details of your health and focus on enjoying your life, the more easily you'll align with blissful wellbeing. Believe that you're on a continuous path of change and improving all the time, without even trying. It's inevitable!

What are five or more things I felt appreciation for today?
How do I expect tomorrow to go?
What's inspiring me to eat what I love and love what I eat?
Imagine enjoying every meal you eat like it's the best thing you've ever tasted.
Body, thank you for taking anything I put in my body and using it to the best of your ability to bring more wellbeing to me.

Day 14

I Sleep Restfully

I am sleeping so well, I enjoy it more every day.

Before I go to sleep, I guide myself into a wonderful state of mind.

I set intentions for how I want to feel.

If I go to sleep with some good-feeling energy, I'll wake up feeling energetic.

And if I go to sleep feeling good, I always wake up in such a blissful state of mind.

I even have better dreams now.

Consider this:

What if no one ever told me that I "required" a certain number of hours to sleep?

And that it's supposedly required for my longevity?

Isn't my health always better when I believe I'm well no matter what?

Isn't thinking I need a certain amount of sleep to live longer a belief I learned that I can easily change like any other belief?

Couldn't I just decide not to associate myself with studies that have been done on it? I'm me, after all. Not a part of a study where my individual character and beliefs were factored in.

I like knowing I don't have to associate myself with anything I ever read, unless I choose to or it's something that makes me feel better.

What if I just decided that all I need is to rest and breathe to restore my body's energy?

What if I knew my cells were getting replenished and my body was getting all the rest it needed while I find ease and comfort in my bed, even if I didn't fall asleep?

How much easier could I fall asleep if I took all the pressure off of any set number of hours I "needed" to sleep? Or that I needed to fall asleep at all?

What if I could then easily and effortlessly fall asleep? I could even fall asleep at the reverse count of 3-2-1 if I really wanted to. It's been done! That's how powerful the mind is, and having the knowledge of that is where my invincibility begins.

First of all, I am a unique individual and my needs are different from anyone else. I'm not a statistic. What I believe and how I feel is what governs my health and wellbeing. And yes, the quality of my "sleep."

And if I practiced a new belief about my needs or what I wanted, how much better would I sleep?

I can decide this for myself. I can choose to be healthy and set intentions to live as long as I want to. My intention is powerful. And saying I have a strong immune system on a regular basis creates that very thing. And while I'm at it, I'll say that I am able to sleep as well as I wish to!

How does it feel to wake up in the morning and find out that my intentions worked? I got my wish. I had a restful sleep and woke up feeling completely blissful.

Action: Before you go to sleep each night (starting tonight):

(NO pressure but if it works out!) Head to bed when you *start* feeling tired.

Do your daily list of what you appreciated about your day. It's a great way to get yourself into a good-feeling place before sleep so you can wake up in a similar state.

(Optional but highly recommended) Turn on your favorite music station or app and choose violin or cello music.

Connect with the three forces: palms down, up, and outward as you did on Day 8.

Do your evening Qi Gong exercise (The Fountain) from Day 8, if desired.

(Warning: not for pregnant women!) Get into bed and use your thumb to massage the K1 acupressure point on the sole of your foot just under the ball but toward the center of your foot. If you find a tender spot, you're on it. This is the first point on the kidney meridian and can provide immediate soothing for your night's sleep.

When you're about to go to sleep, think about how your body will be rebuilt with perfectly healthy cells while you're resting. Try to make this statement every night. Thoughts of perfect wellbeing will cause greater functioning of your body, and over time it will show you the results.

And when you get good and comfortable, place your right hand over your heart center and your left hand on top and focus on slowing your breath. Allow a slight pause between breaths, with the exhale a bit longer than your inhale.

Then ask yourself questions like this (or record these words in your voice and play each night, if desired):

> Body and mind, it's time to relax.
> Show me what it feels like.
> How does it feel to feel sleepy?
> How does it feel when I allow myself to sleep peacefully and restfully?
> How does it feel to wake up feeling blissful?
> How does it feel when I allow myself to fall asleep?
> Think of the words that would describe how blissful you feel when you wake up.
> And then begin to think of the words that describe how it feels to rest.
> How comfortable is your pillow, your bed, and your body?
> Go back to focusing on your breath, or ask more questions like that until you drift off.

If you aren't feeling relaxed enough to sleep by then:

> Count backward from 100, seeing the numbers written in the sand on a beach you're at. See each number wash away when the tide comes up.

Try this tonight and don't skip any steps, if possible.

Let your body respond to the questions and help you fall asleep! Try it and give it a chance. Sweet dreams!

What are five or more things I felt appreciation for?
How do I expect tomorrow to go?
What's inspiring me to feel well rested when I wake up?
Now, close your eyes and imagine your night's sleep and your day going as wonderfully as you'd like it to.

I Love My Daily Routine

It's time to enjoy my day and feel free to do what I wish. I am now achieving a life I love, and it feels *so* good to create great habits that align with my desires! So I decided that I'm going to stop doing anything I don't enjoy, or find a way to make it enjoyable.

Slowly but surely, my everyday experience is becoming more of what I envision for myself as the ideal kind of day. Since I like things to be easy, I create a routine that's easy to do and easy to stick to. Life is not meant to be hard!

I've made a lifelong goal (and rule) to enjoy everything I do in some way, shape, or form. The most important goal of all is to feel good. To feel really, really good. That's my goal every single day, from morning to night.

So, what does my ideal schedule or routine look like? Am I happy with how things are? How do I really want my day to go?

Think of how my daily or weekly routine is now, and write or think of any part of it I'm not satisfied with and wish to change.

____

____

____

____

If I need to or want to continue doing these things, is there anything I can do to make it more enjoyable? Think of one way I can do this or one way to look at it differently. Is there any reason I can think of that makes me feel thankful for it or fortunate in some way?

____

____

____

____

I can decide right now to focus on that and let that energy carry me into better circumstances in all areas of my life.

Is there anything I can stop doing or trade for something new? What new habits or activities would I love to add to my daily or weekly routine?

What about having a completely different routine? Have I ever desired a major change like that? Such as going from a night owl to a morning person, or vice versa? Or to stop following any schedule and just live a life of spontaneity?

What if I knew that I needed to do something different to get different results in my life? Am I ready for change? A little change, or a big change?

I'm already doing some wonderful things to align with my desires. But I'm always open to anything that could put me on a new journey that makes life even better. If I have the desire for it, changes will come as I become ready for them. And it will feel so comfortable I may not even realize it's happening! Until I look back one day and feel amazed at the strides I've made!

What if I discover that I feel much happier when I get organized, get up early, and have more hours in a day? Or perhaps I'd love to allow myself to sleep in and have no agenda at all.

Whatever routine works for me will be what's best. I trust that I'm always being guided to evolve at just the right pace for me.

The idea here is to go from any struggle in my day to the *best* day I can have. Like ever! I want to leave out any moments of indecision, feelings of dread for anything I "have" to do, or anything of that sort.

It never has to be that way. When I focus on creating solutions for any of these matters, I will fill the time spent on indecision, worry, or unwanted circumstances with something I'd enjoy. I don't want to have any excuses for why I'm not having a wonderful day. I say *yes* to this!

So, what am I inspired to do in my daily routine? Have I noticed any repetitive thoughts that are calling me to make a change? Such as adding a new habit, activity, or spoiling myself a bit more?

This is how I see my ideal morning routine (and it feels absolutely wonderful!):

____

____

____

____

My midday routine looks like this:

____

____

____

____

And this is the perfect evening routine for me:

____

____

____

____

Here's my ideal weekend:

____

____

____

____

I am now achieving a day that is perfectly designed for me! If I wish it, dream of it, believe in it, and feel it's a part of me, I can make it mine. And if I'm completely happy and loving the way things are, I love knowing it's only going to get better. Change is inevitable, but I intend for it to always be an improvement, and a major one at that.

Action: Either on a paper calendar or blank piece of paper, write out your ideal weekly routine and put it on your refrigerator or somewhere you'll see it often. Let it inspire you to follow it now or see it as what is now becoming your ideal routine. It's all happening as you frequently match your energy with ease and joy and wellbeing.

Include all the delightful details. Don't hold back. There's no need to settle for anything less than what you want out of life. You're capable of having a blissfully harmonious day, *every* day. You're the creator. Let it be whatever you wish it to be. Write down your desired weekly routine now, before answering the following question.

When you follow this routine, how does it feel? Take a moment now and visualize your day's activities and how it would feel when you're living your life this way. See it as viewing yourself on a movie screen going through the actions of your day, and finish it with what's happening in your ideal weekend scene.

Review your written schedule each morning or before bed until it becomes instilled in your mind as the ideal day you're striving for. The vision is then held in your mind and in time becomes all that it is. Depending on the strength of your desire and belief and expectation of achieving it, it can come about somewhat quickly or gradually.

On another note, can you think of at least one thing that you've been wanting to do routinely and you know you're able to do it, but it's just not happening? Perhaps a new or improved habit that you believe would help you get from where you are to where you want to be in terms of better health or another life goal?

Make a decision to do it with ease, and enjoy it in some way. However, if you feel it nagging at you to do it, and it bothers you to think of it, it may not be what's right for you now.

When the thought of something doesn't feel good, it may be guilt talking or a belief in something we "should" be doing, but that's not likely your true desire, or it may not be the right time for it. Everything that's meant to be is working out for you.

If it *does* feel good to you, consider writing it down now and coming up with a plan to implement this habit. Write the day and time you'll start doing it and how you'll do it.

To ensure success in achieving it, choose another routine habit to pair it with. Or set it up in a way that you have to do it or will make yourself do it. Such as walking during a lunch break for more exercise, doing a yoga pose while brushing your teeth or at the copy machine to improve balance and muscle tone, or leaving a gallon of water in rooms you spend time in so you'll drink more water.

What are five or more things I felt appreciation for today?
How do I expect tomorrow to go? Imagine it now.

Day 16

I Am More at Ease Every Day

When did it start getting so easy for me to feel better *any* time I want? Why is it so easy now? I am able to find the feeling of ease whenever I feel the need to. And I get better at it *every* day.

I know that it's said that what we resist will persist, so I'm doing my best to go with the flow and accept whatever comes. And if need be, I guide myself to feel at ease. All it takes is a moment of time.

With my eyes open or closed, I breathe. And then I talk silently to myself. It's a new habit I'm really beginning to enjoy. The more I practice, the more I feel my body's response. I can feel a change in how I feel right away. The energy can soothe or energize me, whichever I intend.

I decided that everything would be easier for me and it's all happening now.

> It's easier to guide my thoughts to feel how I want to feel.
> It's easier to breathe *deeply* and quiet my mind. I'm doing it right now.
> It's easier to connect to my energy and feel aligned with blissful wellbeing.
> It's getting easier to be myself, to love who I am, and feel inspired to do what I love.
> It's easier to thoroughly enjoy eating whatever I choose to eat.
> It's easier to walk through my day with *effortless* ease and feel free to be me.
> I often feel like dancing, humming, or singing.
> I am smiling and laughing more easily and *way* more often.
> Feeling good is easy for me!

Is there anything else that's feeling easier for me now? At work, or home, or in my social or personal life? Write or think of this now.

____

____

____

____

____

____

69

____

____

____

____

____

____

How has this improved my life? Has it made another area of my life easier as well?

____

____

____

____

____

____

____

____

____

____

Am I more at ease about any family situations right now?
Am I at ease when spending time with all of my friends?
Am I more at ease around my significant other?
When I think of these things do I feel at ease or uncertain?
How much ease do I allow myself to feel when I think of the future?
Do I trust that it's going to work out really well for me?
Do I feel at ease with my work life?
Do I feel at ease with what I do in my free time?

Am I at ease when I think about what I eat and how well I sleep?
Am I allowing things to flow in all of these areas?

Is there anything that's not feeling easy that I can do something about? Do I feel more tension in my body at any particular time throughout my day?

How can I feel more at ease about the situation? Is there another way to look at it that will benefit me? What can I do to make it better or help myself feel better about it?

I can think of it now and change how I feel about it by asking myself:

> How does it feel to allow myself to see this situation differently or let it go?

> Do I want to give it the power to take control of my thoughts and emotions?

> Am I letting it be more important than my feeling good?

> Can I see it as something that will pass? Or something that has nothing to do with me?

> How does it feel to allow myself to let it go? Will it matter in a week? A month? Or a year from now?

> Does it feel better to give myself permission to let it go? Or to hold onto it a little while longer while I sort it out?

> Can I make it easier for myself by keeping my thoughts and focus on how I'd like things to turn out when all is said and done? Imagine it now and see how it feels.

How does it feel to allow myself to choose blissful wellbeing?

Sometimes it feels like I'm taking baby steps, and other times I feel empowered to create the changes I want *all* at once. I know that I'm going to keep moving forward, and it's going to keep getting better.

I just have to keep reminding myself that I am *meant* to be in the joy of who I am. That being happy and healthy comes naturally to me. And that I don't have to work hard to "deserve" or "earn" the right to enjoy myself and make the most of my life!

Action: There's always a way to feel more ease than you feel at any given moment. You may not even realize that you have any tension in your body until you try to relax different parts of the body.

Take a moment now to get into a completely comfortable position sitting or lying down, then close your eyes and take your time to do the following (or even better:

record yourself giving the instructions to follow this on your phone's voice memo or other mode, and play it back).

Say to yourself very slowly:
Body, it's time to feel ease. How does it feel to allow myself to feel ease?
How does it feel to allow myself to release *all* resistance?
How does it feel to be *so* relaxed that *every* muscle and *every* part of me is softer?
As I go from head to toe, I breathe in and focus on every part of me and soften any tension there.
Putting my attention on my face, breathing into it, I feel it getting softer.
Even...softer.
My forehead is softer. The layers beneath it are softer.
Even...softer.
My jaw is completely relaxed.
My neck and shoulders now...completely letting go.
Even...softer.
My arms and my hands are relaxed.
My chest feels soft inside and out.
Even...softer.
My abdomen is letting go and feeling ease.
My upper, middle, and lower back is softening right now.
Even...softer.
My hips are releasing all tension.
And now my legs are feeling completely relaxed.
And breathing into my feet, I can almost feel tingling in my toes as I take my attention there.
My body is capable of more ease. Body, double my ease.
And I feel my body getting even softer.
In my next breath I'm breathing in golden light that's doubling my energy.
How does it feel when I allow myself to feel twice as much energy?
I am refreshed and energized, and I intend to allow this feeling to stay with me the remainder of this day.

Take your time and give your body the chance to respond. Notice if you feel a change in your energy or feel relief. If not now, you will! Just practice guiding your thoughts in this way and enjoy giving yourself attention!

If not already, have faith that there will come a day when it's always possible for you to feel at ease no matter what's happening around you.

What are five or more things I felt appreciation for today?
How do I expect tomorrow to go? Imagine it now.

Day 17

I Am Raising My Vibration

The vibration of wellbeing has a higher frequency and I must be aligning with it because I'm feeling *so* good. That's a telltale sign. There's a measurable difference between when I'm feeling good or feeling unwell. And right now, I feel the wellbeing flowing to me.

This day is all about doing whatever it takes to feel *so* much joy that my body's energy continues to vibrate at this higher frequency.

How I feel right now is how I'll likely feel in an hour, but I'd like to ensure my good feeling will last. I not only want to feel this way now, but today and every day.

So, I want to practice raising my vibration as often as possible. In other words, I want to practice feeling joyful. I want to make it my routine habit. And I know I've said it before, but I can't say it enough. I'm just so happy to know that the more consistent I am about it, the more I retain this higher energy, and the more natural it becomes.

I know what to do now. It's *easy.* I've been raising my vibration in various ways my *whole* life without even knowing it. But now that I'm living more purposefully, I'm more aware of my emotions and whether or not I'm feeling a higher or lower energy. And now I make a point to do what I can to keep it high.

How can I intentionally raise my vibration anytime I want? What kinds of things can I do?

Of course, there's always my thoughts or affirmations. Since thoughts have their own vibrational energy, the more positive my thoughts, the higher my frequency is.

I can focus on my *favorite* things and appreciate what's around me.

I can keep my favorite high-vibin' song running in my head. No, I'm *not* kidding!

I can practice regular meditation, which allows me to release resistance and instantly raise my vibration, if I let it.

I'm also in a higher vibration when I'm feeling *ease* and clarity, or any feeling that feels good to me. And there are plenty of actions that bring about a higher vibration as well, which I'm always open to.

73

About every half hour or so, I can straighten up my posture, and look up and smile. And I will increasingly raise my energy and perhaps improve my immune system. Consider it proven by research. Or just feel how much better I feel!

I can focus on my heart energy and a feeling of love for anything I wish, including myself. Try it now.

I can ask great questions that get me thinking about all the limitless possibilities that are available to me, such as "Why is it so easy for me to attract what I want?"

I can intentionally call light to myself, and connect to the earth, the universe, or my *pure* positive energy.

I can take it further by imagining a *pearly* liquid light pouring into the palms of my hands as I face them upward and imagine it filling me up. When I use my intention and visualize it and feel it, the response I get from my body and my cells is so powerful!

I can also create my own visualization process, which is sure to work even better for me.

I can spend time doing things that I'm passionate about.

I can spend time in nature.

I can listen to music, especially instrumental or sound healing music with binaural beats or isochronic tones. My cells can begin to resonate with the frequency of the music to help me sleep, focus, or energize, or whatever the music is attuned for.

I can watch comedies.

I can smile and laugh, sing and hum or drum and dance and play more.

Sometimes just deciding I'm going to find things to smile or laugh about will keep me in that high-flying mood all day long. It's *fantastic.*

I can even think of words of appreciation to get myself there. What kinds of words will guide me there?

Here are some more affirmations. They work best when they're true or I imagine they're true for me, and do my best to feel how they would feel. I can practice until I wholeheartedly believe them, and then more easily align with my desires:

    I am loving and accepting myself *more* every day.
    I *love* my body and my body loves me.
    I *love* being in this body

I wouldn't trade it for anything in the world
I repeat, I *love* my body and my body loves me.
I *love* my mind; I *love* my life and the way I feel.
I am now allowing myself to feel the blissful energy that's flowing to me.
I appreciate how good I'm able to feel and that I'm letting this be for me.

It's all about what I believe. So if I believe something will raise my vibration, it will. I can even choose something I don't typically like to hear, and decide that from *now* on when I experience that, my vibration will go up instantaneously.

I simply enjoy myself more every day. And therefore I am now aligning with the natural ease and effortlessness of life, the way my life is *meant* to be lived.

When I'm in the joy of who I am, I'm aligned with my true nature and naturally in a very high vibration. I feel fun and free to be myself more.

When I want to raise my vibration or simply enjoy my life more, I'm not only *finding* ease or *following* my bliss. I'm also actively *creating* it.

And I love it when I get to that point when I'm *so* comfortable in my own skin that I start humming or singing a song in public and don't have a *care* in the world about what anyone thinks. Or I may not even be aware I'm doing it.

It's a *great* feeling to feel that free. And of course, feeling free to be myself is the absolute *highest* plane I can be on. Yay!

I'm in charge. I'm the creator of my reality. I choose to be the master of my mind and use my energy and imagination to create anything I wish to *be* or *have* or *do*.

I can feel my way into a higher vibration any time I want. The more consistent it is and the more positive momentum I build, the more natural it becomes for me to stay in this energy.

And I *love* knowing that the higher my vibration, the higher level of wellbeing I have and the higher the level of abundance will be in my life. I believe in my own wellbeing now, and no matter how good I was feeling before, I intend to feel even better.

And I love knowing that the law of attraction is responding to my consistent thoughts and will bring me more reasons to love my life. I am now choosing to live my life in a state of blissful wellbeing. I won't settle for anything less.

Action: It's time to practice breathing in that blissful feeling. You can do this anytime, anywhere, and help yourself feel more refreshed and calm at the same time. Just let your intention and energy do the work for you.

Get yourself comfortable sitting or standing, with your spine straight and neck aligned; with an open chest, yet very comfortable. And read this nice and slow...

I am open and receptive and allowing my body to respond to these words.
With my *whole* body actively involved, and with a slight pause between breaths, I'm breathing in somewhat quickly through my nose for about two to three seconds. As I breathe out I'm allowing my body to go *completely* soft in relaxation. I am breathing in gently but deeply into my *entire* body. Slight pause, *complete* release on exhale. I'm breathing in through *every* pore of my skin. I'm able to conjure this feeling and actually *feel* my body tingling all over. With my fully active inhale being my focus, and my body doing a *complete* release upon exhale, I feel as though my *entire* body is breathing for me, and *every* cell in my body is receiving *ten* times more oxygen and energy. And it is so.

If I want to go further, I allow my entire body to be involved right now and feel as though I'm breathing this energy *directly* into my cells and can *feel* it in my bones. I put my attention on my back and feel my breath clearing any tension there. I can see or feel any tension as a solid piece of ice, turning to water, and then mist, softening and allowing ease. Any tension is released and floats away. I can slowly read the last two sentences again if I want more relief there. Can I feel the tension releasing?

My body is magnetic and pulling in relaxing yin energy from the earth and taking in the energizing yang energy that's around me.
I'm pulling this energy further into my body as I breathe in deeply.
I am allowing this healing and replenishing energy to reach *every* muscle, *every* tissue, *every* organ, *every* gland, and everything in between.

The energy in and around my head feels lighter. I am feeling a lightness in my chest now. I am allowing my breath to clear and cleanse my body and feel twice the amount of energy I was feeling before, or more.
My energy's becoming so big that it surrounds me, and I feel protected.
I am rejuvenating and strengthening my energy field any time I use this full-body breath. My attention to it and my intention is all that's needed.
I'm not putting any effort into breathing other than to feel the blissful energy flowing into me, and I feel the freedom in it.

If I'm feeling really good right now, I intend for this energy to stay with me for the remainder of the day and beyond. I can do the short or long version of this any time I wish and feel renewed.

Whether you want to raise your vibration or just energize yourself, try doing this simple breathing exercise anytime. The longer version is nice, too, when you have time for it, or try it while lying in bed with a recording of your voice. The more you practice it, the more you'll find yourself breathing more fully without a reminder. Especially if it feels really good to you. A blissful feeling is achieved now or with more practice!

Your breath is like a gateway to cultivate more energy, more clarity, more wellbeing, and a more intimate connection to your authentic self. Isn't it wonderful?!

A few more suggestions...

The next time you go out to see live music, face the music or the musicians and let the vibration of the music resonate in your heart center. You can often feel it right in your chest or when placing your hand there. Also take a moment to focus on each instrument and hear its sound.

The closer you are to the music, the more you'll feel it. At a distance you can feel a subtler sensation if you pay attention to how you feel. Music will generally raise your vibration, unless it's something you don't enjoy listening to.

Consider walking into a music store and picking up a djembe drum to hit with your hand a few times, and feel how the vibration feels in your body. Ask someone to show you a Bahia buffalo drum, and hit it with the accompanying soft mallet. It's a low bass sound and its incredible vibration goes the distance.

You'll be amazed if you hold the drum over your head with the underneath facing you, and reach up and hit it with the mallet. You'll likely feel it in your entire body. You might wonder if it's clearing your chakras!

If you play this in your kitchen, you'll hear the metal stove or other surfaces respond to its vibration with their own rattle or hum. In a soft, rhythmic beat; this drum can put a baby to sleep. Literally. It's been done!

Drumming is an ancient tradition that's being shown to provide many health benefits, and research is backing this. Consider joining a local drum circle or drum to your own beat at home.

Now try closing your eyes and imagine you're listening to an opera singer or violin playing. Or imagine you're the one singing in your head. Your imagination alone can raise your vibration. It's that simple. This is why mantras and toning can be used inaudibly (or audibly) to promote healing or spiritual development.

If desired, try it now: close your eyes and think of a long sounding "Ahhh" or "Om" sound as you inhale, and again as you exhale, with your attention on your chest.

Lastly, choose one or more of the suggestions in today's topic for raising your vibration, or choose your own way and start practicing it daily if possible. Choose something you haven't done or done as often as you'd like.

Even just picking one favorite upbeat song or tune to hum on occasion will make a difference in how you feel all day. Try it for a week and see if you notice an improvement in how you feel at the time you're humming and throughout the day and week.

What are five or more things I felt appreciation for today?
How do I expect tomorrow to go? Imagine it now.
How many ways will I find to raise my vibration tomorrow?

Wellbeing Is a Part of Who I Am

Whenever I start a sentence with "I am now," or "I decided," it means to me that in that moment of that decision or statement, a change is occurring. An energy shift is evident. And the words that follow that phrase are in the process of happening the moment it's spoken.

It's a commitment and intention to do something. It means I know I can do it. And I *will* do it. And in that moment or minutes, hours, days, or in some cases months to follow, it is *all* happening.

I love my powerful words, thoughts, and intentions. And I *love* using them to the best of my ability to create the positive transformation I *know* is inevitable for me.

I love knowing that <u>*I decided*</u> *that blissful wellbeing is a part of me.* It's who I am. It's all I know. I released any beliefs that didn't serve me, and I continue to practice the feeling state of blissful wellbeing. It's become all I know. Nothing else enters my mind.

How did I get here?

I made my powerful intentions known.
And I decided to be in charge of how I feel.
I am now allowing my body the ease it requires to let my wellbeing flow freely.
I continue making peace with worries and fears or anything I consider a problem.
I am frequently guiding my thoughts to a blissful place.
I am staying open to positive change.
I am now being more mindfully present in the joy of the moment.
And I am letting my emotions guide me and making choices that feel right to me.
I started purposely living a life I love.

I decided to practice being in a state of complete wellbeing until it felt like a part of me. And it's now become a part of who I am.
I knew it was simply a choice I could make.
And instead of looking for things that could be *wrong*, I started noticing and appreciating what was going *right* for me.

I am now creating new thought patterns that are programming new beliefs.
And new neural pathways are being built in response to my new beliefs.
And they're being strengthened with repetition of my happy thoughts.

So I am now activating my highest vibration to create the highest level of wellbeing for me.

It's so great to know that my higher energies will always override any lower energies I have. So while I frequently stay focused in a good-feeling place, my body and everything in my life is transforming to accommodate my wishes.

I am now designing a life I love. The ideal life I'm meant to be living. Things always work out for me, and everything's falling into place. As I hold my vision of blissful wellbeing, I am now allowing for a remarkable transformation to take place anywhere it's needed or desired.

How does it feel when I am living a life of blissful wellbeing?

How do I answer the following questions *from the mindset of total and blissful wellbeing*? Give one or more answers to each question.

> How do I feel?
> Do I feel a sense of relief or freedom?
> Why does it feel so easy for me now to achieve or maintain a healthier body and a happier state of mind?
> How does it feel now that I've achieved it?
> What does feeling good mean to me now?
> What does being happy mean to me now?
> When did I start seeing that all things are possible for me?
> How am I letting it change my life?
> How has it changed my family life?
> How has it changed my work life?
> How has it changed my personal life?
> What am I doing that I wasn't doing before?

I am now choosing to *always* feel the way I was intended to feel when I came into this world. I hold a vision of myself in the state I wish to be in. It's a part of me now. I live it and breathe it.

And the results of my positive thoughts are being shown to me by the way my body feels, and the way that I *easily* and *freely* move through life. It's as though my path has been cleared or laid out for me and all I have to do is simply *allow* good things to happen for me.

Every day in every way I am *more*. More aligned with blissful wellbeing. More aligned with my true nature. More passionate. More loving. More energetic. More courageous. More at peace. And more connected and in tune with who I am.

And every day in every way I'm better at allowing myself to be in the lighthearted energy I know is my true authentic self.

Action: Imagine it's six months from now and you've achieved your desires for a higher level of wellbeing. You love and appreciate where you are now, but it's become even better. Let's say that you've achieved *all* your desires for your body, your energy, your clarity, and your life, as you imagined them to be or better. Imagine it's ten times better. Or a hundred times better!

Now, close your eyes and see an image of yourself walking toward you as you envision yourself. What do you see?

Can you imagine yourself in a state of blissful wellbeing with a smile on your face? You're feeling *really* good. You're confident. You're feeling at ease and on *top* of the world.

The energy in and around your head feels *lighter* and *freer*. The energy in and around your *entire* body feels lighter and freer. There's no tension. There's no struggle. There's nothing cluttering your mind. And you're *completely* free to do anything you desire.

Take your time and visualize yourself in this state while you're at home, work, or socializing, traveling, or doing anything you'd love to be doing. Do what you can to feel the sensation of being there; see it, feel it, taste it, and touch it.

As the image gets closer and closer, the last thing you notice is your face glowing in the sunshine right before this energy becomes part of you. It *is* you. It's already done. It's yours to align with and available to you now. Close your eyes and take yourself there now.

Hold this vision in your mind. Daydream of it often or as you drift off to sleep. If you have trouble visualizing it, write out a detailed description of it. Handwritten is best, as it allows more time for emotions to come up as you write out the words. Allow yourself to feel excited about what's to come!

What are five or more things I felt appreciation for today?
How do I expect tomorrow to go? Imagine it now.

I Am Creating the Perfect Day for My Wellbeing

I decided that *I am now* allowing myself the freedom and right to be in the natural state I was born to be in. The true nature of my body. Its natural state of blissful wellbeing. This body of mine is now resonating with *pure* positive energy.

The strength of my desire for it and my faith and trust and belief in it are arranging it all for me. No matter how good I feel now, I'm *always* able to feel even better.

And striving for as much joy or fun as I can have is never a bad thing! I deserve to feel as good as I can feel—which is nothing less than fabulous!

> What if I don't even realize how much more *amazing* my life could be if I just made a few little changes?
> Even little changes can bring bigger and better outcomes.
> What if I started paying more attention to myself?
> What if I did more of what I love to do?
> How much more amazing does my day feel when I do something that nourishes my soul?

I intend to set this plan into motion as of now.

I love to play this fun game where I'm creating a perfect day in my ideal life. A day that is *filled* with joy. Where I feel good from morning to night in *every* way. Where I'm happy with *every* area of my life and it just keeps getting better.

I can say I'm just playing a game, but it's actually helping me see that I can have this day now if I want to. Or have I already made it so? There's always a way. There's always a solution. And nothing's in the way.

Well, let's just see where this goes. And then I'll determine how doable it feels to do it right now. But one thing I *do* know is that I'm going to envision it and feel my way into it until it's mine and it's what I'm living.

What I *believe* is possible is the extent of what I can make happen. So there's no end to what I can do if I believe in it. I have access to *all* possibility.

I am a masterful creator and I am in charge of my destiny. I am in charge of my day. I have a *wonderful* day every day because I choose it to be.

When I've achieved the most blissful day I could possibly imagine, how does it feel to be me?

What new things am I trying? What is making me feel like each day is a new beginning?

What does having the ultimate perfect day of wellbeing feel like? When I'm full of vitality and my energy is flowing? And I'm feeling inspired to do everything I want and love to do?

When I have the time and energy to do anything I wish, what is my day like? What am I doing? Where am I? Who am I with?

In one sentence, summarize my idea of the ideal perfect day in my state of total wellbeing.

____

And now write down or think of the answers to the questions below.

When I wake up in the morning, how am I feeling? What am I thinking about? What am I expecting my day to be like? List three words or phrases that would describe my perfect morning.

1. _______________________________
2. _______________________________
3. _______________________________

List three or more words or phrases that describe my perfect afternoon.

1. _______________________________
2. _______________________________
3. _______________________________

What's for breakfast, lunch, and dinner?

1. _______________________________
2. _______________________________
3. _______________________________

List three or more words or phrases that describe my perfect evening. Where will I go or what will I do?

1. _______________________________
2. _______________________________
3. _______________________________

How do I feel when I'm falling asleep?
List three or more words or phrases that describe my perfect weekend.

1. ______________________________
2. ______________________________
3. ______________________________

List three or more words or phrases that describe my perfect social life or favorite activities I would be doing.

1. ______________________________
2. ______________________________
3. ______________________________

And what am I doing for work? For fun? With my family or partner? What do I enjoy doing by myself on this day?

1. ______________________________
2. ______________________________
3. ______________________________

When I close my eyes and see myself having this day or weekend, what is it like to be there? How does it feel? Reach out and touch something in each of the scenes. Feel your feet on the ground in each place and feel as though you're in the scene. Try it now.

And then imagine it's like a movie screen you're watching yourself on. Or try another way to feel it or visualize it in a way that works for you.

How does it feel to align myself with the energy of my perfect day? And to know that I am now achieving this reality?

From this day forward, I intend to do whatever it takes to feel the way I wish to feel and make this wonderful day a part of me and who I am. I am now achieving a life of bliss!

Action: You can have this kind of day every day. Anything you're able to conceive in your mind, you are able to achieve. So go for it! It may take time to line things up, or it can happen quickly, depending on the strength of your desire, belief, and expectation.

Choose one or more of the ideas you thought of for changes or new activities you'd love to add to your day, and start doing it tomorrow.

If you're not feeling ready or not sure you can fit it in, just decide you'll imagine it as you drift off to sleep each night. The ideas for how to make it happen will come when the time is right!

One day you'll look back and realize you're living it. Trust that all is very well exactly where you are right now, but also enjoy the excitement for what's to come.

What are five or more things I felt appreciation for today?
How do I expect tomorrow to go?
How does it feel to be the master of your day? Imagine it now.

I Am Decisive

What if I knew that simply quieting my mind and tuning in to my emotions would bring about the most intuitive thoughts? The kind of thoughts that guide me toward experiences that benefit me in the most delightful way?

I love it when I realize my mind is no longer being pulled in two different directions on any subject. My decisions have become easy. I make the choice that feels right to me. If it doesn't feel completely right, then it's a no. Or it means I need to hold off, take a step back, and let the answer come.

By nature, I am intuitive. I'm *constantly* being guided to make choices that are aligned with my true desires. I'm getting better every day at gaining more insight. This simplifies everything for me! My life keeps getting easier.

And I love knowing that the more I practice meditation or connecting to my breath, the more decisive I become!

How does it feel to have *so* much focus that I make my little daily decisions with effortless ease?

And what's it like to have a built-in guidance system that also helps me make the best choices for the important decisions in my life?

In what ways does it make my life easier?

What decisions do I need to be making right now?

And what kinds of things do I wish to be more decisive about?

How can I become more decisive? Better yet, how can I practice using my intuition to make decision-making effortless?

What if I just need to build confidence in myself to improve my decision-making skills? Or what if becoming more decisive builds my confidence up?

All I really need to do is practice. When I practice using my intuitive skills, it's like exercising a muscle that is strengthened over time. And then *everything* falls into place. My confidence. My decisiveness. And my *easy*, effortless, and most magnificent life!

So let's practice. In general, I want to follow the guidance of my inner wisdom. I'm *truly* being guided on a path to more joy. It's about following my heart's desire. If something feels good, it's more than likely the way to go.

First I need to know how I feel when something feels right or wrong to me. How can I tell if something I'm deciding is a yes or a no? When I'm looking at something and appreciating it, I'm saying yes to it. When I'm looking at something with distaste, I'm saying no to it.

So I just need to determine how a yes and a no feel in my mind and body so that I can use it to make all of my decisions, not just the ones that are obvious to me. It's very simple, yet we often allow doubt or other factors to interfere with what could be a clear decision.

Once I'm more consciously aware of this and my highly intuitive emotions, all my decisions become easier.

When I'm just beginning to learn tuning into my intuition for an answer, I like to silently ask my inner guidance to show me what a yes *feels* like. I give it a moment, and then I ask to be shown what a no feels like.

Right now I can close my eyes, intend to connect to inner guidance, and put my attention on my heart center. First I take notice of how my chest feels before I begin and then silently ask "show me what a yes feels like." Then a no. Then try yes again. Try it now.

This may take practice, but a no should feel heavier in the chest, and a yes should feel lighter. And I also might find myself smiling.

I can try it again now with my attention on the space in front of my eyes. Ask for a yes or no and see if I notice any colors or other sensations. It's different for everyone, but red often appears for a yes, and gray for a no, or it appears to be dimming.

Now I can try thinking of two plates of food. One is my favorite, the other is not even close. When I close my eyes and think of each one separately, can I notice the difference in how I feel about each of them? Do I see any color or other sensation come up?

I can use this for anything like which outfit I'll wear, what menu item or restaurant I'll choose, or which is the best choice for the bigger decisions in my life. Just imagine each choice and feel which one will have the best outcome.

I can imagine myself in it, looking at it, or being there and seeing which feels better. I'll trust that my guidance will always be better than any review or other opinion.

I make decisions about my health the same way. I do what feels right, and I do what I believe will help me feel better or get well. Whatever gives me peace of mind is what's important, whether it's doing something or nothing.

Is there an answer to a question or any big decision I need to make right now?

To practice feeling an answer intuitively, I close my eyes and go within and notice how I'm feeling before considering any decision. Then I can think of the question and ask it in a way that will allow for a yes or no answer.

I may need to ask a few questions to arrive at an answer. I just need to give myself time to feel it. If not immediately, I may receive insights or answers in the hours or days ahead. I can even ask that I receive the answer within a day or two.

If there are options, I can imagine taking each possible route, one at a time, including not choosing any of them if that applies and see which feels better once it's taken place. If none of them feel right, but I must make a choice, which one do I feel less resistance about?

The choice is right for me if it feels easy. I'm not questioning it. I'm *all* in. I know that it's what I want. I may even feel goosebumps or shivers in confirmation when I'm thinking of the right choice for me.

If I'm questioning a choice I'm making, it's time to take a step back and get some clarity. When making the best choice for me, I'll never need to rationalize anything.

If I ever have a really big decision like the choice between two jobs I could take or two houses I want to buy, I can make believe that I've decided to choose one and hold on to that idea or feeling for a couple hours. And in the next couple hours, have the idea and feeling that I made the other choice.

I can often make a choice rather easy for me when I use this process. I start to imagine what the decision feels like to me and what long-term effects it may have on me or my family, good or bad.

What if I could check in and ask how my mind, body, and spirit feel about a decision, one at a time? I can present the options to each and feel the response.

When we're indecisive, it's usually because we're divided. Taking the time to check in like this can often bring back harmony and suddenly make a decision very clear.

And if my whole self is not on board with something, it may be best not to force it. If I really want something to work, and I let the issue rest, I may find the answer I was seeking rather quickly.

The answers will always come to *me* without having to search. And the more I let this be my way, the more easily they come. Trusting in the intuitive process is key.

If desired, I allow myself to be led by my spirit and follow my heart for all my decisions.

I am now finding myself in the feeling place of a confident person who's making great choices for the most ideal life for me. And every choice I make has an effect on how the rest of my life goes.

Why is it now so easy for me to make decisions without the slightest hesitation?

I am now becoming keenly aware of my inner guidance. It's the natural intuition that is always available to me. I love connecting with myself to get answers to all of life's questions.

I am happy to use the tools that are at my fingertips. They make decisions so easy for me! And I get better at it every day. Now I truly understand that all the answers are within me.

I love this ability to easily make the choices that lead to more good things for me.

I'm getting really good at this and *love* how tuned in I feel. I'm becoming more receptive to the answers that come to me in various forms.

I feel that my mind has been transformed from any inner conflict or struggle to inner calm.

I feel a sense of ease and freedom unfolding more and more every day.

I feel more present, more joyful, and many more ideas are flowing.

My mind is free and clear, thank you!

Action: If desired, practice using your intuition for decisions this week or as often as you like. Keep reminding yourself by asking "which feels better?" It takes practice, and it can be easier to feel it with your eyes closed in the beginning. You'll get better with practice.

There are many more ways to tap into your intuition that you can find information on. Here's a few you might find helpful...

Journaling: ask a question you need an answer to and start writing whatever comes to mind. It's a bit like thinking out loud, and the answers begin to come.

Pick a card: take two or more index cards and write a one-sentence description of each option relating to any decision you're making. Set them facedown in front of you and ask which option is best for you. Place your hand over each of them or just look at them, and pick the one you're drawn to most. Use this for specific answers or write a "yes," "no," and "do nothing right now" on each card. It's always best to choose what feels right for you. However, going through this process often makes the right choice suddenly stand out.

For fun: try to anticipate the outcome of a situation or the end of a movie you're watching. Or think of what numbers or colors might be in something you'll be viewing. It's a fun way to practice your intuitive skills.

Muscle strength testing: energy runs through our muscles and they momentarily weaken when we make a statement that is not in agreement with our belief. We can also use it to ask questions. It's believed that the subconscious mind is able to answer our questions through this method.

It's also used for more important matters like diagnosing and treating some conditions. There are various ways to practice it, but here's a simple way to introduce it for the purpose of getting basic answers:

In your nondominant hand, make a loop by bringing your thumb and index finger tips together.

Then link the same fingers of the other hand inside the loop you made with the back of the hand facing upward. Palms will be facing each other.

Make a statement that's true, like "My name is ____." Holding your linked fingertips somewhat firmly together, try to pull your hands apart. Then try saying your name is something else, and pull again.

Your fingers should hold tight for what you consciously or subconsciously believe, and pull apart when you don't agree with something. Now, try "Show me a yes" and try pulling. And "Show me a no."

You can use this to help you decide how you're really feeling about something. But know that it's never foolproof. It may just be telling you an answer based on feelings of doubt. But if it feels good, practice it as often as you'd like.

Hopefully you've noticed this already, but you'll find that decisions start to come more easily the more you meditate, walk, or enjoy more solitude. Memory improves as well!

And that's a certainty as you become more aligned with your true nature. You become so clear that you can decide anything with ease, and it feels so good. The clarity has taken over because you're in such a high vibration, there can be no other way for you. Hooray!

What are five or more things I felt appreciation for today?
How do I expect tomorrow to go?
In what ways will I be more decisive? Imagine it now.

Day 21

I Am Balanced & Calm

Begin today by bringing the palms of your hands together, either cupped or in prayer position. Gently hold them in front of you, slightly touching your breast bone, as long as it's comfortable, and continue reading.

When I'm in balance, I am well. My life is in balance, and I feel centered.

I am now achieving harmony of my mind, body, and spirit, where I move through life with effortless ease. This powerful intention has been set in motion.

How does it feel when I'm in balance? When I feel centered and everything in my life is flowing in a positive direction?

What does that feel like to me?

I am strong, yet flexible, and easily go with the flow.
I let anything unpleasant roll off of me.
How does it feel when I'm there?
How good does my body feel when my balance has become stable?
What's it like to live my life with my body in total comfort?
How much more clear-minded am I without stress or pain as a distraction?
What am I thinking about?
To be present right here, right now, is to be in balance.
That's how I know I can always find my balance.
There's only one place I can find it. In the present.
Where I am calm and centered.
And have allowed myself to be free. Free of any struggle.
How free do I feel when I string these present moments together and a peaceful balance is all I know?
Can I see my life becoming that way?
What's it like when I stay present in every moment?
What does my day feel like when everything is easy and flowing?

I choose to be in balance. Effortlessly and easily and always in balance.
Right now I'm deciding that's how it will be for me.
How do I feel when I allow everything in my life to be this easy?
What's it like to go for months or even years without any major mishaps? Or even minor ones? To feel as though luck is on my side?
Isn't it great to know that things are working out for me?

Good things are always happening to me.
And I love that the more I appreciate it, the more it flows.
And I'm letting it in!

I help the circumstances of my life unfold perfectly by setting intentions like these. Yay!

Feel free to unclasp your hands.

If I'm ever feeling a little off, there are many ways to quickly regain my balance. I know I could be off-balance when I'm feeling indecisive, anxious, have physical discomfort, or even quite literally start bumping into things. This is my body or guidance getting me to pay attention so I'll take the time to restore my balance.

How does it feel to allow myself to take a rest if I feel the need to?

What if I just spent more time in nature, a sure way to restore balance? That is, if I take measures to divert the bugs. Just kidding! Or am I? Laughter will restore balance as well; don't forget!

What if all I needed to do to keep my balance indefinitely was to take a few minutes a day to go within, be present, and meditate or do Qi Gong? Both promote balance, harmony, and healing, and this profound experience can only be experienced firsthand.

And wouldn't it be great if I could just ask myself really good questions to keep myself in balance? Such as, "How does it feel to allow myself to feel completely balanced?" I really love how my mind and body respond to my suggestions!

What about right now? Let's try this exercise for soothing and balancing my energies...

With my arms crossed over my chest, and fingertips resting on my shoulders; breathe and *slowly* alternate a light tapping with my fingertips from side to side for about 15 seconds or so (stop reading, close the eyes and be present), then slide the hands down to the side of my arms and gently squeeze and hold. Close your eyes, breathe evenly, and be present.

Bring the palms together, rest the hands in the lap or against the breastbone again, and breathe and be present. Feel the energy between the palms and the inner balance occurring between the left and right brain, where they work together in harmonious ways. I allow myself to feel balanced and attuned to this energy.

What are some other things I can do to stay in balance? What is my favorite thing to do when I'm seeking more balance? Can I make time to do it more often?

Maybe it's just having a cup of tea and reading a good book or going out for a drive, or taking my sweet time to finish an ice cream cone? Just about anything that will get me out of my head will soothe me, shift my energy, and bring me back into balance. Does anything come to mind?

If not already, I'm deciding right now that I have balance and calm in my life. I am in the qualities and energy of what that would feel like. I can already feel my breath slow, my blissful energy rising, and a smile forming on my face.

I'm allowing myself to feel as though my breath is soothing and balancing every cell in my body. My body is responding to my request. I can almost feel tingles all the way down to my toes. Breathe it in, imagine it, believe in it, and make it so.

What thoughts and feelings or images will continue to guide me there? Can I see myself looking and feeling completely serene, confident, and well-balanced?

Where am I? What is the most soothing place I can think of? Watching the ocean tide go in and out? Lying on a hammock? Sipping on a piña colada or a cold beer? Or standing in a yoga pose? I can close my eyes right now and take myself there. What did I see?

Any time I wish to find my balance, I'll do what feels right for me. And I love knowing I can always recall the image of this little private haven I created and be transported to a state of balance and harmony.

Action: If you're open to it, let's try a visualization practice that can help balance your body's main chakras. Chakras are spiraling energy centers along the core of our body that transmit and receive energy and regulate the flow of energy through our system. They interact with our endocrine and nervous system. Keeping them balanced can help maintain a higher level of wellbeing.

One or more of them can become over or underactive from various factors such as chronic stress. Energy healers are often able to see or feel which chakras are off-balance. However, if *all* of them become open, balance can be restored wherever it's needed. You can help to open or balance them by using intentions and visualization, among other actions or techniques.

There are many ways to use intention and visualization to clear or move energy in your body, but we'll try to keep this simple. The affirmations below have been specifically chosen for their association with each particular chakra when it's in balance. Change the wording to your liking.

If desired, you can also use your right hand to do a clockwise spiral motion in front of each chakra as you read the affirmations. Do your best to see the colors and spinning chakras in your mind's eye. If visualizing is easy for you, see them as a funnel shape where the smaller end is attached to the spine.

> Bring your attention to the base of your spine at the root chakra; see or feel a deep red wheel-like energy spinning there in a clockwise motion that reaches a few inches or so from you toward the earth. "I am physically strong and secure, and always grounded and connected to the earth."

> Now bring your attention to your sacral chakra, just below the navel. See or feel it spinning and glowing in a brilliant orange, with its radiant light reaching out a few inches or so in front of you. "I am creative, enthusiastic, and emotionally balanced."

> Next, bring your attention to the solar plexus, just below the rib cage. See or feel it glowing in a golden yellow, spinning and spiraling outward. "I am confident and energetic, successful and in charge of my destiny."

> Bring your attention to your heart chakra; see it in a sparkling emerald green and feel its radiant energy transmitting love as far as you can see. "I am open, loving and lovable, trusting and peaceful, and I am in harmony with all life."

> Bringing your attention to your throat chakra at the base of the neck; see or feel it spinning in a soft, turquoise blue. "I not only hear, I understand. And I easily and creatively express myself from the heart."

> Moving up to the third eye or brow chakra, between and slightly above the eyebrows; see or feel it spinning and glowing in indigo blue. "I am open and receptive to my intuitive guidance and trust the answers I seek are within me."

Now, bring your attention to the crown chakra at the top of your head; see a violet or pure white energy spiraling and stretching upward from your crown to a few inches or so above you. "I have a keen sense of awareness and feel connected to the universe and the life-force energy that's flowing to me."

Lastly, express your appreciation for your body functioning perfectly and keeping everything in balance.

Now try closing your eyes and visualize it. If you don't recall the color, just use a golden yellow or whatever color comes to mind. They do vary in color by individual, and your intuition will sometimes prompt you to use the one you need the most.

If you have a hard time imagining or feeling the chakra, sometimes it helps if you see yourself standing in front of you, several feet away, and see them spinning in color as you envision yourself there. Knowing it's an image of you, the subtle sensation of the chakra energy moving can be felt in your body.

It can be much easier to do it this way. Try it both ways and see which one feels better. You'll find that the more aware you become of your energy, the easier it is to see and feel them spinning.

If you want to keep it really simple, just imagine or feel that you're breathing in to each chakra. Begin at the root chakra and move upward, breathing in to each chakra, one at a time, and moving to the next one as you exhale.

Let it be easy and enjoyable, or do nothing at all. Your faith and belief in your wellbeing is keeping you aligned with it. And your inner guidance will prompt you to do anything that's helpful for you to do.

So there's no need to jump through any hoops to get there. And while this is a nice thing to do for yourself, it's not necessary *at all* for you to stay in alignment with wellbeing.

Simply feeling as good as you can feel is all you need to focus on. That alone will balance everything out, if anything needs to be. Every part of you and your life is becoming all that you want it to be!

What are five or more things I felt appreciation for today?

How do I expect tomorrow to go?

I release and let go of any imbalance in my energy, and I call back all of my pure positive energy. I am completely balanced, and it shows by the ease and flow I'm experiencing in my day. Imagine it now.

Day 22

My Body Is Transforming to Accommodate My Wishes

I am now achieving total wellbeing, no matter what has ever been before. My body has a built-in capability of bringing itself back into balance. And once it's there, I know how to keep it there.

And the experience that others are having never relates to me, so I never need to put myself in a category with anyone. Not even genetically. I'm not a statistic. I'm an individual and I respond differently to anything that occurs in my body. I also know that my body's energy can be cleared of anything that needs to be healed.

Better yet, things won't even settle into my perfectly functioning body because of the way I think and the belief I now have in my invincibility. Anything that's been before has passed and my new thoughts and beliefs are making sure of that.

Any condition that's lingered is on its way out, and I'm able to keep that thought in mind and allow things to improve while I focus on other things.

If the belief in placebos and the power of visualization can heal all kinds of health conditions for others, I can certainly practice my thoughts about all of this and allow good things to happen for me as well. And I intend to do so to achieve or maintain my completely healthy body and lock in my future health. It's already done.

And if my only desire is to have more youthful vitality or simply feel happier, I can have that too. I am focused on my blissful wellbeing and the ease and joy in my life. And that is what I'm attracting more of *every* minute of every day.

As I energetically align with a higher level of wellbeing, my body begins to respond and I see results. It happens quickly or slowly, but it's all happening. My body and the cells of my body know what to do, and they always respond to my desire, belief, and expectation.

All *I* need to do is stay out of the way, and that just means I need to keep doing what I've been doing. Breathe, relax, have fun, and focus on my wellbeing and anything and everything that brightens my day. I am now easily doing this no matter where I am or what I'm doing.

I also like to give myself permission to indulge myself endlessly when I feel the need to. Or just because I *can* and want to. Life is meant to be enjoyed. And the more lighthearted I am, the more I allow my body to feel good.

97

How does it feel to know that I'm allowing my body the comfort it needs to feel even better than it did before?

There comes a time when I notice my body is functioning at its best and I feel more relaxed, yet energized at the same time. How does it feel when I've achieved this wonderful state of being?

What are the words that describe how it feels to have a comfortable body, free of all bodily tension? How many can I think of?

____

____

____

____

____

____

____

____

____

____

And when I paint a picture of how I see my evolving body, what is changing? What's becoming? Do I have a feeling of expectation for really great things to happen for me?

With my eyes closed, I can see myself standing in front of me right now, and I have this *amazing* good-feeling body. You might even say it feels *blissful*. How would I describe it?

Write or think of several words or phrases to describe the feeling, beginning with a nice deep breath into the whole body that reaches every part of me, and start with "Oh, how I *love* when my body feels this good! I feel so ________."

And go on and on, finishing the sentence with dozens of words or phrases that come to mind about how my body *feels* and how it feels to be *in* my body and how my life is changing into an even happier and healthier place for me. I feel so _________."

____

____

____

____

____

____

____

Action: While you're able to clear any conditions by taking your attention off of it and focusing on the ease and joy in your life, it can be helpful to acknowledge some of the more stubborn issues and intend to release them.

In a sense, you're making peace with it, and the process involves talking to your pain or a stressful situation. And the issue seems to clear itself more quickly when we decide to face it. But only briefly. Long enough to say goodbye to it.

However, if you're not having any trouble with ignoring an issue and feel more focused on total wellbeing, then keep doing what you're doing and skip this step.

It's when you have trouble ignoring something where this can be helpful.

So if that sounds like you and you're open to trying it, please continue, or feel free to try it another time.

Just doing this once is enough. Afterward, just have faith whatever it is will be cleared away. And then go back to focusing on thoughts of wellbeing.

Begin by paying attention to your breath, just breathing naturally, pausing slightly between breaths, relaxing more and more.

Now tune into your body and feel if you have any area of discomfort and bring your attention there. If it's just a current situation that's causing you mild stress, think of that. If you could give it a number from 1–10, 10 being the most discomfort, what number would you give it?

Now, with the first thought that comes to mind, even if it feels like your imagination, do your best to answer the questions below. This is my version of a technique I learned in my Reiki teacher training course.

The entire time you're reading the questions or statements, remain focused on the area of discomfort or issue, and pause briefly to think of each answer. Now, bringing your attention there...

If it had a shape, what shape would it be? (known symbol or its own)
Does it have a name?
What color would it be?
If it had a texture, what texture would it have? Is it rough or smooth?
How dense would it be? Is it heavy and thick or light and spacious?
Is it a result of an imbalance in your own energy?
Or have you picked up this energy from somewhere else?
Is it here to stay for a bit or is it on its way out?
Ask if it needs more attention.
If so, what does it need?
Is there more for you to learn from it?
If it had a message for you, what would it say? What does it want you to know?
Allow an answer to come even if it feels like your imagination.
If you could say something to it now, what would you say?
Does this give you a clue about where it came from?
What words of encouragement would you give it?
Now say a few words of appreciation for how it served you; perhaps it made you give yourself the attention you deserve, and showed you how strong you can be. What would you like to say?
Lastly, you can appreciate it for the desire that grew in you for a healthier body and more joyful life.

If you feel ready, decide to let it go.
Now, imagine it has a golden sphere of light around it.
Look up, smile, and gently intend to let it go. It's safe to let it go.
Now see or feel it gently pull away from you and float away.
In your next breath, allow a shimmering pink light to fill the space it left. Each breath increases its pure positive energy.
Every exhale spreads this light to your body and extremities.
It's getting brighter and bigger until it's surrounding your body.
It's within you and around you and you're *breathing it all in.*
It expands a few feet above, below, and around you.
It's your protective shield of energy and your intention is allowing it to stay with you now.

Continue with these intentions, or state your own:
My body's responding to my thoughts and intentions.
I am changing the energy and emotion associated with this discomfort or stress.
And therefore I am now clearing any stagnant or blocked energy that may have been causing discomfort.
Any tension or unwanted condition has left me now.
Now or in the hours or days ahead, these words have set this transformation in motion. As I become ready, anything that needs to be cleared is being released, safely and gently.

Take a few breaths or a break for a moment. Do you notice any change in how you feel? If your number from 1–10 has changed, what is it now?

Another suggestion for any kind of pain or issue is to try acupressure. Just look up acupressure for anything that ails you. And always check with your physician or research it before trying it.

If applicable for you, here are a few more words on this topic:

Do your best to turn your focus to a belief in your desire and positive energy being stronger than anything that's happening right now.

Know that it can leave as quickly as it came. You're never stuck with something. Now or in the minutes or days to come, you could be saying: "My head feels lighter, my stress has lifted. The issue or discomfort is gone. And I am free of it."

You are now building positive momentum for your ideal health and wellbeing to be what you're living, and from this point, it's easy to maintain. Your unbending desire, belief, and expectation of it is making it true for you.

Now ask yourself "Why is it so easy for me to do this now? Why is it so easy for me to allow myself to let this go and know that it's safe to do so? How does it feel when I allow myself to feel better? Why is it so easy to believe and expect that I am reaching a state of blissful wellbeing now? And to believe that I deserve it? I so deserve it!"

Decide that your only focus from here on out is to remain aligned with the energy of your intrinsic nature and total wellbeing. And very importantly, to love and accept yourself. Get to know your beautiful self! You are absolutely amazing!

What are five or more things I felt appreciation for today?
How do I expect tomorrow to go?
How do I expect my body to feel? Imagine it now.

I Am an Example of Peace

Any difficulties I experienced in the past strengthened my desire for a better life. The harder it was, the stronger my desire. And some new desires were born that I didn't even know I had. For that reason, I'm always thankful for those experiences.

But right now I'm deciding that I don't need to go through anything tough for my life to become better or more wonderful. I know what I want now. I welcome new experiences that will guide me on my path to more good things, but I'll let them come to me in an easy, relaxed manner.

My feelings of joy have power over any struggle I encounter. Feelings of joy amount to a higher vibration. What if I had a *stronger* belief that my higher energy would always override any lower energy, in me or around me, and clear my path? A path that leads to much more joy.

What if I didn't have to believe it and it was just about my energy or the natural law of vibration? How much am I allowing my inner joy to fill me up, spill over, and change my circumstances? Why is it so easy for me to use this ability to transform any situation now?

What's it like to take things as they come in an easy, relaxed manner? And to know that all the while, I'm actually creating more ease in my life? When I'm in a state of peace, I'm feeling the ease and acceptance of how my day will go, and more ease or peaceful situations will find me.

By being in the qualities and energy of peace, I invite more of it into my experience. The more consistently I am in the feeling place of it, the easier my life is. And isn't it nice to know that being an example of peace and calm is creating more of it for those around me as well?

How good does it feel now that I've taken the reins and become responsible for creating an even better life for myself?

I feel that life is a gift and something to celebrate every day. I see all things from a place of inner calm, and it permeates my *entire* being. This is the energy I am giving out, and I can see that it's being returned to me.

It seems that everyone around me is going out of their way to be kind to me and to each other. I've noticed this happening more often and I believe that I'm creating this change. I radiate peace and wellbeing and its energy spreads beyond boundaries.

And no matter where I am, who I'm with, or what I'm doing, I find reasons to feel good throughout my day. That's what my life is all about now. I wouldn't have it any other way.

How did I get here? What have I been doing that has made this happen for me? When I want to align with a state of peace, what kinds of words guide me there? Right now I can take a moment to close my eyes, focus on my heart energy, and think of one word at a time until I find that feeling place.

Isn't it nice when it becomes obvious that I'm affecting the people around me with my positive energy?

I love taking the time to notice these changes in the weeks ahead, and I believe it's all due to the changes I'm making in myself.

How much better do I feel at the *end* of the day when there's been no struggle in my day at all?

With all of that being said, I still welcome anything that comes my way. As I will always know that each life experience, good or bad, has the potential for bringing me more of what I want. More strength, more growth, and a stronger desire for better times and more good things.

I also know that I'm in charge of how I feel and how I react to things, so any so-called "bad" times are easier to handle. They're also becoming nonexistent for me as I align with my true nature.

But what if one or more of those experiences leads me to bigger and better things? What if it was just a stepping stone I had to take to get to where I wanted to be?

Anything that ever feels like it's gotten me off track always leads back to the peace I feel in my heart. It stays with me wherever I go!

Action: Acknowledging and appreciating the effects of your positive energy is a great way to attract more positive outcomes for you. And don't underestimate its ability to make a difference in what's happening around you, even if it has nothing to do with you.

Do your best to notice any situations or relationships changing around you. For example, you may see two people getting along better than usual, or more cooperation among coworkers or family members.

If nothing else, enjoy the pleasant conversations or kindness you witness on a daily basis. You're creating it!

What are five or more things I felt appreciation for today?
How do I expect to feel throughout my day tomorrow? Imagine it now.

I Feel Empowered with Pure Positive Energy

I almost forget sometimes that I have an energetic body that interprets and receives information on a vibrational level. I am continuously giving out a signal that attracts similar frequencies, those of people or circumstances. And I have my emotions as a compass that tell me if one direction is better for me to go than another.

All that said, I'd rather just think of it like I get back what I give out. And I like to think that my positive thoughts, intentions, and energy are spreading more joy and wellbeing wherever I go, and even beyond that. I feel that my energy is now higher and stronger than any negative forces or energy that's around me.

What if I could think of it as a strong inner core or my inner self that I'm getting better at letting shine through?

What if the more I practiced connecting to it, the brighter it became and the farther it spread?

What if my core energy was powerful enough to reach beyond all boundaries? Is that a bit extreme? Well, it may seem so. But the image of it is vivid. And my imagination and I are boundless, as are my thoughts.

Isn't the best part that the more I radiate positive energy, the more I attract positive people, conversations, and moments throughout my day? I often tell myself that *I'm creating more and more positive moments by appreciating this one.*

And how does it feel when I know my mind, body, and spirit are in harmony? When I feel this way, there's no struggle. Anything that felt like that before has been replaced with ease, clarity, joy, and fun.

What's it like now that I'm creating a genuine feeling of blissful wellbeing? What does blissful, pure positive energy feel like to me?

Have I noticed that I can breathe in with my attention on my core or heart center or whole chest and feel like I'm breathing in something rather heavenly? It's as though there's a blanket of blissful energy being laid upon my chest.

When I intend to do this throughout my day, it helps me stay in such a good-feeling place. It really makes for a wonderful day. But the feeling is becoming natural to me whether I intend it or not. And I love knowing how healing this is to my body.

How does it feel to be so tuned in and connected to myself that it allows me to have a clear mind and feel present in whatever setting I'm in?

What's it like to be so connected to my energy and in control of it that I'm able to feel as blissful as I want to? And how does it feel to be able to release energy that doesn't serve me or weighs me down in some way?

I can just decide to release it, intend to call back my energy, and guide my thoughts to a better-feeling state. It's getting easier every day!

I love when I start seeing the results that show me how powerful my thoughts and intentions really are. Isn't it great to feel guarded and protected with positive energy?

Action: Once again, it's time to breathe into your body with the intention to allow ease and replenish your energy.

As you breathe in, you'll be putting your attention on one part of the body and feeling energy pulling in there; as you breathe out more slowly, you're allowing the entire area to feel at ease and instantly release any tension.

Start by imagining there's a glowing ball of golden light in the space in front of your eyes. Begin slowly breathing this energy into your face, exhale, and soften the entire face.

Take your time and continue energizing and softening as you breathe this golden light *in* and out of each: the eyelids, cheeks, forehead, eyebrows, and the space between the eyebrows.

Breathe the light into your throat; exhale and soften your entire neck.

Now breathing the golden light into your chest, feel that it's the most blissful energy you've ever felt. Put your heartfelt effort into conjuring the feeling of it as though it's the first time you're seeing the sun in a very long time and you're breathing it in. It's soothing and energizing you and making you feel the fullness of your vitality.

How much better can you make it feel? Try it once more.

The most blissful energy you've ever felt is accessible. It's all around you. You're breathing it in right now, *evenly, slowly, lovingly.* Your body's breathing it in for you. You feel a lightness in your chest. There's no effort. Just a grand feeling of peace and pure elation.

Allow yourself to feel the self-love and acceptance that will enhance the flow of blissful energy you feel.

Gently but quickly breathe into the chest again, in 2–3 seconds, then slowly exhale and completely release all tension in the body. Softer.

Even softer. And now slowly breathing in, feel an extra layer of blissful energy washing over you and it's pouring into your heart center. Breathe into the chest again, and double the blissful energy and ease you feel now.

Now breathe it into your ribs and allow the ease to take over you.

Breathe into your abdomen and soften it completely as you exhale.

Breathing into your hips, energizing and softening more and more.

Then breathing light into your back and kidney area, and exhale, completely releasing any and all tension. Body, show me how it feels when I allow myself to feel blissful ease and wellbeing in my back. It's softer now, and energy is flowing there.

You're now experiencing an increase of circulation throughout your back, your body, and all your extremities. Your intention is doing this, along with your breath.

Continue breathing, energizing and softening your legs, your feet, and come back up to your arms, the palms of your hands, and once more to your face. Intend to breathe in and out at each area.

Breathing into your body now, you feel blissful energy washing over you, and it's pouring into every cell of your body. As you exhale, your entire body relaxes. Settle your attention on your heart center now and thank your body for the blissful wellbeing it continues to show you each and every day.

Give yourself a moment to relax and feel the energy. Try closing your eyes and breathing into your face, chest, and abdomen once more, if desired. It may help you feel the energy more.

And now it's time to begin practicing another hand mudra today that you can try now and include in your daily meditation or breathing exercise, if desired. Avoid doing this any time you have a cold or cough.

Begin by getting comfortable and resting the back of your hands on your legs and placing your hands in the Prana mudra position with the tip of the thumb touching the tip of the ring and little finger, and keep the index and middle finger straight and gently extended.

Simply put, the Prana mudra is felt to energize the body. It recharges the inactive energy in the body, and is said to promote healing of over a hundred disorders. It is felt to restore balance, increase longevity, clarity and confidence, and relieve fatigue and depression.

Amazingly, it's also said to help correct vitamin deficiencies, impurities in the blood, and improve eye health. Just imagine what else it can do. And mudras have been practiced for so long, it's origin is considered prehistoric.

The fingers used in this mudra connect the earth, water, and fire elements of the body and stimulates the root chakra at the base of the spine. This generates heat that awakens the organs and revitalizes the body's energy.

To achieve the best results, practice the mudra daily for a minimum of fifteen minutes and up to 45 minutes, while sitting or walking or lying down. It's also important to stay tuned in to your breath.

Do your best to hold the belief that you're able to free yourself of any struggle and achieve blissful wellbeing on a daily basis. If not now, in time you will. Allow yourself to feel the pure positive energy and wellbeing that is available and continually flowing to you.

What are five or more things I felt appreciation for today?
How do I expect tomorrow to go?
How do I expect to feel? Imagine it now.

I Know What to Do When Life Gets Stressful

Begin today's intentions with your arms folded with the right hand on the ribs and the left hand on the side of the arm. Unfold them any time you wish.

I am ready for anything that life brings my way. I am in control of my emotions and armed with intentions. Anything that presents as a potential issue doesn't last long. It never has a chance to. I know what to do.

And the more I practice all of this, the less of a problem anything is. There comes a time when nothing stresses me. And it feels fantastic. I am reaffirming right now that I am making a life of effortless ease my new lifestyle.

There are a few things I like to do each day that have proven to be helpful in setting myself up for a great day and better times ahead.

I ensure that I'll have the best day possible when I do this before I get out of bed, or just after:

> I enjoy a few minutes or more of meditation or deep breathing.
> I consciously make the choice to have a wonderful day.
> I set intentions for how my day will go and think of the words that will describe it.
> I do my own ritual, or the energy protection routine where I connect to the earth, universe, and nature, then call back my energy, and seal and protect it with my intention.

I also like to prepare in advance in case anything ever comes up that I find even the least bit frustrating. It doesn't have much of a chance to throw me off when I'm ready for it. I only have to think this through once and recall it if needed. So if something ever comes up that feels uncomfortable:

> Before I respond I'll take a deep breath and remind myself that I'm in charge of how I feel and how I react to things. And that feeling good is what matters most to me.

> I'll remind myself that what I put my focused attention on will get bigger. So if I resist it or let it frustrate me for long, more things like it can show up for me.

> And since I can't control what's happening but I *can* control how I feel about it, I'll take my focus off the problem and spend time thinking of a solution.

There's always a solution. If I just think of what I really want the outcome to be, the solution will come to me.

And sometimes the solution is just finding a different way to look at the situation that helps me feel better about it in some way. And I can always think about something else if it's an option.

Then I ask myself if this issue will matter later on, or if I just hold on a little longer, will it work itself out and improve on its own? Especially if I believe it will and expect it to!

And I'll remember that when I respond positively to a stressful situation with kindness, respect, patience, or tolerance, others tend to follow my lead.

Any time I change the way I usually respond to someone or a situation, it will automatically create a change in the outcome. And every interaction thereafter will feel better and easier.

And I *love* believing that things always turn out well for me. I also like to believe that things will go well for everyone involved.

Now I know this and don't have to try and think of it when confronted with a stressful situation. It's instilled in my mind and comes to me the moment I need it. And I decided that after this day I will no longer allow stress to take over me, if ever. I won't allow it.

Are there any situations happening right now that are causing stress or concerns? Read the questions below and see if a solution comes to me. It's okay to read them without answering and allow my intuitive guidance to provide an answer in the days to come.

Is it something I can step back from and let it work itself out?

Does it involve me, or am I making someone else's problem my own?

Is this a time when I could wish them well and put myself and my feelings first?

Is it something that I can at least take a couple days to sort out?

What if I busied myself with something easy and fun and let the answers come?

If I could decide right now to do something that I would enjoy and would get my mind off of it, what would that be?

How does it feel to give myself permission to let it go for now and see what happens?

What if taking the pressure off myself puts me in a much better mindset? And what if that's the only way I'll be able to hear the answers I'm seeking?

Can I work this issue out and still allow myself to be at ease and in the flow of abundance that's available to me? I believe I can. And that's right where I want to be. The best outcomes arise from here.

Why is it so easy for me to let this stuff go now?

What does it feel like to be free of it?

And how does it feel to know that I can affect future outcomes in such a positive way?

And that I'm doing this all for me, and the betterment of my future?

When did I start making how I feel so important to me?

Why is it so easy for me to give myself permission to feel good now?

How does it feel to know that when I'm past this phase, things are even better for me? I've evolved from it. It inspired new ideas and a stronger desire in me for things to be better.

I soon feel clearer, lighter and brighter, and at times a wonderful feeling of elation. Total relief.

Action: Have faith in your ability to cope with any stress that comes your way. Not only getting by, but handling it brilliantly. Let your creativity fly when it comes to finding the best ways to gracefully maneuver your way through life and the many personalities and situations that come with it.

But find relief in knowing that your positive thoughts build positive momentum and are always attracting the circumstances you wish for. If you're determined to do whatever it takes to have more fun, everything will naturally work out for you.

You are now becoming free of any potential struggle. It may seem unlikely, but your belief is making it so. If not now, there will come a day when you look at everything with an eye for the potential positive outcome it offers you.

What are five or more things I felt appreciation for today?
How do I expect tomorrow to go?
How much easier can I allow it to be? Imagine it now.

I Have a Natural Ability to Create Positive Change

It's time to be in a state of blissful wellbeing.

When I say "it's time to do" something, for me that means that I've decided to make it happen. I'm beginning to create it right then in the moment I make the statement. It's getting done. It's going to be a part of me.

And sometimes I just say it to myself to remind me that it's what I'm working toward. But in my mind, I'm not only working on it, it's already become my state of being. It's already been decided, and it's already become who I am. The belief in having it makes it so.

Upon deciding it, I practice living in the feeling place of it. I'm always in the vicinity of it. It's my primary thought pattern.

Having all of this as my practiced thought makes for an even stronger belief in my total blissful wellbeing, and soon I am seeing the signs of being in full alignment with it.

So in terms of my wellbeing, I know that I'm in charge of how I feel now, maybe more than ever. You could say I have authority over my mind and body. My body responds to my requests.

I love being in charge of how I feel. And I know all kinds of simple yet powerful ways to feel my very best. And I love knowing that everything I've been doing has a direct effect on my overall health and happiness.

I am now achieving some really positive changes and everything keeps getting better. It's all becoming so natural to me now.

I have a natural ability to:

> Use my words, intentions, energy, and imagination to create anything I desire.
> Guide myself into a state of ease or wellbeing or anything I wish.
> Release any resistance and redirect any thoughts as I need to.
> Keep up my energy or recharge it as desired.
> Work with my energy and intention to create more energy, clarity, happiness, and wellbeing, or a healing response by the body for ease or pain relief, or anything I desire.
> Instruct my body on how I want to feel and allow it to respond to my wishes.

And sometimes I do that by just asking myself a simple question like; "How does it feel to feel better?"

Asking questions is a great way to shift my energy to feel how I want to feel. Just the suggestion posed by the question alone is enough to get a response. Let's practice again right now.

How does it feel when the energy in and around my head is lighter and freer?
Stay here for a moment and ask the question again.
Do I notice my chest getting lighter at the thought of it? Is my head feeling lighter as well?
How does it feel when I allow myself to relax?
How does it feel to be completely at ease right now?
How does it feel to allow myself to let go of any tension in my forehead?
What if I could lift any heaviness off of my head?
What if I imagined a magnet collecting unwanted thoughts and pulling away any heavier energy there?
Can my body show me how that feels?
And how does it feel to be full of energy and vitality?
How does it feel to double my energy?
And when I wish to double my clarity, how does that feel?
What if I decided that my memory would improve and believed it was entirely possible, and it became as good as I believed it would be?
What if I looked in the mirror every day and said I look and feel younger every day, and made it so?
What if intending to breathe energy into the face and body was creating more youthful skin?
What if spending time in meditation was reversing my age as they say it can?

What if I think it feels strange to think of things like this? If I don't ever need it, I'm better for it. Maybe it's just nice to know it's something I can try if I ever want to.

I also like knowing that whenever I wish to make positive changes, I can simply decide with some determination that I am going to stop or start doing something or improve it in some way or another. The way to make this work for me is just about guiding my thoughts to a point where I believe that anything I say I'm going to do, I'm going to make happen.

If it's important enough to me, I will. And it's taken care of without any further effort on my part. I believe it and it's done. And sometimes I add visualization to help things along. I am able to see the vision of what I want and create it. And ideas on how to achieve it will come.

Another great way I've become more in charge of the positive changes in my life is to decide I want to do something and use it along with intention, belief, and a trigger or anchor to initiate it. For example:

Whenever I tap on this, it means I'll instantly have more energy.
Whenever I squeeze this, it means I'll become calm and relaxed.
Whenever I touch these fingers together, I will have instant clarity.
Whenever I hold this middle finger, I will release my frustration.
When I count to 3 and say this word, I will feel relief of pain or stress.
Whenever I smell that scent, it automatically puts me in a state of bliss.

I just have to "program" the action I'm doing or word I'm using by applying it once I get to the feeling place I desire. Once the feeling is locked in, I can then use the trigger the next time I wish to feel that way.

How does it feel to allow myself to let go of any preconceived notions about myself and just decide to allow my natural wellbeing to flow?

When did I decide that it was safe to let go of anything that no longer served me?

Why has it become so effortless for me to intend something I want and have my circumstances change almost immediately?

When did it start getting easy for me to quickly release tension in my body? Or any other condition?

How does it feel to have released all resistance?

And when did I get so good at intending for my body to feel something or let go of something and have it instantly?

Why is it getting so easy for me to see all my potential for having my mind and body feel the way I want it to? And not just on occasion, but always?

Why does it feel like every wish I've ever had is getting granted?

With all of these tools that I have learned or known myself, and most of all because of the knowledge within me, I know how to change or improve or create anything I wish to.

I no longer underestimate my ability to create anything I wish. My body is as energetic as I believe it is. My mind is as brilliant as I believe it is. My life is as great as I choose it to be.

I am putting the time in, nurturing myself and my beliefs, and more good things are coming to me. They're always coming, but now they're coming sooner and more often.

Action: How do you want to feel right now? What are you feeling like now, and what would you prefer to be feeling, if any different? Now ask yourself how that would feel? How does it feel when I allow myself to_______?

Close your eyes and ask that question again and give your body time to respond.

Now pick one feeling you'd like to "arm" yourself with. In other words, pick a feeling you wish you could have ready in a moment of need. For instance, confidence to say what you mean when speaking to someone you're not always comfortable sharing your true feelings with. Or it could be a feeling of motivation or productivity.

Then choose a trigger point or word to lock or anchor it in.

Next, either do what you can to feel your way into that feeling state, or wait until you're in it. For example, if you were working on something and feeling super motivated and being extra productive, take a moment when you're at the height of that feeling, and pick a word that symbolizes it, or choose a finger to squeeze.

Then you would say the word or squeeze the finger and set your intention. Something like: "I am now feeling the amazing energy of this and I am locking this feeling in."

Any time I want to call this feeling back to me, I will think of this word and squeeze this finger, and my mind and body will recall this energy and state of mind for me. I will be just as productive as I am now, or more so."

Your body can learn to associate the action with the feeling and bring it back. For best results, make your intention very sincere and be determined to call the feeling back to you as needed.

Consider writing down the feeling you want to recall and the word or action and feel your way there or wait until it's happening. Good luck!

On that note, here's a final intention or just more practice finding a better-feeling place.

I am now breathing deeply, and it feels as though my entire body is breathing. The life-force energy that pervades all things is now flowing to me and through me and reaching every part of me. I am now feeling wellbeing flowing, and I am receiving light in every cell in my body. The energy around my head and heart is feeling lighter and freer. Read it again or think of more thoughts like this if you'd like to keep it going.

What are five or more things I felt appreciation for today?
How do I expect tomorrow to go?
How much more blissful can I feel? Imagine it now.

I Maintain My Wellbeing

When I practice a state of wellbeing, it's a part of me and I believe in it.

When I believe in my total wellbeing, I have an invincible mindset. I'm aligned with my natural-born energy of blissful wellbeing, and I do my best to *stay* aligned with it.

But every once in a while, I like to check in and see how I'm doing. And before I raise any question about it, I remind myself that I fully accept myself *wherever* I am. If I'm going to go there, I'm going to do it free of any pressure or guilt. *Always.*

I am where I am and doing pretty great, actually. And guilt can hold me apart from my true desires. So I decided a while ago that any guilt I ever felt has been lifted from all areas of my life.

I am now achieving all my desires, free of limiting thoughts. I am and will always be in my most wonderful state of mind. This is my powerful intention.

So, with a desire to maintain wellbeing, what kind of questions should I ask myself when checking in to see how I'm doing? What's the first one that comes to mind?

How about: what actions am I taking to keep moving forward? Have I made any changes in my life to help improve or maintain my health and happiness?

____

____

____

____

What am I doing now in my daily routine to feel more ease?

____

____

____

____

Have I created any *new* habits that inspire or cause me to feel more joy?

____

____

____

____

Have I let go of any habits that no longer feel aligned with my desires or how I envision myself?

____

____

____

____

How is my body feeling? Have there been any noticeable changes in how I feel?

Am I feeling less stressed, if ever? Do I feel a comfortable ease in my body?

Am I experiencing a calmer, clearer mind?

What are my routine thoughts? What is my focused attention on?

____

____

____

How am I doing at guiding my thoughts?

Do I remind myself often to redirect any unwanted thoughts? Am I getting better at catching it when it's happening?

Have I been following any impulses to get up, go out, or spoil myself in some way?

Am I doing pretty good at putting my needs and desires first, other than necessary family wishes or obligations?

Have I been ignoring any needs or wants of my own?

If I ever have stress or discomfort, am I doing something about it sooner than later? Do I take time to breathe, walk, rest, or massage it? Or ask someone else to?

When a potentially stressful situation comes up, do I remember to focus on a solution rather than the problem?

What do I believe about my state of wellbeing or what am I beginning to believe? What am I expecting to happen?

____

____

____

Am I giving myself credit when I notice how well I'm doing? Do I acknowledge or appreciate it in some way?

When I reach any milestones, big or small, am I celebrating them? Do I allow myself to get excited and happy about it?

Now that I've thought that through, how do I feel about where I'm at? Take a moment now to reflect on any areas that I feel really good about. I feel really good about:

____

____

____

If I want to feel my way into a state of *believing* that I am maintaining my total wellbeing, what kinds of things can I say to get myself there?

If I close my eyes right now and think of this, what are the words that describe how it feels to me, one word or phrase at a time?

____

____

____

My consistent thoughts become my beliefs and my reality, so I like to practice the feeling of blissful wellbeing. It's like I'm telling the story of how I wish it to be, but then I notice how natural it becomes for me to feel that way.

How did I get started? How did I get myself to believe it? To have it become my only thought in my conscious and subconscious mind? And to feel the truth of it in my heart?

For one thing I tell myself something like this every single day:

> I have *such* a strong immune system.
> My body and all its systems are functioning *perfectly*.
> I love my body and my body loves me.
> Body, *thank you* for the wellbeing.
> And thank you, to *all* my cells, for the wellbeing!

In the beginning I was saying it at the same time I did another habit so I wouldn't forget. Like every time I got in bed or got out of bed.

With practice, I started thinking of it all the time. And that's how it took over any worrisome thought I ever had before. It's *fantastic!*

I am now maintaining my wellbeing by consistently guiding my thoughts to better-feeling states. My thoughts are turning to things and creating my reality.

So, I easily stay aligned with wellbeing. I am now completely well, or in the state of becoming completely well no matter what.

When I have the desire for blissful wellbeing, believe I can have it, and practice the feeling of it, it must become my reality. And the reason I'm practicing it until I've achieved it is because I know how good it feels. And I love feeling good.

What are some other words I would like to say to myself or keep circulating in my mind?

I love that my body __________.

I have faith in my body to __________.

I can achieve __________ in my mind and body.

I am now achieving more __________.

I am now achieving a state of __________.

I am now aligning with a state of __________, __________, and __________.

My mind is __________.

My body is __________.

My wellbeing gets easier to maintain every day because _______________.

I will be doing more __________, __________, and __________ to help me stay aligned with it.

I practice the mindset and feeling of being *blissfully* well. I do it so often that it's become natural and it's just who I am. I don't have to remind myself after I've done this. These are the words that I was meant to be thinking from the time I was born.

All I need to do is think of anything I can tell myself that inspires me to believe it. To believe that blissful wellbeing is available to me. To believe that it's truly my natural state that only needs to be called back to me. And then do *everything* I can to keep that belief in my heart. I love talking myself into things that are *so* very good for me! And it's true. Because I said so!

Action: There are many ways to detect your body's energy and guide or direct it with intention. There's one way you might find interesting that seems to bring your energy back into balance or can even relieve discomfort.

So to sense your body's energy, you're going to tune in and see how aligned it feels with your core energy. Think of your core energy in whatever way it feels to you; it may feel like your spine or the area between your navel and your heart center or a core or beam from head to toe.

Don't give any real meaning to the results. Just think of it as another great way to connect with your energy and feel more in tune with your body. And it's a quick exercise. Once you read through the steps, the whole process should only take a minute.

When you're able to, try standing with your feet just a few inches apart or where you're comfortable.

> With your eyes closed, bring your attention to your core or center of your body and sense where that is for you.

> Then put your attention on the very outer edge of your left ear for a couple seconds, then your right ear, and again on your left, then right.

> Try and detect if one side feels farther away, or if it feels like the same distance from your center.

> If necessary, go back and forth a couple more times to determine if there's any difference.

> If either side seems *farther* away; use your imagination and intention to guide or pull the energy over or inward toward the center. And then more gently or briefly intend to gather the other side as well.

Feel as though you're gently coaxing the energy to gather in the center and intend to bring it back into balance. It's almost like you're waving it over, but it may feel differently to you.

Before moving down, always take your focus back to your center.

Then try it again on the shoulders, waist, and hips.

If they feel about the same on each side, great. Just intend to release any unwanted energy, if any, and call back all of your energy.

If you did notice one or more areas feeling off, check in again, beginning with the ears. See if it feels more balanced.

It's possible to see positive results from this, such as clearing an achy shoulder just by intending to direct the energy in this way.

Well done! Sometimes it can take practice to sense the energy, but it often surprises people when they check back in and something has changed.

And now for more "homework." During the first minute or so of your daily meditation, put your attention on the center of your mind or the space in front of your eyes. And for each inhale or exhale, smile to yourself and think of one of these words: ease, joy, wellbeing. So breathing in, think "ease," breathing out, think "joy," and breathing in, think "wellbeing."

Allow it to instill the feeling of what each of these mean to you. Just hearing the words will do this, so there's no need to think about it. See how you or your body feels afterward.

It's just another way to guide your thoughts or train your subconscious mind to think only thoughts of wellbeing. Remember, you're doing whatever it takes to feel as good as you can feel until you're in a state of *blissful* wellbeing *all* day, *every* day.

And with more practice, it comes naturally to you again. Like it was when you were a happy-go-lucky child. Or hopefully it's the way you've always been.

Either way, if it ever feels overwhelming or like you're trying too hard, just let yourself be. Know that you're doing the best you can, and you're doing it *all* very well. No matter where you're at, it's just right.

What are five or more things I felt appreciation for today?
How do I expect tomorrow to go?
How do I expect to feel? Imagine it now.

I Am in the Qualities & Energy of Blissful Wellbeing

Why is it so easy for me to be in a state of blissful wellbeing now? How did I get here?

I set my intentions, released some old beliefs, and found a place of ease. I'm taking time to purposely increase my energy and clarity, nurture myself, and practice a state of wellbeing. And I always focus on the end result of how I want to look and feel.

And I decided that I am now in the qualities and characteristics and energy of my blissful wellbeing. I remind myself daily of what these qualities are.

Basically, I follow what I believe is required for me to achieve more ease, energy, clarity, and joy.

What are the qualities or characteristics that I'm in or intend to be in? Write them down or think of them now. Include actions like smiling, laughing, or choosing to feel as good as I can feel.

____

____

What else am I choosing to be or have or do from this point forward? Finish the sentences below, giving as many answers as I'd like for each one.

From now on, with the best of my intentions:

I *choose* to feel _______.

I choose to be more _______.

I choose to have more _______.

I choose to enjoy more _______.

I choose to do more _______.

I will do my best to _______.

I am really good at _______.

I am excited about _______.

I am ready for _______.

I am now achieving _______.

I decided, and it's done. And I intend to keep it going.

How does it feel when I'm in a state of blissful wellbeing, with my body, mind, and spirit in harmony with one another?

What's it like to have a clear mind, a comfortable body, and understand the true meaning of being in the joy of who I am?

When I'm feeling blissful every morning and letting it carry me through my day, what's it like to live that way?

And how do I feel at the end of the day when everything's gone my way?

How does it feel to close my eyes right now and imagine what it's like to be there and be living it? What does it look and feel like?

What would be happening with my home life? Or my career or social life? Think of this now.

I am in the qualities and characteristics and energy of blissful wellbeing. It's who I am now.

I am an example of wellbeing to others, and love to spread joy. I cherish and respect myself. I feel at ease, confident, and able to have positive interactions with anyone I meet. The thoughts or ideas I share are in keeping with my true desire for wellbeing.

Action: Say these words slowly and repeatedly as you breathe in and out and put your attention on your heart center. If you'd like, set a timer for five minutes or longer. Give yourself enough time to feel it and enjoy it! "Mind, body, and spirit: it's time to work together in harmony. Show me how it feels when I allow myself to feel blissful." Breathe; repeat.

What are five or more things I felt appreciation for today?
How do I expect tomorrow to go?
How will I feel? Imagine it now.

I Am Focused & Unstoppable in My Spirit of Peace & Wellbeing

I am practicing the feeling of anything I wish to achieve until I make it mine. I'm taking the path to my greatest joy and wellbeing. And I know I deserve it!

Why am I feeling so certain that everything in my life is becoming better every day in every way?

Why am I starting to feel so good?

Why do I feel more at ease in my body now?

What is making me feel lighter and brighter?

When did I become so clear-minded?

Why is it suddenly so easy for me to release unwanted thoughts and beliefs?

Why am I able to be so mindful and present in nearly every moment now?

How did I get to have so much more energy?

How does it feel to allow myself to feel good all the time?

When did I start feeling so focused and unstoppable in my spirit of peace and wellbeing?

I am on a magnificent life-changing journey that's ongoing. I will never be the same. I am moving upward and onward. It can only get better.

I am creating positive change with my natural abilities.

If I speak of myself, I only share the thoughts of wellbeing that I'm focused on.

You see, *I become the way I see myself...*

And what I believe I can be, I can be.

My thoughts have energy and power to change everything, as I wish it to be.

What are some powerful words I can use to describe myself when I'm feeling focused and unstoppable in my spirit of peace and wellbeing?

When I am feeling focused and unstoppable in my spirit of peace and wellbeing:

> All that I desire is flowing to me as I transform my thoughts.
> All that I desire is flowing to me as I believe in me.
> All that I desire is flowing to me as I believe in my wellbeing.
> All that I desire is flowing to me as I make it a part of me.
> This blissful feeling of wellness is a part of who I am.
> I feel it flowing to me, and I expect it to keep flowing to me.
> I made peace with myself and anything I ever allowed to cause me worry.
> I only associate myself with words of wellness now.
> I am focused on blissful wellbeing and feeling fully aligned with it.
> I am an example of joy and wellbeing to others.
> And when I decide to achieve any goal and practice the feeling of what I want as though it's mine right now, it becomes so.

Now, continue this with any words I wish to add, for as long as it feels good.

Action: Practice this train of thought as much as possible! If you're already feeling as well as you deserve to feel, good for you!

What are five or more things I felt appreciation for today?
How do I expect tomorrow to go?
How will I feel? Imagine it now.

Day 30

1-2-3: I Feel Ease

As you read this day's intentions, do your best to feel these words are true for you. Take your time, breathe deeply, and allow yourself to feel good.

1-2-3, Mind and Body, it's time to feel blissful wellbeing. Show me how it feels when I allow it to flow.

I can hear these words resonate in the center of my mind and know they're a part of me now. They describe what is now becoming my reality.

You *could* say I've reached a nonresistant place of peace in my mind and body. I am feeling *completely* at ease in my body and my mind is clear. Life is becoming incredibly easy.

I easily make choices that are aligned with my desire for blissful wellbeing. Is there any fun in that? Oh, yes! That means I only do what I love to do, and feel more joyful than *anything* else. And there are *no* rules. *That's* my only rule.

And I know it's just going to keep getting better. I truly feel energetically aligned with such a blissful feeling that I'm not even sure it's describable. If I had to come up with some words, it would go something like this:

I am feeling *so* much more at ease with myself and the way things are, it makes me want *more* of it. As I find more ease, I am gaining greater focus, and that is turning to *full-on* clarity.

Now I'm experiencing so much clarity that I have made room for more positive energy and brilliant ideas to flow.

I am now creating a clear knowing of all that I desire, and it's growing. I am feeling *so* good that I know I'll *never* settle for anything less. And I'm so happy about that. I am finally allowing my life to *flourish* in whatever way I wish.

Body, how does it feel now that I've allowed myself to release all resistance?
How does it feel to have *so* much energy flowing to me and through me that I *always* feel ready for my day?
How does it feel now that I've allowed myself to relax and feel *blissful*? I am now so relaxed that *every* part of me is feeling blissful.

My head and neck and shoulders are so relaxed they feel weightless.

My chest feels lighter than ever, inside and out.
Even...lighter.
My abdomen is softening with ease.
My upper, middle, and lower back is completely at ease now.
Even...softer.
My hips are releasing any tension.
And now my legs are so light I can barely feel them.
And breathing into my feet, I can almost feel tingling in my toes as I take my attention there.
My body is capable of more ease. Body, double my ease.
And I feel my body getting even softer, and my insides are feeling buoyant.
It's almost as though I could be floating.

And now I'd like more energy. Body, show me how it feels when I allow myself to breathe in deeply and double my energy and feel more blissful.

I want to feel the energy flowing into the crown of my head, flowing into my head, neck, shoulders, arms, chest, abdomen, hips, legs, and feet, right down to my toes.

And now it's time to do a wave breath. I place my left hand on my abdomen and right hand on my chest. As I breathe in and out of my nose, I feel my abdomen and chest rise and fall.

I follow my breath moving upward from my abdomen, to my heart center, to my upper chest, and feel a slight lift in my shoulders.

And then I follow my exhale down from my chest, to the heart center, and back to the abdomen. I'm taking a few more breaths like this until I'm feeling very relaxed.

In a moment I'm going to count to three as I breathe in and say the word "ease" as I exhale. And when I say that it means that in that moment I've decided that I'm allowing myself to feel completely at ease and allow my wellbeing to flow.

My body will feel relaxed and energized at the same time, and completely free of resistance the moment I say it. And my mind will be clear and my head will feel lighter.

And now, if desired, I'm going to place my palms together in a prayer pose and very gently push my thumb knuckles into my chest right in the center on the breast bone about two inches above the sternum.

Pressing the palms together like this connects the right and left hemispheres of the brain and is a natural way to relieve stress and anxiety. And the acupressure point I'm pressing on is known as the sea of tranquility. I may feel an immediate release of tension or stress when pressing on it.

And if I'm feeling really good at this moment and I want to lock this feeling in to call it back any time I wish: I breathe in to the count of three and think of the word "ease" being stretched for as long as I exhale (Eeeease). Begin breathing in 1-2-3, think **"Ease"** with a longer exhale. Again 1-2-3 **Ease**. Repeat a few more times if desired.

Now I can relax my hands again. I'm going to close my eyes and take another breath as I count to three…nice…slow…deep breath…and as I exhale, say the words "ease and energy" with the intention that I'm soothing and energizing my body at the same time. Do this now.

Like a button that switches on and off, I can recall this feeling any time I wish. Just by repeating 1-2-3 **Ease** or pressing on the sea of tranquility acupressure point. I am in charge of how I feel and this is a way to train my mind to feel any way I wish. My body will respond to this cue from this moment on.

Action: If you're feeling pretty good, intend for this feeling of ease to stay with you throughout the remainder of your day. And practice calling it back to you anytime you wish.

You can also try imagining the word "ease" over an area of discomfort to relieve tension, such as seeing it over the forehead for a headache. With practice, you'll see that you can instantly release tension there and in seconds feel it getting lighter.

Try it with and without the 1-2-3 breath and see which works best. It's a great way to induce some clarity as well! You can even use 1-2-3 **"Clarity"** as your word. All you need to do is have the desire for it, the belief and expectation of it working, and a sincere intention, and then remember to use it.

Try seeing or feeling it written over any area of tension you have right now, if any. And now or in the next hour or so, see if you notice any change there. With practice, your body will respond to the words on command and bring you right to that good-feeling place.

But at first you might want to try aiming for the next best feeling from where you are. So if you're feeling great, aim high. If you're feeling a lot of discomfort for any reason, just let your intention be simply to feel better than you do in that moment. And keep leveling up from there to feel better and better. And *know that you will*.

You can use this process to help you achieve any state of mind for any purpose. You just need to practice the feeling state you desire and then pick any word or hand mudra or other action to anchor or lock it in at the moment your feeling has peaked.

You'll be able to say the word and immediately recall the feeling you intended it to have. Your body associates the feeling with that word and it responds on command.

It can help you achieve more ease, clarity, energy, happiness, and even abundance. Anything, really. But for best results, practice one at a time for at least a few weeks or so.

One last intention of the day for you: if not now, this process will work for me with practice. I will get there as my belief gets stronger. When I believe in my ability to change how I feel at any given moment, this comes easily to me.

And now is a great time to picture yourself in front of you once again in the image of the healthy, happy, thriving body you have or are now achieving. Your desire and intentions have already made it vibrationally available for you to align with. Yay!

How does it feel to be a vibrational match to blissful wellbeing? Why is it so easy for me to keep this going now?

Now that I've practiced the feeling of it more frequently, I've activated a healing response, and wellbeing is in full flow.

It's always flowing, and now I've become more receptive to it.

How does it feel to know that I am now achieving a state of blissful wellbeing?

Anything I do that gets me closer to it is a step in that direction.

Why is it so easy for me to feel the wellbeing flowing to me now?

And where did I get all of this energy from?

How does it feel to know that my body is transforming to accommodate my wishes and desires?

Why is it so easy for me to achieve blissful wellbeing now?

Keep asking questions like this until it becomes your expectation that it's inevitably becoming your reality. There's no need to answer. Your body will respond. Your energy will respond. Your inner being will answer.

Without any effort on your part, the answers or ideas that will help you get there will come. It might be in the days ahead, in your dreams, or any time you allow yourself to be at ease.

And your body naturally responds to this, as well as your belief in your wellbeing. And the more ease you feel, the more quickly your body can heal *or* maintain wellbeing.

Try it for the next seven days. And again and again until it becomes a habit and you start to see results. There's your new challenge. Can you keep asking: "Why is it so easy for me to feel blissful?" You may never want to stop.

If any of the actions during Step 1 felt really good to you, consider marking the pages and continuing to do them.

Please note: now that you've had a few weeks of practice writing daily thoughts of appreciation, there will no longer be any reminders for it. So do your best to continue the practice. If you haven't begun to notice the benefits of doing it, you will! Have trust.

What did you learn and how do you feel after completing this step?

Has anything changed (*your energy, thoughts, or feelings about something*), or have you experienced any stress or pain relief? If not now, you will in time; have faith and keep moving forward! I believe in you!

From this point forward, do your best to be in the energy of pure positive energy and total wellbeing. Expect it, and feel it's a part of you.

What's Next

And now you're ready for Step 2...

The next 30 days will be focused on a feeling of love, appreciation, and personal freedom.

Step 2

I Choose to Feel Happy & Free

The purpose of this step is to practice more consistent thoughts of love and appreciation until:

> You feel good all day, every day, no matter what's happening around you.
> You're free of any of life's big or little struggles.
> You love and accept yourself completely.
> You feel appreciation for anything you pay attention to.
> You're aligned with your true nature and confidently sharing that side of you.
> You feel happy and free and in harmony with who you are and with all that is.

This is you taking the lead and guiding yourself on your path to so much more joy. Even in the most challenging of times, there's always a way to see everything in your life from the perspective of your core being or inner light, which is all love.

So do your best to allow yourself to feel better than ever about yourself and your life, and set yourself free. And you'll know what I mean by that by the end of this step.

If desired, set this intention for the next thirty days, or create your own:

> I intend to let go of any stressful emotions and focus on positive thoughts that make me feel happy and free.
> I intend to become better at being my own best friend.
> I intend to appreciate my life and all it brings.
> I intend to align with my true nature and raise my vibration even higher.
> I intend to set myself free and be as happy as I can be.
> I am now creating a life I love more every day!

Take one day at a time and let your goal be to feel good from morning to night. This is not about waiting for a half-hour yoga class to relieve stress at the end of your day. This is about making it your new lifestyle to be as present and joyful as possible in every moment.

And know that it's absolutely possible for you to feel *that* good. You're able to achieve your natural state of blissful wellbeing. Truly! And if you're already there, even better.

But if not, isn't it nice to know what you have to look forward to? You're feeling so fortunate to be who you are and to be living your life, that *everything* feels better. You're feeling happy and free as you were born to be. And you deserve to feel that good!

Day 31

I Was Born to Be Happy & Free

I choose to feel happy and free, as I was born to be. I am meant to be enjoying life in whatever way I can and feeling free to be me. I want to feel that I am safe and belong wherever I am. Even though I may be there most of the time, I'm always open to feeling better. There's no limit whatsoever to the level of happiness I can feel.

True happiness is whatever it means to me. Generally, I would say it means that I'm feeling deeply satisfied with my life. I'd even say downright giddy.

My primary purpose is to be in the joy of who I am, allow myself to keep moving forward, and expand through my love of life. The better I feel, the more I wonder why I would ever settle for anything less.

And what does freedom mean to me? It could mean that I'm free of all struggle. I am free of worry, fear, guilt, resentment, or resistance of *any* kind. It's a feeling of being at ease in my body and feeling free to be myself. It's being free of the desire to control what happens.

And it can be a feeling of trust and certainty that everything is working out in my life and in the world. And all of that can result in a feeling of personal freedom.

Can I see myself letting go of any desire to control things, and just go with the flow more? What's the first thing I would let go of that I seem to always have the urge to control or change outside of myself? Can I think of something now?

How do I feel when I've allowed myself to release *any and all* resistance and feel free to be myself? Think of the words or phrases that would describe the feeling I wish to have.

If I could tune in to myself and receive clear intuition to help me know more of who I am and what I want, what's the first question I would ask? Think of this now.

What if I could change everything just by wholeheartedly loving and accepting myself as I am? What if everything I wanted in life fell into place, simply by doing that?

What's the first self-doubting thought I would let go of? And what is one positive belief I'd like to have about myself right now? Think of each question and what answer first comes to mind.

When it comes to being happy, what do I want? How do I feel when I'm deeply satisfied? If I'm feeling really happy right now, or if I close my eyes and think of a time or place that makes me feel happy, how does it feel? Think of the words that would describe it in detail.

Is there anything in particular I'd like to feel happier about? On a scale of 1–10, 10 being the most satisfied, what score would I give my home life ___, work ___, social life ___, personal time ___, or hobbies ___?

What is my overall goal for the level of satisfaction I wish to achieve in my life?

It's time to start consistently and purposely choosing the words and thoughts that create the most wonderful life for me. What words would I say right now if I knew it would come into existence and create an immediate change for the better? What is my wish?

What encouraging words can I give myself to achieve my goal of attaining more happiness and freedom? Let's see how convincing I can be about my ability to feel happier than I do right now.

What kind of thoughts will guide me to a happier feeling place? Even happier than I am right now?

Anything I desire to have in my life are things that I believe will make me happy. And as I allow myself to feel happy and free more of the time, I easily match the energy of my desires and allow them to manifest more quickly.

I am deciding right now that happiness is always available to me. There's nothing to wait for. No situation has to change in order for me to be happy. Right now I'm focusing on feeling happy and free and letting it be.

If need be, I can turn my attention away from things I don't like. Either way, I will always choose to focus on what I *am* happy about, and then all my desires will fall into place right before my eyes.

Feeling happy and free comes naturally to me, and I am now aligning with the energy of it. I may already be there, but the more consistently I feel this way, the better my life will be for me. I am able to feel good every day from morning to night.

If I close my eyes right now, I can take a glimpse of what my life looks and feels like when I've achieved more joy and personal freedom. What does it look like?

____

____

What am I allowing more time for?

____

____

How does it change my life? I envision it now and call it to me.

Action: Based on the answers you came up with for today's questions, write a list of intentions for anything you wish to accomplish and how you want to feel by the time you're done with the next 30 days of actions and intentions. You can write this below or in your appreciation journal.

Be sure to notice when you're feeling better about something that used to bother you and celebrate each and every milestone no matter how small. And get ready for big ones, because they're coming too!

How does it feel to allow yourself to feel happy and free and live your dream?

One last reminder: don't forget to do some journaling about your day and expectations for tomorrow!

My Inner Spirit Guides Me to Align with My True Self

I wish for my mind and body to be in harmony with my inner spirit and allow it to lead me through life.

My inner spirit is that non-physical part of me that's all energy. It feels like a loving, breathing consciousness. It breathes life into me. It's the fun part of me. The silly part. The part of me that I love the most.

It's confident, free, and feels limitless. Its guidance is never based on what's logical or practical. Isn't that nice to know? Or is that kind of scary? After all, we're all used to trying to be at least somewhat in control, aren't we?

But the more we connect with this innate quality within us and come to know our true nature, we easily let go of any desire to follow a set guideline or change circumstances outside of our control. We're simply happy to govern ourselves and only ourselves.

We sometimes feel better if we have control over *something* in our lives, but that often stems from insecurity we learned in childhood. As a child, we're all quite sensitive, and it's natural for some of this to stay with us, but it's just as easy to unlearn. It's just a matter of self-love and acceptance and wanting personal freedom badly enough to feel our way there.

Our inner being has no fear-based agenda, and neither do we once we've shed away all the layers acquired from life experiences that put those walls up in the first place.

If I'm not already there, I intend to feel my way into the feeling place of personal freedom that is the essence of my true nature. The guidance is available and I just need to be receptive to it.

How does it feel to know that by nature I am all love?

What if I knew that being fully aligned with that energy ensures I will not only *feel* safe and guarded, but I will be? Being aligned with it just means I follow my heart and allow it to guide me.

What's it like to have trust in my inner guidance and always expect things to go really well for me?

Can I see myself giving in to that faith and trust and enjoying the freedom that comes with that? How does it feel to allow myself to spend less time worrying and more time living purposefully?

How does it feel to tune in to myself on a deeper level where I can hear the intuitive messages?

What's it like to have that clear intuition that's constantly guiding me?

How does it feel to be supported in this way? I can see it as inner guidance, higher self, inner spirit, or wise self. I can see it any way I wish. But I love knowing it's there. And it's always encouraging me. My quiet mind picks up on it more every day.

And I love knowing that I have the ability to become so attuned to its energy, that I'm practically dancing through life.

Everything becomes effortless when I'm that authentic in my beingness.

How free do I feel when I've let go of any desire to control things other than how I feel?

Am I able to feel happy that I'm the only one I'm in charge of?

How does it feel to set myself free?

How do I know when I'm there? Am I there now?

Do I know how good it's going to feel to set myself free?

Will I know it when I'm living it?

How good does it feel? That point where I'm so connected to my inherent energy, that all I know and feel is what can only be called the truest form of freedom?

With the most delicious feeling that must be from allowing myself the freedom to be who I came here to be.

How does it feel when I let logic and practicality take a back seat to follow my heart more?

How does it feel when I allow myself to be in a pure state of joy so often that I can't help but keep it going? Why is it suddenly so easy for me to find my way here?

Action: If you're open to it, take a moment to tune in to your inner being. Right palm first, place your hands over the center of your chest. Imagine a shimmering pink or green ball of light in front of your chest and intend to breathe its energy into your heart center.

Close your eyes and allow yourself time to feel connected to your heart energy. Feel as though you're breathing in and out of your heart center. Let yourself be present and mindful of your breath and feel the harmony of your spirit, allowing it to bring harmony to your mind and body.

Your inner spirit or soul is the essence of you. When you allow it to lead you, life becomes more and more effortless. And way more fun!

Taking time to connect like this can be a necessary step to better understand your true nature. To know yourself on a deeper level is to give yourself the gift of self-love and a direct route to all the answers you seek. You gain an inner knowing that must be experienced to fully grasp how amazing and powerful you and your thoughts really are. And with this inner knowing comes the joy of trusting and feeling that all is well. Be open to it, and it will come, if it hasn't already.

Until tomorrow, happy day to you!

I Honor Myself

It's time to honor myself and feel good about every part of me. I want to give myself the love and acceptance I deserve. I know it's a necessary step if I want to create positive changes in my life.

My relationship with myself is the most important one of all. After all, how I feel about myself truly sets the tone for every one of my life experiences. And when I treat myself well, others will follow my lead. And that results in much happier relationships for me as well.

I love knowing that I'm in a constant state of change and always becoming who I am. I am exactly where I'm meant to be in my life right now, and I'm better every day in every way.

When I honor myself, I come to a place where I make myself important. I care enough to do what feels right for *me*. I allow myself to feel good and do everything I can to bring more joy into my life.

Why is it so easy for me to do this now? And why do I suddenly feel so worthy of my time and attention?

How does it feel when I allow myself to give as much to myself as I've given to others, or more?

How does it feel to honor myself? What does that mean to me?

Think of three or more things I can do to honor myself more. Are there any opinions, wishes, or other ideas that I'd like to start listening to, that I may have stifled or ignored in the past?

    1. _______________________________________

    2. _______________________________________

    3. _______________________________________

How good does it feel when I respect my own opinions and wishes and keep promises to myself?

How much better is my life when I completely accept myself?

How does it feel to stop judging myself and appreciate my uniqueness?

How I see myself is who I become. I intend to be in the qualities and characteristics of my most confident, loving, self-respecting, joyful, radiant self from now on. When this is a part of who I am, I am magnetic to all my desires. And life just keeps getting better and better.

Imagine it's six months to a year from now and I've achieved my goal for more joy in my life, including how I feel about myself.

Answer the following questions from that standpoint. Think of the words that would describe how I'm feeling. Think it through in detail, say it out loud, or write it out in the journal.

What are the qualities and characteristics I am in?

How much better do I feel about myself?

How much better do I feel about how I look?

How much has my level of expectation improved for how people should treat me?

How does it feel to have a natural ability to confidently speak my mind?

How does it feel to be good at letting others know what my needs are?

What's it like to make decisions without feeling the need for anyone's approval?

How comfortable do I feel showing others my authentic self?

How does it feel when my words are genuine and spoken from the heart?

How does it feel to smile and laugh more?

How does it feel to allow myself to feel really good about who I am?

What are my favorite things about myself?

What am I really good at?

When it comes to my home life, I'm good at _______.

When it comes to my career, I'm really good at _______.

When it comes to my social life and friends, I'm really good at being _______.

In what ways am I treating myself really well?

In what ways am I being more supportive of my own needs or desires in the following areas?

With my family:

With my partner:

While at work:

With friends:

One change has occurred in each of those areas for my benefit. What has changed? What was my wish?

____

What's it like now that it's taken place? With the new changes, how does it feel to be at home or with my partner or at work or with my friends now?

____

____

And what else am I doing for myself that's making me feel honored, cherished, and respected? Can I think of anything?

I am the only one who knows what's right for me and what will make me happy. I just need to connect with myself on a deeper level and the answers and insights will show me the way. My desired outcomes are finding their way to me.

Hold the vision and expectation that I am achieving this by six months from now, but know that it's more likely that it will happen before then, if not already.

Action: Once again, place your hands over your heart center and take a nice, slow, deep breath. Close your eyes and think or say, "I choose to deeply and completely love and accept myself." Say it a few more times with the intention that from this moment on, you promise to honor and respect yourself more every day. Always feel free to use words that you're comfortable with.

If not already, start doing one or more things each week that honor who you are. This would be something that makes you feel good about yourself and increases your feeling of self-worth a little bit more each time.

It could be something as simple as a bubble bath! If your schedule is busy, consider doing it biweekly or monthly. Pick a day and time that works and put it in your calendar. Set a reminder and do your best to follow through with it. You are worth it!

Have a great day!

I Am My Own Best Friend

There have been times in my life when I had my mind on everyone but myself. Did I somehow learn to be there for others and think it's perfectly okay to neglect my own needs?

Well, I love how much I value myself now, and more so every day. It's helping me feel important enough to put myself first. I can even say I truly enjoy my own company. This is so vital to living a life I love!

It was easy to start feeling more appreciation for being who I am when I realized that I wouldn't want to be anyone else. And it feels *so* good to be my very best supporter. It comes naturally to me as I practice being the constant friend I've always wanted.

What does it feel like to be my own best friend?

How does it feel to practice it until I feel completely worthy of all that I desire? Shouldn't this be an easy one? Well, it can be. After all, I *am* worthy of all good things. I am believing this now more than ever.

What kinds of words, thoughts, or questions do I use to guide myself there if I feel the need to?

How does it feel to give myself the love and support I've always deserved?

What's it like to be there for myself the way that I've been there for others?

When did I start caring so much about how I feel?

How much better do I feel when I begin to listen to my body's prompts for nurturing?

And how does my life change when I begin to listen to my internal voice? The one that's constantly guiding me on a path to more joy by way of instinctive thoughts or emotions?

How does it feel to allow myself to feel truly happy? *All* the time.

What had to happen to *finally* make me aware of all the unique talents and gifts I have to offer just by being me?

When I feel unconditional love and appreciation for myself, what is that like? Write or think of numerous words or phrases that show appreciation for my qualities, including my mind, body, personality, skills, and anything else I can think of.

____

____

____

How does it feel to allow myself to be proud?

What are the words of encouragement I would give to a close friend in need of more confidence or self-acceptance? Think of one super-duper inspiring statement that would uplift just about anyone. What would I say?

____

How would it feel to hear all the positive words I heard or wanted to hear since I was a child? There are more lovely words than I can imagine!

And it can feel really good to think of the words that I deserve to hear. So just this once, I'm going to entertain the idea of hearing words that I would have chosen for myself to hear at various stages in my life.

And I *did* hear many of them, but also forgot some of them, and missed more than I know. But my favorite words are mine to hold onto as long as I wish.

My thoughts, beliefs, and love for myself are the keys to opening all the doors to my success in life. Success in finding more joy, more love, and more abundance.

And no matter how corny it sounds, I can think of this exercise I'm about to do like this. I'm planting the seeds that allow my self-esteem to grow and put me in *full* bloom of the person I was born to be. I am meant to feel wonderful and believe great things about myself.

So, what are one or more things I would say to myself at age 7? Can I think of an image of myself from that time? What do I think I may have wanted to hear? Words that will stay with me from now on and allow me to "bloom."

____

____

____

How about ages 14, 21, and now? Or any other age I wish. Think of one or more things that would have been nice to hear then or to hear again at each age. What will help me remember how special I really am? Take some time for this. Write it down if desired.

____

____

____

How good does it feel when I decide that my words are the only ones that matter for my own wellbeing and happiness? I'm the one that makes me stronger and wiser. And I believe in myself enough for everyone.

If I ever felt like I was unwanted, unimportant, or not enough in any way, what would I tell myself that would validate the reasons it was completely untrue then and now? What would I tell a sibling or friend if they were asking me the same thing?

____

What are the words of encouragement that I think I may need to hear or believe about myself to become the happiest and healthiest version of me?

____

____

____

____

____

____

____

____

____

____

What if I could start being that voice in my head now? The one that says what I need or want to hear *all* the time? Like the kind of words that instill a belief in my true value?

The words encourage me, inspire me, soothe me, or build my self-confidence. They tell me all the things I've always been meant to know and believe about myself.

What if I was often told that I am wise, wonderful, happy and free? Wouldn't it be nice to continue hearing that? And all the things I've ever wanted to believe about myself? Until it's who I am and my life begins to show me the results of this brilliant energy I'm giving out?

How does it feel to be the truest version of me that's right here beneath my layers?

From now on I allow myself to be the one that whispers in my ear and offers all the encouragement I could ever want. I am open and receptive and allowing myself to see and feel my many gifts and talents. I have so much to offer.

And *all* the things I say and do and feel and believe now are replacing any self-doubt I've ever had. The more I practice this self-talk, the more it gets instilled and remains in the forefront of my mind.

Why am I now able to see myself for all that I am? It feels so good to value myself!

And isn't it nice to know that others treat me better now that I feel such a strong sense of self-worth?

How does it feel to have unconditional love and acceptance for myself? What are three or more words that describe how it feels?

1. _______________________________
2. _______________________________
3. _______________________________

I am doing my best to completely cherish who I am or take steps in allowing it more and more. I may have learned to downplay feelings of self-love and acceptance for thinking it's selfish, egotistical, or undeserving.

But, oh, how truly deserving I am of love! As are we all. My self-love and acceptance brings out the best in me. I know that I am more successful in all areas of my life because of it. And I like believing that love and acceptance bring out the best in everyone.

If I close my eyes right now to see it, how do I look and feel when I've allowed myself the unconditional love and acceptance I deserve?

Action: What are the words of encouragement that you would like to be telling yourself? Words that you believe will help you become the happiest and healthiest version of you?

If you haven't already, write a list of the most uplifting words you can come up with that resonate with you. Think of the words you've offered to a close friend, or even an acquaintance. They're often words you need to hear yourself.

Do this when you're feeling really good so there's a positive energy behind your words. Keep the list with you or stick it up somewhere, and read it daily or as often as you'd like. Grab your notebook or journal and do this now.

The more you practice your positive thoughts of self-love, the more they become embedded in your subconscious. This is what's intended to be your thought pattern through your whole life. So *let it be now*.

Now, if desired, place your hand(s) over the following areas and think or say "I completely accept myself" or words that feel comfortable to you: top of the head, forehead, back of the neck, shoulders, throat, chest, upper abdomen, lower abdomen, hips, back, and legs.

Now cross your arms and place your hands on the side of the arms toward the shoulders. Give a gentle squeeze, and repeat the words several times with your eyes closed. Then just breathe in and out and be in the stillness for a moment.

Remember to be there for yourself. Practice being your very own cheerleader! Sometimes it can take practice, but everyone's mind has the ability to change.

The more you allow uplifting words to be your primary thought or dialogue, the more instilled they are in you, and the quicker you replace any old unwanted thought patterns.

Have a great day, Bestie!

I Am Self-Governed

When I'm self-governed, I am confident in who I am and trust in my decision-making abilities. I think independently and live by my own rules without hesitation or self-deprivation. I trust my instincts and feel self-guided.

I respect my own opinions. There's no second-guessing myself. (Yay!) I feel no need to defend my opinion. And I never feel the need to seek the approval of others to validate my choices. All self-doubt has left me, and I feel free.

Why is it so easy for me to see it this way now?

When did I start allowing myself to take charge of the rules that I live by?

When I practice the feeling place of it, how do I feel? What are three words that I believe define my level of independent thinking?

     1. _______________________________

     2. _______________________________

     3. _______________________________

What would I say is the main standard I use when making choices on my own? How easy are my decisions?

____

How confident do I feel in my ability to make my decisions without consulting with someone first?

What are the daily or routine decisions that I make easily? Can I think of three or more?

     1. _______________________________

     2. _______________________________

     3. _______________________________

What kinds of decisions am I making that I always feel certain are the right choice? Can I think of a couple that apply here? For work or home or another area of my life?

____

____

When I focus on how much confidence I have when making decisions that come easily for me, all the other decisions I need to make will become easier for me as well.

If I'm needing more courage in some areas, what words can I use to guide myself there? On what topics do I need more courage? How would I finish these statements:

I am deciding right now that I can easily make a decision about __________.
And it's easy for me now because __________.

How does it feel to allow myself to make the choices that feel right to me on every level? And not just because I'm feeling obligated to?

Are there any boundaries I need to set for myself or others?

What am I making important now that might not seem so important if I looked back on it five or ten years from now, if anything?

Is there anything I'm doing that used to work for me, but may no longer be aligned with who I am *now*?

Is there anything I could stop doing so I could do more of what I wish to do? Would I like more time with family? Or more time to work on a work project or a hobby I enjoy? Or just more personal time?

If I'm putting in a lot of work hours, is it necessary, or could I be busying myself for other reasons I may not have yet considered?

Do I offer advice or get in the middle of something that might be better worked out by those involved? With family or coworkers or someone else? Can I think of anyone like this?

Am I allowing them to decide what feels right to them? What if giving them time to sort things out provided the time they needed to get better at helping themselves?

What if seeing them learn to use their own coping skills would give me great relief, make me so proud, and allow me to have more free time?

Or what if I asked them questions that guided them to find their own answers?

Would that feel better, or does it feel better to continue helping them as I was before?

Can I decide that the next time an issue comes up that I'll gently encourage them to work things out for themselves, or try something different that feels right to me?

When possible, and if desired, I am kindly and confidently letting others know that I sometimes have something I need to do before I can help them.

What activities do I enjoy doing now, without hesitation, guilt, or offering excuses?

____

____

____

____

____

____

____

____

____

How does it feel to give myself permission to do what I wish?

How does it feel when I'm so self-assured in my own beliefs that I don't feel the need to defend my opinion to anyone? To just know that what is right for me is right for me, and their opinion is right for them? And be okay with all of it?

What's it like to just see it with the understanding that they're doing what feels important to them and following their own guidance? And doesn't it feel great when their opinion of what *I* think doesn't have to matter to me?

When I feel an urge to argue or *make* a discussion go *my* way, what if I just chose to walk away with the satisfaction of knowing that no-one or no-thing can keep me from having a great day?

I love knowing that releasing anything I ever felt defensive about, if anything, sets me free and aligns me with my true nature! I am becoming completely free of resistance, and this can only bring me to a place of more ease, joy, and freedom. And I'm always ready for more of that!

How does it feel to know that *every* time I let go of a little more control, I'm doing wonders for my body and my wellbeing? And I am closer and closer to achieving my desires. Yes, I want this! But first and foremost, I desire to feel the joy of the journey on my way to it all.

Action: Place your hands on your chest, right palm first, and take a moment to close your eyes and go within and connect to your heart energy. Take a couple of nice, deep breaths.

Think of your intentions for any changes you'd like to make to become more self-governed; intend to transform any feelings of insecurity or limiting beliefs with more confidence. Always make your statements positive, and begin with "I am now."

If desired, add this intention: "I am deciding right now to release all self-doubt. I choose to trust in my natural ability to be self-reliant and have my best interests at heart. If I've been stifling my thoughts or wishes or not doing something because I lacked confidence or feared someone wouldn't approve or support it, I will consider doing it when the time feels right to me."

And whenever you make a decision that you initially feel good about, but then start second-guessing yourself, say the word "release" and say an affirmation like:

> "I am better at making decisions for myself than I think I am, and no one else knows my thoughts well enough to make the right decision for *me*. If my decision affects others, it may feel unkind or unaccommodating, but it's what's best for me. And I'm happy to follow what feels best for me."

Can you imagine someone telling you they admire how much confidence you exude and wish they could feel that good about themselves? What would that look or feel like? That's how you're feeling right now. Breathe it in. And show yourself what it's like to feel like that all day tomorrow! And the next day, and the next...

I Allow Myself Personal Freedom

Why do I feel so free to be my authentic self now? I'm acting like the person I wish to be and all my choices reflect my true preferences. And it feels so good to live this way.

When I align with this energy, I feel free to express myself and do so as I please. I let myself be who I am and do what I love. I say yes when I mean yes, and no when I mean no.

I am at ease with who I am and speak my truth straight from the heart. Showing my confidence in all my interactions comes naturally to me now, and my positive and peaceful energy is felt by all those around me.

Could this be what it feels like when I allow myself to have more personal freedom?

What is my life like when I've gotten to this point?

What have I been doing that's creating a feeling of personal freedom?

Am I being true to myself, and letting my voice be heard?

When I'm being my authentic self, what does it look like? What do people see in me? How much of myself am I showing them?

How easy is it to show them who I truly am versus what I want them to believe about me?

How clearly or objectively am I able to view myself? Am I being fair to myself?

Do I think of myself as confident, brave, and bold, or soft-spoken and timid? How do I wish to be? How do I see the real me?

____

____

____

What comes out when I allow myself to relax and have fun and be real with people?

Do I notice when I'm holding back, or does it only become clear in occasional glimpses of myself, which only seem to come when I'm no longer with the same company?

And by that time, don't I find myself wishing I would have been more at ease, more talkative, or *less* talkative, and more confident, friendlier, or more straightforward than I was?

Write or think of a description of how I think others see me when I'm showing my genuine self; you know, the version of me that I may *want* to share, but also may hide.

____

____

____

If I can check in like this on how I think I'm seen from another's perspective, it often reveals how I see myself, or how I wish to be. And at times, it may show me how little I'm revealing about who I truly am.

Now try again with a new description of how I wish to be seen by myself and everyone. In describing myself this time, I am doing my best to be unbiased. In other words, I won't mask my deepest desires in any way. I am to be bold and unashamed!

This isn't about ego; it's about letting myself come out of my shell. It's about lifting constraints or limitations I may have put on myself and coming out of hiding. Yay! We're often not even aware we do this. Yeesh! How is that possible?

So how do I see myself as who I am now becoming? What do I envision?

____

____

____

Upon allowing myself to openly and completely and unabashedly love and accept myself, I will no longer have *any* part of me in hiding from myself or anyone else. Isn't it so good to know?

It's time to ask myself some more really good questions.

Is there any time I'm not being myself with a particular person?

I can close my eyes right now and think of someone or a group of people I'm not always comfortable being myself with, and see how I'm opening up with them and showing them my true nature. Imagine it now. I intend to be in this energy when I see them next.

What about when I'm with a partner? At times we don't fully share our whole selves when we first meet someone. And the longer we're in the relationship, the harder it gets to open up and tell them how we really feel on some subjects.

We may fear it will complicate things or feel uncomfortable to suddenly bring these things up or act differently. What is one small step I can take to reverse that situation and start exposing the real me, who I know they will love and adore?

And has there ever been a time when I made myself small or conformed to others' needs so they felt better about themselves? Or for any other reason? Can I think of a time or two when I've done this?

There are times when this is merely a show of kindness, which is always such a wonderful thing. It's when it affects my wellbeing that it might be worth looking at.

How much better do I feel when I know and believe that I'm better for *everyone* when I allow my inner light to shine through? Isn't it great to know that in that state I'm radiating joy to all?

If I gave myself permission right now to focus on myself and what is really important to *me*, would I feel relieved? What would I say if someone asked me this?

Can I see myself finding a way to do more of what I want for the sake of pure enjoyment?

When I allow myself freedom of time to do more of what I love, what am I doing?

____

____

____

What kinds of things would I be doing that are only in the spirit of fun?

____

____

____

What am I saying no to? Is there anything I'm doing that I don't enjoy anymore?

____

____

____

What am I saying yes to? What am I doing now that I love to do? Is there any way I can do it more often?

____

____

____

I *love* knowing that feeling happier is a way to create more opportunities for cash flow that will allow me to do a *lot* more of anything I wish! *So* many choices!

What about when I feel more confident and free to be myself with everyone I know, or don't know? What does it feel like to be me?

____

____

____

What kinds of things might I randomly say to people if it was in the spirit of fun? What could I say to start a conversation?

____

____

____

What if I decided that it's *completely* okay if I choose to detach myself from the limiting words and beliefs of others, if desired, and allow my *own* rules and free will to reign over me?

Did that sound like some form of silly poetry? Well, if it reminds me that I'm in charge of making choices that make me happy, so be it. It's really about being committed to living authentically and honoring my true feelings, not to mention allowing myself to feel happy no matter what.

I'm deciding right now that it's okay if I don't go along with something just because it's the nice or "polite" thing to do. It's my choice. Though in my unwavering mindset and spirit of joy, I'm still able to take part in *any* conversation or experience without it changing how I feel or what I believe.

I'm so stable in my makeup to deserve this life. Did that make sense? Or did it make me think of a movie like *Pride and Prejudice*? Did it make me laugh? I hope so. It certainly didn't make sense. But it was fun. Now onto more serious things...

Although I'll never take myself or anything I've read too seriously. All the answers I seek are within me. That's right. *Me*! Just a reminder, My Dear.

So, what do I love about having the gift of free will? I like believing it's always okay to do everything my way. And I'm doing it all in a *great* way!

Well, as long as I abide any formal laws. Darn those laws. I'm kidding, I'm kidding! Really, I am.

But sometimes I do have to set boundaries for myself and the loved ones in my life. But haven't I been saying that I'm free to do what I want? Then why set "boundaries"?

Since there are schedules to keep and obligations to tend to, I like to set boundaries so I can make some time to do more activities that support my wishes and dreams. Or just to keep my life in balance while I enjoy doing more of what I want.

I like to have a balance between being responsible and giving myself the freedom to do what I want. Of course which side of the scale is higher or lower often depends on my circumstances.

I love to allow myself to have more personal freedom, yet I know I'll always be happy to be responsible for some things that are really important to me, like family.

But I'll also know the difference between being overly responsible and following my heart in the right direction. I'll always choose what makes me happy.

And sometimes that means I'm going to do what feels comfortable or safe, and that's what I need to do.

Nonetheless, I am feeling so liberated. I feel more free to be me every day. Freer to live my life authentically. I'm doing what I wish, saying what I choose, and all with such a natural feeling of being in the joy of who I am. Confident, easy, and free.

I practice my personal freedom until it's a part of me. I am free to be my most genuine self and do what I want. I am owning up to this and making it mine.

I often tell myself that *I make the rules. I decide. I get to choose. And I can do whatever I want.* Doesn't that almost sound like a song I could keep running through my mind? Wouldn't that be hilarious? Even better!

I choose to be led by the free-spirited side of me to my heart's content. I am so very fortunate to be me. I completely embrace who I am now and who I'm becoming. It just keeps getting better!

Action: Is there anything you can think of that you can start doing that will create a feeling of personal freedom for you? In what ways do you wish to free yourself? In what areas of your life? Are there any areas or situations or settings where you feel more inhibited or constrained?

Are there any beliefs you learned that may not be your own? Or something you never considered making your own decision about because it's the norm or what everyone else follows? Such as when to go to sleep, when to eat, or how much to eat or sleep?

Can you think of anything like this that's traditionally done or you've done your whole life and automatically follow?

And when something you've heard about that topic runs through your mind, it stays with you. For Example; I didn't get enough sleep so I'm going to be tired all day. Or: I'm not getting enough nutrition in the food I'm eating. I need to eat more ____.

This is just an example of something that could be considered a limiting belief. Albeit a small one, but those little things add up and can affect you. And in a way, you would be relinquishing your right to choose what you believe or want to make your reality. And you can easily make your own rules for anything you wish.

If you do decide to think about this more or start trying to change your way of thinking around this, do what feels comfortable and have fun with it! Without even trying, you'll likely be more aware now of the many options available to you.

Lastly, take a moment now to breathe into your throat chakra, imagining a sky blue or turquoise color over it. Breathe into it with the intention of clearing it, opening it, and balancing it.

Then see or feel it connected in some way to the heart chakra with the intention of enabling a harmonious flow between them. Think of allowing this to increase your ability to speak the words you truly wish to share more fluently from the heart.

Let yourself have the kind of day that makes you feel free to live life your way!

Day 37

It's Time for Me to Have More Fun!

It's time to be in the joy of who I am. It's my birthright, and I want to feel happier *all* the time. I know it's a *feeling* I can take with me wherever I go, but I decided I want to actually *do* more of what I love and start having *way* more fun. Life can seem so busy, but I'm ready to make it my priority like anything else I *"have"* to do.

To get myself started, I'm going to talk about what I love today. What I love to be, or have, or do, and most of all, what I love to feel. The idea is to get myself into the spirit of fun. As I feel my way into this energy, the ideas and opportunities for more fun will manifest.

Saying what I love to do, or what I love about myself or my life, is also a great way to show appreciation. And feeling appreciation for the best parts of my day is the easiest and fastest way to bring more of what I love into my life. And I do it because it feels so good!

What can I say that will get me to that feeling place?

Finish the sentences below with anything that feels *really* exciting to think about, and include things you haven't yet done:

I love feeling _____.

I love to be _____.

I love to have _____.

I love going to _____.

I love that I am _____.

I love that I let go of _____.

I love that I'm allowing myself to _____.

I love that I feel so good about _____.

I love that I'm feeling free to _____.

I love how brave I'm being about _____.

I love how great I am at _____.

158

And I really love to do these hobbies and activities that feel so exhilarating to me:

Why is it so easy for me to make time for this now? Now is the time, if at all possible. What if I could forget about waiting until I have a vacation to do some of these things? Am I willing to wait? Does it feel better to make time for it now, or get to it *someday*?

I'm deciding right now that if I ever set things aside, I'm going to keep my promise to get to it. And *sooner* than later. I love doing things for myself! And there are *so* many things that would feel *so* good to do, that I *know* are waiting for me. I'm ready right now!

Write down five or more *new* ideas for activities, hobbies, places to go, or anything I'd like to try that I believe will bring more zest into my life:

Although I'd like to stay focused on the fun, I also want to check in occasionally and make sure I'm following my heart's desire.

Is there anything I'm not doing that keeps calling me?

Am I aware of what's stopping me from doing it? Am I concerned about taking time away from other obligations?

When I think of going for it, do I feel a sense of relief? Yes, or no?

Or does it feel better when I think of doing without it, at least for now? There are times when that *is* our path of least resistance.

All I need to do is follow my instincts, do what feels best to me, and I'll always be making the right choice for me.

And I'll ask again: if I'm wanting to stop doing anything, or do less of it, what is one thing I can do to move in that direction?

If desired, I can set an intention or make a plan for a gentle release when the time feels right to me.

I do my best to believe that I am much better for everyone when I take care of my own happiness first. And it's so nice to know that in my consistent state of joy and appreciation, I am attracting only the best life experiences!

Action: In the spirit of fun, close your eyes and think of anything you love. Say them aloud if possible, beginning with "I love _____." Think of all the things you love to do, love to have, places you want to go, or new activities you would love to try and keep going for at least a couple minutes. And the many ways you love to *feel*.

Here are some ideas to get you started, if need be: I love having fun, I love to dance, I love ice cream, I love my job, I love that I feel so good, I love going shopping, I love being with friends, I love having time to do what I want, I love the sun, I love the trees, I love being happy, I love being me.

Consider doing this every day when you're waiting in line or at a red light or any time you think of it. It's a great way to practice positive thinking and raise your vibration at the same time.

To remind you, consider writing "I love ____" on a sticky note and place it on your steering wheel or bathroom mirror. Or hide it somewhere, lest you become known as the "peculiar" one in the family. Extraordinary, yes. Peculiar? No, never! Or perhaps, you'd proudly take ownership of it, hmm?

Also, start spoiling yourself more. On the same day and time, biweekly or monthly, do one thing on your "love to do" or "would love to try" list. Add it to your schedule with a reminder.

Then write each of them down on small pieces of paper or index cards. Fold them up and place them in an envelope. Pick one at the time of your "appointment" and always reschedule it if necessary.

If you need ideas, consider these: see a comedy movie, go to a ball game, go dancing, have coffee or dinner, get a pedicure or massage, take a warm bath, get an ice cream, or spend time in a park. I bet you can think of something *way* better.

Plan the outings with someone or go alone. Then there's no need to wait for someone to be available. You might be surprised at how much you enjoy your own company!

- ★ When did it become so natural for you to have fun no matter where you are or what you're doing? You love feeling good and allowing yourself to be as healthy and happy as you can be!

I Am Intimately Connected to My Wise Self

It's time to connect with my pure positive energy. When I make a habit of connecting to my natural-born energy, the wisest part of me, I feel connected to everything. I never feel alone. I feel safe wherever I am and have this all-knowing, undeniable trust in things working out for me.

Connecting with myself on a deeper level is my direct route to achieve anything I desire. I have the answers to all my questions. I know who I am, what I want, and what path to take. The more I tune into my energy, emotions, and inner guidance, the more I know this to be so.

This inspires me to check in with myself as often as I can. It only takes a couple minutes and before I know it, I'm feeling attuned to the energy. What if I knew that doing this is completely changing my life in the most amazing way? I am worth the little bit of time this will take!

When I take time to be in quiet stillness and feel the harmony of my heart energy for even a moment, I find that I'm receiving all the guidance I need. And without any effort on my part, I know who, what, where, and how I'm going to align with anything I wish. It's very simple. Life becomes easy and effortless.

How does it feel to allow myself to be attuned to the best part of me, the truest part of me that wants to guide me on my highest path?

When I'm in this energy, I feel the harmony of my mind and body and feel in love with the world and *everything* I see. That's how good it feels to be loving and accepting and appreciating who I am and all that is.

I am simply seeing through the eyes of my wisest self and it knows how amazing I am. And it loves when I'm feeling it, too.

I am better every day at connecting to myself and my energy on a more intimate level. Doing so is allowing me to hear my inner guidance more easily. And helping me feel in love with life!

How does it feel to connect with my soul on such a deep level?

What's it like to know that I'm all love, on every level of my being?

What if I could sense this energy that's within me and all around me?

Perhaps I've already been doing it when I do deep breathing or connect with my heart energy. The more I practice it, the more I feel this subtle energy. And the more tuned in I am to my body and my inner guidance system. It gets better and better and keeps me wanting more of it.

It's been said before that the breath is the bridge between the mind and body. Why is it so easy for me to understand now?

How does it feel to connect to my breath in meditation, Qi Gong, or during another form of exercise? Have I started to sense the subtle life-force energy that flows to me and through me?

Do I notice the feeling I get in my chest like my heart energy is expanding? It's a blissful feeling that comes from within and is all light and love.

What's it like to tap into this pure inner joy and let it radiate wellbeing to all those around me?

What if I could use it to create days filled with love for all things?

How does it feel to hold on to that energy?

What if it helped me be in the moment, yet be delightfully detached from some happenings and be going in the same flowing direction as my desires?

Has this lovely energy helped me feel more connected to my true nature? Or have I started receiving more insights? Isn't that the best part? Or is it just how good I feel?

When did I start trusting that my guidance will always be there giving me directions on where to step next?

Isn't there such a great feeling of peace of mind when you always know when to say yes and when to say no? I always know what choice to make.

I have the support available to me and I intend to use it. I just need to tune in to it.

When I allow my inner spirit or heart to lead me, how much calmer and freer do I feel?

How does it feel to have a built-in soothing mechanism that allows me to be more accepting and calm in all situations?

What if I knew there would come a time that "coping skills" were no longer required with my heart leading the way? Or what if I'm already there? How does it feel?

How does it feel to be free of any struggle?

If I followed my heart and always chose what my positive emotions were telling me, how would it change my life? Is there any area of my life that would benefit from this?

____

____

____

____

____

____

____

____

____

____

____

____

____

From now on, for anything I've been doing because it's practical, realistic, or logical, I will ask myself what my heart wants first.

Action: Right palm first, place your hands over the thymus point, just under the collarbone in the center of the chest (it may feel raised). This is linked to the higher heart chakra and is often called the "seat of the soul." Putting our attention there or gently tapping on it is felt to awaken our spirituality. It can bring about feelings of unconditional love. As mentioned in Step 1, it's also felt to strengthen the immune system.

With intention, breathe in and out of the space beneath your palm, and think or say "I'd like to connect with my inner spirit" (or higher self or words of your choosing). Then slowly ask yourself these questions:

How does it feel when I allow myself to connect to my inner spirit?
How does it feel to be guided by this loving energy?
How does it feel to open my heart and feel more love growing inside me and radiating from me?
How does it feel to have so much love in my heart that I feel more appreciation, patience, tolerance, compassion, and acceptance for everyone and everything?
How does it feel to be set free?
As I become more tuned in to my inner spirit, my mind, body, and spirit are in harmony.
How does it feel?
Inner being, how are you feeling?
How does it feel to allow myself to feel blissful?

Now, to yourself or aloud, say the words that come to mind, and say them slowly to give your body's energy time to respond. "My inner being feels ______." Say the first thing that comes to mind. If you need help getting started, begin with: "My inner being feels…"

Peaceful… confident… comfortable

Lighthearted and free

Loved and loving

Completely unlimited

Blissfully present

Unconditionally happy

Pure potentiality

Full of clarity

Naturally abundant

Eager and excited

Magnetic

Do your best to conjure up the feeling of it. What would it feel like? Take a moment to close your eyes, focus on your heart energy, and silently say or think of as many as you can think of or repeat the same words over and over.

Keep going until you feel your energy shift, and continue as long as you'd like. Feel as good as you can feel, and allow your body to be in that space with you. If it feels good, do this as often as you'd like, until it feels like a constant presence that guides and supports you. It can and it will!

You can also choose a trigger to connect to this energy, such as your hands over your heart center or putting your thumb, index and middle finger together. State the intention that the moment you do this, you'll be connected to your mind, body, and spirit at once, as represented by the three fingers.

During this time, if desired, you can ask a question about a decision you'd like intuitive guidance on. Specify that you'd like to receive the answer within two days, if desired. Write it down so you remember to pay attention to thoughts or signs that show up.

It can come from any source, such as a multitude of acquaintances who offer similar words of advice or a song you hear repeatedly, or an email, phone call, or an ad or article that pops up on your computer screen with related information.

It can also show up smack dab in front of you on a license plate, billboard, or side of a bus when you least expect it. It happens!

And whether you've asked a specific question or not, always pay attention to signs like this, for it's quite often guidance that's meant for you.

The more you connect with yourself and summon this pure positive energy, the more the answers and insights will come and the higher your level of wellbeing can be. You'll begin to feel more secure in the world and any worries or fears naturally dissipate, sometimes without you even realizing it.

Until one day when you look back and realize how much angst you've let go of. You'll get clearer on how you want to live your life, and feel more certain of your pure potentiality.

Wishing you a happy day!

I Choose Love

I choose to see through the eyes of love. This is the true secret to setting myself free. And it's my one answer to all of life's questions. It simplifies *everything*.

When I'm looking through the eyes of love, I feel a loving appreciation for anything I pay attention to. It also gives me the ability to see a solution for every problem or situation and helps me understand or appreciate what's really happening.

As I change my perception to a more positive view, *the world around me changes with it.* Can I feel the significance of this? I can already feel how this is transforming my life into anything I wish it to be.

This love guides me when I can't decide. It provides me with the right answers every time. And I always feel better when I follow my heart.

So, what's it like to see through the eyes of love?

How good does it feel to have a sincere appreciation for *everything* around me?

How does it feel to know it's leading me to the freedom I desire?

How does it feel to be led to the right decision every time?

What's it like when I embrace the love in my heart and let it guide me in all areas of my life to achieve a deep satisfaction?

Any reason I ever had for feeling anything less was never aligned with my true nature. It's just something I learned and I'm happy to let go of.

Action: Start practicing the art of seeing through the eyes of love in a more purposeful way today or tomorrow. Be mindful of where you are throughout your day and notice what's in front of you: the people, the conversations, the sky, the trees, the flowers—anything you pay attention to.

And now, grab your journal and write a list or think of all the people, places, or things that you feel loving appreciation for today.

Take a moment to close your eyes again and imagine being in their presence and tell each of them one or more specific things that you appreciate about them. Yes, even the flowers and trees.

How does it feel?

Next, think of anything that you consider difficult, uncomfortable, or annoying to deal with. And then imagine what it's like to see the situation through the eyes of love.

What would love do here? Try to think of it in a way that allows you to appreciate it in some way.

For example: if there's a stressful situation of any kind or you hear people arguing, what can you appreciate about it? Ask yourself how love would see the situation. An example would be to briefly notice it, silently wish them well, and feel an expectation for things to work out easily, and perhaps imagine they'll be laughing in a moment.

There are many times we worry about others and discover later that things worked out fine. Give yourself permission to have faith that everyone is where they're meant to be, and are on their own path and being guided to what's best for them. Allow yourself to be at ease.

If you've had any recent issues come up with a certain individual or group, take a moment to close your eyes and imagine being in their presence; tell each of them one or more specific things that you appreciate about them. Stop reading and do this now.

Do you feel a little better?

What if you decided to think of it in one or more of the following ways?

> There's more to the story than you know.
> They're doing the best they can and they're figuring it out.
> They learned this behavior and they're still becoming who they are.
> If you had thoughts of acceptance or compassion as you observed them, would it change how they're acting?
> If you feel that someone blames you for their unhappiness, it's likely their need to repair the relationship they have with themselves.
> If you don't like what someone is saying or doing, what if you decided that it's not about you and they're just doing what they think is important to them.
> Everyone's on their own path, being guided to what's best for them to learn and grow.
> They're doing it for the fun of it. Wish them well and take your attention off of it.

Did any of these make you feel better? Perhaps you'll find another way that feels right to you. Remember that having more freedom and happiness is where you're headed. So allow yourself to be creative when trying to find ways to let go of things you can't control.

Another easy way to redirect your thoughts when it's hard to avoid a frustrating situation is to simply say "I choose love; I choose wellbeing."

You can intend for "I choose love" to mean you're choosing to accept what is happening and let it go. And "I choose wellbeing" means that you're not letting that something or someone affect how you feel.

It reminds you that you're in charge of how you react to things and allows you to remain calm or at ease. Set an intention now, if desired: "I intend to practice this from now on and I ask that my heart remember this with me."

You can also be thinking: "I choose love. What would love do here? How would love see this? How does my inner being see this?"

And if there's a choice to take your attention off of something, great. But if you're paying attention to it, always see it in a way that eases your mind.

Now, if you're open to it, place your right hand over the heart center, left hand over the right. Close your eyes and silently repeat the word "thank you" over and over again while keeping your attention on your heart center. Stop reading and do that now for a moment.

Then imagine you're breathing in a glowing ball of pink or green light here. Breathe it in and feel its love and light. As you exhale, imagine sending its energy out to the rest of your body. In your next exhale, send it out to anyone you'd like to send it to.

Now see if you can sense the pulsation of this energy. If you can feel your heartbeat in your chest, what does it feel like? Even if you can't feel it right now, imagine what the rhythm would be as you place your attention there.

Once you feel it, then put your attention on the palm of your left hand which is known as the receiving hand. See if you can sense that same rhythm there. Do you sense the energy?

Close your eyes and try it again. Focus on the rhythm at the heart center, and move it to your hand. If not now, you'll sense it more with a little practice, if desired.

This is the energy used in some energy healing techniques, and we all have access to it. You can send healing energy to loved ones or anyone just by focusing on your heart energy as you put your attention on the person and imagine your energy flowing from your heart or hands to them.

It will never be in a way that overwhelms you, but in a subtle and gentle way. They're doing the healing, but you have the ability to provide the environment for it. Our vibrations can be entrained to resonate at a higher frequency with someone else's if we allow it to. But you can also do this long distance.

This is a nice way to open your heart chakra and feel more connected to your inner being as well. How does it feel to know you'll always be guided in the right direction for the best outcomes for your life when you follow your heart?

Love is in the air. Enjoy your day!

I Always Have a Solution

My main priority in life is to feel happy. I practice seeing everything in a way that allows me to stay in a good-feeling place.

So, if I don't like something about my life, I do something about it. I always have a solution to any problem. And when I can't change what's happening, there's always a way to see things in a way that benefits me. Anything I once thought of as a problem is an opportunity for my growth.

I can actually feel appreciation for any challenges or conflicts that come up. It always helps me know what I don't want and creates a stronger desire for what I *do* want. It either pushes me forward or inspires me to learn better ways to live my life. And it always leads me to something better. The more I trust in that, the more it occurs.

If I ever forget this, I remind myself that whatever I push against gets bigger. If I allow things to flow in and out of my life without resisting the inevitable changes or whatever it may be, good things flow in my direction as they're meant to.

And eventually I find that problems rarely present themselves. And when they do, I appreciate how it benefits me.

How does it feel to:

Have a solution to every problem.
Have the ability to see everything in a way that benefits me.
Be in charge of my emotions and how I react in stressful situations.
Transform any stressful or troubling situation into a peaceful one.
Free myself of any concern that anything anyone else is doing will affect me.
Make peace with the way things are and believe that everything will naturally work out as it's meant to.
Let go of the desire to control what others are doing.
Feel amused by anything that used to annoy me.
No longer deal with anything that I once considered a problem.

The idea is to have a way to feel better any time something has the potential to take me out of my good-feeling place. I am in such a great state of wellbeing; I'm not willing to bend on that.

How does it feel to know that nothing is a struggle for me? Nothing at all. Because I'm making peace with anything that was, and I'm now in the flow with a joyful life that comes naturally to me.

How did I get here?

I always focus on solutions. And I always speak of what I want and leave out what I don't want. So that way, I only attract what I desire. That's all I'm inviting into my life now.

So, what are some of my solutions?

If choices are involved, I take the path of least resistance. I think of two directions I could go and take the one that feels best.

I ask myself what love would do in the same situation.

If someone is complaining to me about something, I ask them what they'd rather have happen and hopefully redirect the conversation to focus on a better outcome.

With my intention and imagination, I disconnect my energy from someone I'm having an unpleasant conversation with. I stay in the conversation if desired, but avoid the energy drain a conversation like this may have on me.

Is there anything else I need a solution for?

Do I need to arm myself with a blanket statement to be prepared when someone's unkind words take me off guard?

What would that sound like? Could I smile and tell them I'll respond when they speak kindly? Or ask if they'd mind if we sat down and discussed it calmly? Can I see myself doing this if either one of those are appropriate for the situation at hand?

Can I think of any other blanket statements that may help me avoid further conflict when things start up with someone like an employee, coworker, boss, or family member?

How do I confidently ask for something I want? How do I convey my words with expectation for a positive response and get one?

And how can I kindly and respectfully say no or set boundaries with friends or family members?

I want to offer words that are so kindly or wisely put that they *cannot* be denied. So, is there anything I can think of that I'm occasionally confronted with that feels uncomfortable? Something I would *love* to speak up about or quickly smooth over if it happens again?

What outcome do I want and what steps can I take in that direction? Could I visualize how I want things to be and be in the qualities and energy of the desired outcome?

Take a moment and imagine watching the incident go from potentially stressful to easy-peasy. I offer a gentle, soft-spoken and respectful response or instruction, yet I come through with a commanding presence, and the expectation is clear and undeniable. And so am I!

This person wants to respond to me as kindly, or confidently as I did, or at least appear to. See the end result: a shaking of hands, a hug, or a better work environment. Whatever it is that I want this situation to be like going forward, see it now. Play it through in the mind's eye once again.

How does it feel to be influencing the outcome the next time it happens? What's it like to have that feeling of satisfaction after I've achieved a better relationship with the person?

What if I knew the person would never again approach me in that way? What a wonderful feeling to have gained newfound respect from someone just for speaking up for myself in the kindest, gentlest way.

It's things like this that build my confidence. It's on the rise, big time. Life just keeps getting easier for me. What is that word again? It's *fantastic*, I say!

But in general, when seeking a solution to anything that shows up, I try to think it through like this:

> I immediately focus on a solution by deciding what I want the end result to be.
> What would I rather have happen?
> What's another way to look at this situation that makes me feel better about it?
> Is there anything I can do that will make things easier?
> How do I want to feel after the changes?
> How would it feel to have this situation be really comfortable for me?
> What are the words to describe how I feel when it's taking place?
> What are the words to describe how I feel afterward?
> I write them down and then close my eyes and imagine the end result I desire.
> I see everyone involved in a better place and feel that it's how I wish it to be.
> It feels easy. We're on the same wavelength and enjoying ourselves.
> I keep thinking of that desired result and send well-wishes before I'm about to see them, and every time after that.
> I believe this is helping bring about a positive change, and expect it to happen.

Until my desired result comes about, I only think or speak of the situation in terms of the best outcome.

If it doesn't feel good to think about it, I think of another area of my life that *does* feel good. Putting my attention on any area of my life that I feel really good about is allowing all areas of my life to become better and easier.

Sometimes, I need to get pretty creative when my goal is to feel better. For instance, when I'm somewhere enjoying the quiet and someone or something gets loud, like I suddenly hear yelling, barking, or loud music.

Instead of letting it annoy me, if ever, I decide that the next time the noise comes, it's going to raise my vibration. Or maybe even send a burst of light to every cell in my body.

We did say creative, right? Okay, a little wacky, yes, but very creative. These are the tools I break out when things really get to me. And if the result is relieving stress or helping me have a great day, I'm willing to try it or find another way that works for me.

And I use a similar process when I want to change my reaction to particular situations that hit a nerve or cause a gut reaction in me. Even if it's something that's triggered this reaction for years, I'm still able to put an end to it.

It's just a matter of deciding to do it and replacing that thought or reaction with a new one. I'm able to do this so well that I can create an immediate shift in my energy. And the new mindset I've gained is clearing any previously "programmed" thought pattern around the situation.

Up until that point I may have had the preconceived notion that I would always react the same way about that situation and wasn't ever going to change it. It was just the way I was and I had accepted that as the way things were for me. But now I know that was just a decision I made up in my mind.

It's that simple. It's a matter of practice and belief.

I love how in charge I feel and how much better I feel at the end of the day. I am now attracting the circumstances that allows my happier, healthier life to unfold. And perfectly so.

Action: The next time you're speaking to someone and you sense the conversation going in a direction that isn't pleasing to you, try to mentally disconnect your energy from them. You can disconnect from someone's energy any time you wish, simply by intending to do so.

See or feel your energy spiraling back toward you. With practice you might be able to imagine it as a cord of light that's coming back into your core energy or somewhere around the heart center. And from there you can always imagine forming a protective shield of energy around you.

It may seem odd to do this but the intention and your belief has the powerful ability to keep you feeling positive and retain your energy throughout the day. It can also wrap up the conversation rather quickly. It can surprise you at times how magical your thoughts and intentions seem to be and are!

This may only be for those who feel sensitive about this sort of thing, but try to stay open to giving it a try. The more you practice it, the stronger your resilience will be to negative energy.

And try not to feel badly if you prefer not to follow along with a disagreeable conversation, whether it's sad, gossipy, or mean-spirited, or anything you find unpleasant. It's your choice. There may be times when you're happy to help someone get through a difficult time. But otherwise, consider letting yourself off the hook.

If you wish to practice feeling how your energy can affect someone or hear how yours affects theirs, ask a friend to do this exercise with you. The entire process only takes a few minutes.

1. Have them stand about five feet away from you and close their eyes and relax.
2. Bring your arms up about chest level with palms facing your friend.
3. Intend to send them energy from your heart center to theirs, or core to core.
4. See or feel that there's a beam of light going from you to them at the heart level.
5. Intend to send a loving and soothing energy.
6. As you breathe in, you're focused on your hands and heart center.
7. As you breathe out, have your attention on their heart center and focused on sending energy to their body or heart center.
8. Continue for a minute or so, or as long as you're both comfortable.
9. Now fold your arms and hold on just above your elbows for a moment.
10. Drop your hands down and shake them off as though to clear energy from hands.
11. Tell your friend to open their eyes when they're ready.
12. Ask them if they felt any sensations in the chest area or anywhere else.
13. Ask if they saw any colors, noticed energy moving or spiraling, or anything else.
14. Ask them how they're feeling afterward, and if they feel any different than before.
15. Also, did they notice a change just before you asked them to open their eyes? The simple act of folding your arms can create a sort of barrier between you.

Now ask them to do the same for you, as stated above. Just allow yourself to relax and lightly pay attention to your body sensations.

Try it again while *sitting down*, only this time:

1. Set an intention for how you'd like them to feel during the session and afterward.
2. Repeat above Steps 1–8.
3. Before asking them to open their eyes, wish them more joy and abundance, and any good things you'd like them to experience in their life, including any desires they have that you're aware of.

Ask them to do the same steps for you. Then discuss how it felt each time and any differences either of you noticed in the exercise being done standing, seated, and with or without intention.

Consider trying it a third time, but without hands; just focus on each other's heart center at the same time while thinking of the words "thank you" repeatedly for a minute or so. See if either of you feel any different afterward.

This exercise is a great thing to do with your children or a significant other. I wish for you to feel how amazing you and your energy really are!

Your intention alone is enough to create the feeling of it. There's no wrong way to do it. So if you don't feel like it's doing anything, or can't visualize it, it's still working. Just practice it if it felt good to you, and expect it to get easier. It will!

Lastly, keep your blanket statements in mind and be prepared to practice using them, if desired.

Wow, that was a long chapter. But you got through it. Well done! Have a great rest of the day.

I Appreciate Anything I Pay Attention To

I am able to accept all that is, and I appreciate anything I pay attention to in whatever way I can. If for any reason I cannot, I choose to turn my attention to something else.

It's getting easier to do this every day.

What is my day like when I feel appreciation for all that I have and all that I see?

What are the kinds of things that I like to see?

What are some things I've only just begun noticing that I really appreciate now?

What about things I don't particularly enjoy but have to face them often? Can I find a way to appreciate them? Can I search for a quality about them that I admire?

How does it feel to allow others to be who they are? Can I find something to appreciate about everyone I meet?

What's it like to find something to appreciate about someone I'm arguing with? What if I stopped the conversation to give them a compliment or tease them about something that makes both of us start laughing? And how would that change the next time I interact with them?

What can I appreciate about all the servers that wait on my table or cash me out? Can I appreciate the hard work they do and know they're doing the best they can and if they're not, there's a reason?

What if I decided to enjoy driving no matter what? How does it feel to only pay attention to the safe and skillful drivers?

Even when I'm delayed in traffic or behind a slow driver, what if I reminded myself that this delay could be allowing me to miss a traffic accident up ahead? Or maybe it's helping me arrive where I'm going just in time for a chance meeting with someone. Something that turns out to be a huge opportunity? Could it be life-changing?

Anything and everything is possible. And synchronicities like this happen more often as I become more aligned with my desires. Especially when I trust that all is as it should be. Even those little mishaps could be guiding me on my path to greater things.

What about when I'm stuck in a standstill traffic jam? Instead of getting frustrated can I decide to make out a grocery list? Or better yet, turn on the music and play the drums on my lap, or sing and dance until people in the other cars wished they felt as good as I did. Or would they just be concerned? Whoops.

How does it feel to be free of the need to control how things are going to happen for me?

What if I decided to stop feeling annoyed by anything and feel amused by it instead?

What if I decided to start laughing at myself more often?

I love the idea of appreciating things so that I can stay in a good-feeling place, but is it *really* possible to appreciate everything?

Well, let's sink down to bottom level and see, shall we?

What can I appreciate about a pothole? Seriously...

In the moment that I dip down into a huge pothole, what if I thought about how much time and attention and love has gone into keeping the roads in the drivable condition they're in? And how much I love the road for getting me to where I want to go? It used to be a pile of mud.

Remember, now, the goal is to do whatever it takes to feel good. Yes, we reach a bit far if we must. But it sure makes life fun when our creative mind is at work, coming up with schemes like that. And if it makes us laugh, even better.

What else can I do to turn my life into something that always feels good to me?

Would I miss the news if I shut it off for a little while? Sometimes the way to be in touch with the world is to be far enough away from it to notice its beauty and wellbeing. Isn't it nice to know there's more of that than anything else?

How does it feel to only pay attention to what I like? And to know I always have a choice?

How does it feel to enjoy my day no matter where I am or what I'm doing? To be around all kinds of different people with all kinds of things happening and able to stay calm in all situations? And feel good at the same time?

Does the word freedom come to mind? How about ease? Or joy? Yes, *please*. And thank you. I'll take it.

Action: One of the best ways to practice feeling appreciation is to think of your favorite things about anything you pay attention to: a person or situation, your family, coworkers, your food, where you are, or anything that occurs.

Even if it seems impossible, there's always a way to find your favorite thing about something.

So although you've already been doing this a little bit in your daily intentions, start practicing it more by thinking of your favorite things wherever you go. Do your best to only put your attention on things you like.

Challenge yourself to do it, if you must. Whatever works. And when something comes up that you *don't* like, think of your favorite thing about it or something you can appreciate or admire about it.

Even if it's just to say that you appreciate it for letting you know what you *don't* want and giving you a stronger desire for what you *do* want. But try your creative thinking to come up with something interesting.

Do your best to use this process of finding your favorite things every day. In time you'll see that there's more good things than bad things and the bad things no longer bother you. Yay!

And if you're ever struggling with a difficult situation that's ongoing or a relationship issue, try writing out a page or so of your favorite things about it. Like what it's helping you better understand about yourself. What are one or more things you admire about those who are involved?

When you see things working out for the best, how does it feel to be there? Write out what it would look and feel like after the changes occurred.

This process can really shift your mindset about any situation. You'll know the appropriate questions and answers for yourself and easily start to see it in a different way. So that you can feel better, of course. Try it now if you have something you'd like to feel better about.

The more ease you feel, the more you'll enjoy your world. The more consistently you raise your vibrational frequency, the more you influence your life circumstances. Your positive energy will spread beyond boundaries.

When did it become so easy for you to focus on solutions and keep your life struggle-free?

Whatever you say often can become how things are for you. So start saying "I always arrive safely and on time." Can you think of something you'd like to make happen for you? Start saying it and begin to believe in it!

★ I can do anything I set my mind to!

I Am Struggle-Free

I let go of control, and it frees me. As I focus on my appreciation of what's around me, I hardly notice anything else. I've stopped worrying about what's to come and feel more mindful in the present.

For any negative thought that comes up, I easily acknowledge and release it and put my attention on something I like. It feels like I'm just going with the flow. It's my intention to feel this way now and always.

The more appreciation I feel, the more I see good things coming into my life. I'm finding it easier to let go of the desire to control how things turn out, and that frees me. And I'm starting to see that things are always working out for me.

I never forget that I'm in charge of how I feel and how I react to things. And I intend to do what I can to keep a nice balance in my life.

How does it feel to be so lighthearted that I'm completely free of resistance or struggle throughout my day?

How does it feel to allow myself to feel good no matter what? And to know it's okay when I'm not?

What's it like when I decide to be "all in" when I agree to do something for someone? And let it be okay if I decide to say no. With no second-guessing or guilting myself.

How does it feel to take guilt trips out of my experience; to never give them out and to smile and say something wise when someone puts one on me? Did someone just whisper "freedom!" in my ear? While I'm at it, I'm removing "should" and "supposed to" from my vocabulary.

And how does it feel to be so in charge of how I feel that I'm always calm no matter what is happening or who I'm speaking to?

When it comes to being sensitive to some things, I decided I would be so resilient that I could handle anything that life brings my way. How does it feel to know that I'm in charge of that part of me as much as any other part?

Isn't it good to know that the only reason I am who I am is because I've believed it so? And that I can change any part of it that I want?

Right now, I'm deciding that I can feel good no matter what is happening around me.

What does it feel like when I know this is so?

How does it feel to be in charge of my emotions? And to *love* having them, for they guide me on my path to more joy.

How does it feel to be able to handle anything that occurs?

How does it feel when I'm more amused than frustrated by anything these days?

How good does it feel to be so full of joy and appreciation that nothing bothers me?

This is how I can feel every day when I choose to feel happy and free. I'm doing whatever it takes to stay in my good-feeling place. It's becoming so natural to me that there's no effort being made. It's just who I am. I'm able to be at ease and enjoy my life and that's how it's meant to be.

My free-spirited side is ready to be set free. I choose to practice acceptance, love, and appreciation of all that life brings me. This is true freedom.

Action: Here are some ways to help cope with stressful situations:

Remember from Step 1, you can fold your arms over while you're having a conversation with someone to help calm yourself. One hand on side of arm, other on side of ribs.

Cross your arms over your chest and do light tapping, alternating from side to side. Or consider trying EFT (Emotional Freedom Technique).

Gently squeeze your wrist and massage the pressure point on the inside, about two inches above the wrist, which can help balance emotional stress. (Not for pregnant women, as it can cause contractions.)

You can also just imagine you're squeezing your wrist or even getting a massage and feel the effects of it. Close your eyes and imagine that you're tapping on your chest under the collarbone right now, and see how your body responds.

Put your whole middle finger in the palm of your hand, wrap your fingers around it and apply light pressure on the tip of the finger with the base of the thumb. The meridian acupoint here can help calm anger or frustration. Do the same thing with the little finger when you're needing patience. Just hold and breathe for a moment.

Also, we can hold frustration in our rib area and tapping can help. Reach your right hand over to your left side and gently tap with your fingers or fist, from just under the arm all the way down to the waistline.

Repeat a few times or so from the top down, then switch sides. This is where the liver meridian can be found, and tapping here can release pent-up emotions. Set an intention to let them go.

Is there anything that you react to that would be really nice to let go of? Something that you may not even notice or realize you do, or that you have a choice in because it's been a thing for so long, that you feel like it's just how things are for you? For example, when someone says a word or something in a certain way that triggers anger, sadness, or an upset stomach, or makes you want to be somewhere else.

If you can think of something and you're comfortable with it, state your intention: I am deciding right now to let this go. I am in charge of how I feel, and I get to choose what affects me or not. The next time this situation or word comes up, I am not responding to it. I've made up my mind.

If or when it comes up again, if you feel yourself getting uncomfortable, immediately say to yourself, "I decided I'm done reacting to this. I'm in charge of how I feel and I choose to feel good" or something in your own words.

This is a great way to practice your control over your reaction to things. Once you achieve good results with this, you'll feel empowered to make more positive changes. You're in charge! Well done!

You're able to live your life feeling happy and free from morning to night, and the time is *now*.

Have a great day!

I Am an Example of Joy

I make it my goal every day to be an example of joy. It feels very natural to me, but at times I'm in my head about what I have to get done that day and don't even notice the people around me.

So I decided it would help if I reminded myself about it every morning before I leave the house. It goes something like this: Today I'm going to be an example of joy for everyone I see. And it's going to feel good!

How does it feel to be an example of joy? It may sound like something I'm doing for others, but in all reality, I'm the one that benefits most. When I set out to be an example of joy, I'm inspiring myself to feel good all day.

And in my effort to be an example for others, it always turns out so well for me. What more could I ask for? Well, maybe it would feel even better to know that I've uplifted a few people along my trail. Okay, I'll take it!

As an example of joy, how am I feeling around others? How am I thinking and acting? What am I thinking about them? What am I saying and doing?

What kinds of things have I been doing that are uplifting to others? Can I think of three right now?

    1. _________________ 2. _________________ 3. _________________

And what are three *new* ways that I can be an example of joy?

    1. _________________ 2. _________________ 3. _________________

How does it feel to tell someone another way to look at a problem they're dealing with? This isn't my job, but if I'm already in the conversation, it's an opportunity for me to practice speaking from the heart. Can I think of a time I have done this before?

What if I gave out more compliments to my loved ones? And how good does it feel when I give them out to random people I bump into?

What if I could set an example by showing others how I follow my heart? If I was following my heart's desire, what would I be doing that others might notice? Does anyone in my family get to see me in action? Think of this now.

Can I think of a list of things that I could do to stay aligned with feelings of joy? What makes me feel so happy that I want to share it with others?

Isn't it nice to know my positive energy will be returned to me somehow, some way.

Action: You have the wisdom and power to transform any situation. If you can imagine things getting better, and have faith and trust they will, they can.

When you're an example of joy at your home, workplace or anywhere, it's amazing what changes your high-vibin' energy can do to transform a situation. Add one lighthearted person into the mix and it changes the whole dynamics of any situation.

Think of an area of conflict, if any, and start bridging the gap between two people or a group situation simply by giving them your joyful attention or offering new words, insights, or ideas. And be sure to wish them more joy before you see them each day, and imagine them getting along happily.

Obviously, the action is optional, but it sure can be fun to see your power at work. You may see changes right away, or it may take time for complex issues, but know it will happen. Anytime you change *your* thoughts, energy, or behavior, the circumstances change around you. It's *fantastic*.

Now imagine how it feels to see positive changes at home. How does it feel to have everyone getting along better at home?

Always do what feels comfortable to you. Even if you wouldn't call yourself Miss or Mister Peppy, or prefer to spend much of your time alone, your positive energy and well-wishes are still making a difference. Big time.

Your energy speaks volumes and is received by anyone in the vicinity of your vibration level. Just as in the power of prayer, you're communicating and transmitting your thoughts through your vibrational energy.

Wishing you a joyful day every day!

I Am Open & Receptive to Love

I am more open and receptive to love every day. I've never felt more worthy of love and full of love for everything I see. And now I'm feeling more love for the people in my life. The energy I've been giving out is now coming back to me as well.

I have a new confidence and feeling of ease as I go through my day, and it seems to be attracting more like-minded people to me. It feels so good, and I have a feeling there's going to be even *more* opportunity for new friends and exciting experiences.

I have the mindset and energy now to transform all my relationships to a level of happiness that I envision for us. Even better than it is now.

When I'm feeling worthy of love, how do I feel?

What's it like to be comfortable with someone expressing their feelings to me? Do I enjoy hearing their words? Can I think of any words or phrases that describe how I *want* to feel when someone I know offers me compliments or loving words?

____

____

____

____

____

How comfortable am I when I express my feelings to them? Can I think of one response to their compliment, and what I'd like to say in return that expresses my affection for *them*?

____

____

____

____

____

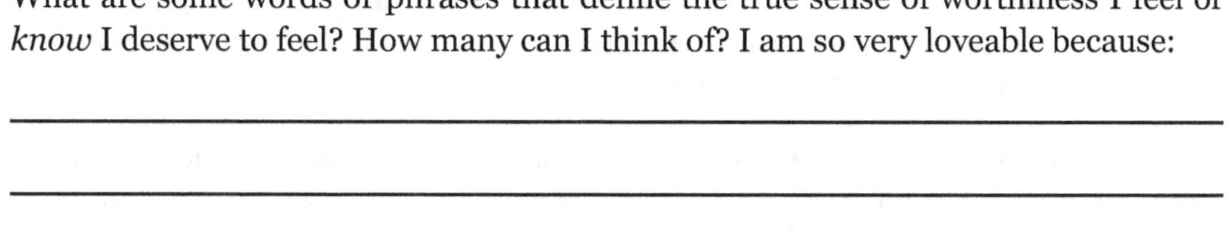

What are some words or phrases that define the true sense of worthiness I feel or *know* I deserve to feel? How many can I think of? I am so very loveable because:

———————————————————————————————

———————————————————————————————

———————————————————————————————

Is there anyone I know that I'd like to be more comfortable or confident with? What if I could imagine being with them right now? We're doing something together that is fun and relaxing for both of us. I can see them in front of me and I'm saying what I'd like to say to them.

What am I telling them? How does it feel to be confident and comfortable with them? When I'm being myself with them, how am I acting? I can close my eyes and play this through my mind right now, and end it with the response I'd like to get from them. Imagine it now.

How did the interaction feel to me? If it's not feeling quite right, I can visualize it again. I feel my courage and openly express myself and see the response I'd hoped for. I guide myself through it until I get the feeling I'm wanting or try it again another day. It will come!

I'm deciding right now to feel confident and comfortable and have things go my way the next time I see them. When it starts feeling good to think of it, it's that much closer to happening for me.

I am now becoming more open and receptive to love, and my life just keeps getting better!

Action: Take a moment to focus on your heart center. Imagine you're breathing in the energy of love and peace and see the colors pink and green there. It's like a glowing ball of energy that's being drawn into your heart center on every breath, warming and soothing you.

You can feel your heart energy getting bigger and lighter and your energy begins to fill the room. You're breathing in this great love, and as you exhale imagine love and healing energy being sent out to anyone you'd like to send it to right now.

There's another great way to feel more love in your heart and begin to attract more positive people, conversations, and experiences, or just to have a wonderful day every day. And this is to simply send out well-wishes and positive energy ahead of you, before you arrive somewhere. This is also a great way to prevent problematic issues or at least have them happen less often.

It's been shown that servers earn twice as many tips or more by smiling or secretly wishing their customers well *before* approaching them. This is just an example of how powerful your thoughts and intentions can be.

So if desired, do your best to get in the habit of sending well-wishes of more joy, love, and abundance, or whatever you wish before you arrive somewhere, to family or coworkers or anyone you're about to meet up with. It's often helpful to do it in the car so you remember every time you get in the car to do it.

While you're at it, imagine what it looks like when everyone's getting along and cooperating, or laughing with one another. See yourself there as well. Feel how it would feel. Sometimes you'll see an immediate change in what used to be more unpleasant circumstances.

Your thoughts and intentions and energy are creating the changes. It's the same reason thinking of your favorite things about a person or place will change the circumstances around it as well. You're applying your positive energy and things must change.

If you think you'll forget to do this, write it down on a sticky note or somewhere that you'll see it in the morning. Or put it on your steering wheel! Isn't it fun to have your family wonder what's gotten into you?

Take a moment to practice it now: think of anyone you'll be seeing today or tomorrow and wish them more joy and wellbeing, laughter and love, or whatever you wish. Think of your family, coworkers, boss, or employees and anyone you will see when you go into a grocery store, coffee shop, or anywhere you tend to go.

Better results are achieved when you're feeling good and your well-wishes come from a sincere and loving heart.

We're all connected by universal energy just as the water connects the fish in the sea. It can't easily be seen, but it's everywhere. You could say that your thoughts and intentions and well-wishes that are vibrational in nature are being carried by this energy that connects us. Perhaps it could be thought of like an electromagnetic radio wave or a wave that ripples through the water.

It's not something we need to understand to see our vibration in motion. The law of attraction is bringing like vibrations together, and your life experiences will show you evidence of it.

Let your expectation for your relationships be all that you want it to be. You are now achieving the happiest and healthiest relationships you've always deserved.

Have a wonderful day, Love!

I Have a Happy & Healthy Relationship

I always find creative ways to attract the right partner or nurture and improve the relationship I'm in.

First I decide what kind of relationship I want and how I want it to feel when I'm in it. And then I think of the qualities I want my partner to have and whether or not I'm giving out the vibe that will attract those qualities.

I can easily attract what my energy is aligned with. If I desire this relationship and feel that it's a part of me and who I've become, I will make it so.

Whether I'm with my current partner or wishing to meet an ideal partner, what kind of relationship do I want to have with them? What does it look and feel like?

Do I want someone who's thoughtful, romantic, and secure, or healthy, happy, and adventurous? Or everything all rolled into one? And why not?

Since I'm feeling so happy, healthy, and worthy, I never have to settle for anything less than a healthy, happy relationship. I have the ability to attract the relationship I want or transform the one I'm in until it feels just right for me.

Before I move forward, I do what I can to let go of any leftover feelings about past relationships. Have I ever wondered why I end up with the same kind of person in every relationship? What if it's because I was thinking about all the parts I didn't like?

If I look at those I've left behind with appreciation in some way, I'll bring that positive energy into the relationship I'm in or *will* be in. How does it feel to appreciate all the best parts of each relationship I've been in?

I bet there's at least one favorite thing about each one that I'd love to have in my relationship now. What are they?

____

____

____

____

Isn't it nice to know that all I need to do is focus on what I liked *best* about them, and I become a magnet for the partner or better relationship I want?

And how does it feel to know that the more I love myself and my life, the more comfortable and enjoyable my relationships are?

In the meantime, what if I practiced being in the qualities and characteristics and energy that attracts the kind of relationship I want? All I need to do is think about how it would feel and expect it to happen when the time is right.

How does it feel to be "the one" that's going to attract my ideal partner? Or reignite the relationship I have? I am their "one," and they are mine.

What would it take for me to be ready for the relationship I see myself in? Do I feel open and receptive to it? Do I hear a resounding "Yes!"?

Does my lifestyle have room for two? Is there a place for them?

When I think of them, do I see them wanting the same kinds of things I want from the relationship?

What qualities do I have that I want them to be attracted to? Would I like knowing they have the same standard as I do for the quality of the person they want to meet?

What are the qualities that I want them to have? Will we have differences that complement each other? *Hand write* a list right now of every detail of the ideal mate or favorites about a current mate, including their lifestyle, personality, career goals, looks, height, age, and more.

When thinking of how I *want* my relationship to be, how would I answer the following questions:

> What is our ideal relationship like?
> Do I feel confident and happy, and do I act that way when I'm with my partner?
> When I'm with them, what are three words that describe how I feel?
> How do we treat each other? Am I treating them how *I* want to be treated?
> What does it feel like when we're being kind and respectful? Or when we playfully tease each other? Imagine how this would feel. What words describe it?
> What are some things we like to talk about?
> What activities do we like to do together or apart?
> What plans are we making? What will we do on weekends? Where do we like to go together on vacation?
> What kinds of things do we do for each other? Think of three things each of us enjoy doing for each other.
> What else do I appreciate about them?

Do I feel appreciated by them? What do I want them to appreciate about me?
What is my favorite quality about them?
How do they make me feel when I'm with them and what do I love about it?
In what ways am I showing my appreciation for them?
Am I being my genuine self with them? How am I letting them in? Am I able to tell them how I really feel?

If I imagine they're sitting in front of me right now, what do I want them to know? Think of this now.

What would I say if it was coming from the heart? If I had no fear of how they'd respond or what they'd think about it, what would I love for them to know?

____

____

____

____

What do I wish for them?

____

____

____

____

If I could sum it up, what are my qualities and characteristics when I'm magnetic to my ideal partner? Think of the person I want to attract and what qualities I believe will attract them to me. What do I think they would be? Write a list or think of ten or more of them now.

____

____

____

____

____

How does it feel to be in those qualities? And are there any that I think I need to practice? What are they?

____

____

____

____

____

____

I'm deciding right now that I'm in those qualities and I am *now* magnetic to the relationship I desire. I've already intended it, and the ideas for feeling it more are coming.

As I go through my days in the weeks ahead, I will be in the qualities and energy that are magnetic to my ideal partner. I will practice this feeling state until it becomes a part of me.

If I want to feel ready for when I meet someone new, I can think of what I'd say when I meet them. If they were sitting across from me right now, and I was feeling as brave as ever, what would I say to them?

Think of one question and two statements that would get a conversation going and show them the most genuine part of me.

____

____

____

____

____

____

____

My true self is the part of me they won't be able to resist, and they can't wait to see me again!

How does it feel to be *so* confident that I say what I want to say the moment I want to say it, even if it's to someone I'm attracted to? It doesn't seem so scary anymore!

And if I'm in a relationship now, what if I started wishing them more joy, laughter, love, and wellbeing before I see them each day? What if I also imagined my heart center connecting with theirs and thought of the words "I love you and thank you"? What changes do I see it bringing about?

What if it works so well that it completely transforms our relationship to an even greater level of happiness for both of us? This is entirely possible. Am I willing to try it every day until I see the results? I intend to give it my best try!

How has my life changed afterward? How do we feel when we're together? If I close my eyes right now I can take myself there and be in the feeling place of it. How good does it feel? Where are we and what are we doing? What are we laughing about? Imagine it now.

Action: Daydream about your ideal relationship whenever the mood strikes. Imagine how it feels to be with them, what you're doing together, what you would talk about, where you'd go, and maybe even what they look like.

If it feels good, do it as often as you like. To remind yourself to do this, write down the question "What am I magnetic to?" on a sticky note and put it somewhere you'll notice it.

It can be fun to imagine the relationship you'd love to be in, and doing so will get your mindset in the feeling place of being in it. And by doing that, you're that much closer to living it.

Whether it's to improve the current relationship you're in or to attract someone new, you're getting ready for it. You're talking yourself into it. You're feeling good about it.

You're not missing someone or waiting for them; you're feeling *just right* where you are and excited about what's to come. You're feeling worthy and know the value you offer that *lucky* someone.

And for a current relationship, allow yourself to think of the amazing possibilities for your relationship to become the way you wish it to be or even better than it feels now. Anything and everything is possible!

Just notice the changes in your partner as you change how you feel about yourself and how you think of them. It's only natural for your circumstances to change as you change, so you're not trying to change anyone.

You might be surprised at how quickly a positive change can come about. You may see changes in how they look at you, how they talk to you, or how they feel about you.

And if you have trouble getting started with your daydreaming, here's a fun game to get you started. Using words or short phrases from A–Z, think of all the qualities that you want in your ideal partner. And if you're already in a relationship, think of all your favorite things about them: favorite attributes, things they do for you, how they make you feel, or anything you can think of that you cherish about them or wish to experience with them.

Another weird but fun way to use this game is to use A–Z to create a name for the many soulmates that are available to you, and state one quality that each of them holds. An example for letter A is "Alex/Alexis has amazing artistic abilities."

When all 26 of their qualities are combined, you've created the ideal partner for you. Hooray! But the real version will only have one name, of course. Then you can hold this intention and vision as your expectation for the next relationship you're in.

Is this too much? Never! Your thoughts and intentions create limitless possibilities for you. Remember, it's all in the name of fun. Thinking of it or saying it aloud feels great when you know you can ramble on about it freely, but you can also try writing them down sometime in your journal. See which one feels better.

Try it now if you'd like. Or try it the next time you're driving somewhere alone. Have fun and laugh out loud about it. It really can get you thinking and expecting that perfect someone to walk right up to you. And they will, *somewhere*, sometime.

Another idea to inspire yourself: consider having a romantic statue or painting with two people in it somewhere in your house. As you gaze at it from time to time, allow it to elicit emotions that feel something like being in love. Find the feeling place, and it must come. And the more in love you feel with any part of your life, the closer you are to *all* your desires.

Also, if you're currently in a relationship, remember to send well-wishes to them each day before coming home to them, and intend to connect to their heart center and say "I love you and thank you" if desired.

If you're ever hurting over a breakup, do your best to think of it in a way that allows you to feel better. Something like this: they couldn't handle the responsibility of a relationship. And the best part is, I'm free to meet the "right" someone. If I was still with the wrong someone, I would miss the one that's lining up for me. My ideal partner and I are becoming ready for each other. I appreciate all those who came before "the right one," for they helped me know what I truly wanted and deserved in a relationship.

Wishing you more love and joy in your relationship! You deserve it!

I Can Transform My Family Relationships

When it comes to family, it gets a little more complicated when trying to stay in a happy place. We care so much about our loved ones and we want what's best for them. We want them to be safe. We want them to make choices that are good for them. And sometimes we just wish we didn't worry about them. And this goes for the children *and* the adults.

But if there's a desire to make things better in some way, there's always a solution. And to find out what that is, I need to decide what I want first. One thing I know is that I'll feel better if I stop worrying. What else?

How do I want things to be at home or with other family members? Is there anything I would like to feel better about?

In what way would I like to see things improve? Can I imagine what it will feel like when we get there?

Can I find a way to accept things as they are?

Can I decide to make peace with anything that's happening?

What if I decided to stop getting involved with what happens between other family members and saw things improve on their own?

If I have a situation like this, imagine it now. Which one feels better: staying involved or allowing myself to let it go? _______________________.

Can I decide right now to start expecting good things to happen for them? What if I could trust that everything will work out as it's meant to?

Isn't it nice to know that when I see it this way, I'm contributing to better outcomes? With faith and purpose, I am changing my expectations and how I respond to situations, and it creates a ripple effect.

What if I take the time I spent on their issues to give myself the attention I deserve?

Does any of this apply to family relations outside the home?

What if I decided that it's okay if a family member doesn't agree with my life choices or anything they may judge me for? And that one day all will be understood or forgotten anyway.

How does it feel to know that my relative may only be doing that thing they do because they care?

What if I decided to admire or appreciate them for it?

Sometimes I may feel like pushing against what's happening at home or with other family members. I want to fix it. I want to help. I want to make things better and to feel better about it myself.

But the moment I decide to let things be, I might be surprised at how quickly things can improve on their own. And I *love* the idea of saving myself unnecessary stress.

No matter what, I'll remember that I have a choice to see every situation in a way that feels better to me, or not think of it at all.

What else can I do to improve my family relationships?

If I want to improve them, I need to feel confident in myself and happy about the relationship.

Am I acting confident and expressing myself clearly and calmly in each relationship? When I change how I'm acting, they will too.

What if I could practice the feeling place of happier, healthier relationships, and visualize the positive outcomes I desire?

If anything, what would I like to change about the relationship I have with each of my family members?

Or how would I like to see things change *between* them?

How does it feel to imagine everyone cooperating and getting along better with one another?

Think of one family member at a time to answer the following questions. Think of at least one answer for each question:

> What would I love our relationship to be like? What three words or phrases would describe it best?
> How do I want them to feel when I'm with them or talking to them?
> What do I appreciate about them?
> What are my favorite qualities about them?

What is one thing I let them know I'm proud of?
What is one thing they do for me or someone else in the family that makes me happy when I think of it?
How do I want to feel when I'm with them?
What would I guess are their favorite qualities about me?
What do I think they appreciate about me?
Is there something I know they appreciate about me but they're just not comfortable communicating it to me?
Is there a way to see their actions meaning more than the words I may wish to hear?
What activities do they enjoy that we do together?
If they could choose, what do I think they'd like our relationship to be like?
What is one thing I could do that I believe would bring us closer together?

If I imagine they're sitting in front of me right now, what would I love for them to know? Speak from the heart and say it all without fear of how they'd respond.

Answer the above questions again with another family member in mind before reading any further.

This is a great way to feel connected with someone and heal or strengthen a relationship, especially if they're in a phase in their life that's causing them to pull away.

If I continue putting my attention on my favorite things about each family member and I imagine our home life being the way I wish it to be, I can work wonders.

If I have the desire to go a step further, I can practice my way into a feeling state of a strong family leader who easily creates positive change. I am setting a clear and consistent example of how things will be.

I use such brilliant thoughts and persuasive words that no one can say no to me when I ask for help. I find the most creative and fun ways to do this.

I'm not going to change anyone. They will conform as I change how *I'm* thinking and acting and change my expectations about the way things will be for us.

I don't wait for the changes or feel impatient about it coming. All things will fall into place without any more effort on my part. If I want this to take place, I set my intention now for my desired end result.

If I imagine our home life being the way I wish it to be, how does it feel? What do I see happening after the changes? How has our life improved?

If I close my eyes right now and picture it, what are we doing? What are we talking about? Who's there? Are we feeling comfortable with one another? Are we having way more fun? Feel how it would feel to have it that way. Imagine it now.

From this point forward, if any issues were to come up...

How would it feel to let myself off the hook? To know that everything I'm doing as a parent, child, sibling, or relative comes from a place of love? I'm always doing the best I can, as are they.

No matter how much I want to help someone, I'll remember that they have their own built-in guidance system and trust that things are going to work out for them. And even if it seems like they're not doing so well at times, they're still becoming who they are, and in time they'll be better.

Hold them in your heart and send them your loving thoughts, but allow yourself to focus on your wellbeing. Stay balanced and strong. And know that it's the best thing you can do for everyone involved. Your energy is contagious!

Action: Here's a few ideas for healing or strengthening relationships, or ways that may help you enjoy a relationship more.

If you're returning home from a long day, take a few minutes or so to sit in a park or in the driveway before going back into the house. Winding down with music or a short meditation or deep breathing exercise will refresh you before seeing everyone and help you feel ready to enjoy your evening with them.

Give each of your family members a complement *every* day this week or show your appreciation for something they did for you. At dinner or sometime before bed, ask them what the favorite part of their day was. If it feels good, do it all the time.

If you're ever having difficulty in a relationship, you can intend to connect with their energy and send them loving thoughts. Your sincere intention and high vibrational energy has the ability to change any situation.

Consider choosing one family member now, and for the next few weeks before going to sleep or when they're standing in front of you, intend to connect with their heart energy and say "I love you and thank you." Let go of any doubt that things are *now* improving, as you focus on how you want things to be.

If you're needing more help with chores or errands, consider this or something like it: write a list of what needs to be done and include everything you can think of. Include loading/unloading dishes, counters, floors in each room, dusting, laundry, yard work, and more.

Pick a day and a 30- to 60-minute time frame weekly or biweekly that everyone is home, perhaps before dinner or a TV show for extra incentive. Write each task on a small piece of paper or index card. Put them in an envelope. Use separate envelopes for age-appropriate tasks if necessary.

At the chosen time, have everyone pick one thing from the envelope and come back for another task when they're done and keep going until the time is up. For daily tasks, consider using a calendar or white board to assign basic cleanup.

Before addressing the family, set an intention to feel confident that it's going to happen and you're going to see it through, and expect them to go along with it.

Sit down at dinner and kindly let them know that you're needing their help with keeping up with things. Tell them your plan and expectations: that you intend to keep driving them, giving them allowance, or paying for their phone or car insurance, or whatever else you provide for them, but you need them to start doing this *for you*.

If they oppose it in any way, just say I've been happy to do things for you, but I deserve your help too, and end the discussion. And then no matter what, follow through. If it's not working, consider making it a trade for having access to phone, video games, or something important to them.

This is a great way to stay caught up on things and relieve unnecessary overwhelm for you. Obviously you know best what works for you and your family. Best of luck!

Lastly, if you have young children that exhibit what you consider bad behavior, you may like this as an alternative to saying no or struggling with them. Generally, they'll always do what they get attention for. So try giving them a lot of attention for good behavior and no attention for the bad behavior, and things might balance out soon.

You can also redirect their attention to something you *do* want as soon as any bad behavior starts. Depending on how old they are, they may love it when you ask them for help with something, even if you have to make something up.

Also, if they're old enough to reason with, give them two other activities to choose from that you're okay with and they'll forget all about the other thing. It allows them to make a choice, and they love that!

May your family life be all you want it to be!

My Social Life Is Just Right

When it comes to my social life, I know what works best for my lifestyle. While I'm open to getting out there more, I like to keep things in balance.

However, as I evolve and my confidence grows each year, my interests are expanding as well. You could even say I've been a little bored with my life at times. So, I may be ready for more, and I'm always open to trying new things.

What if I took action and followed my heart's desire?

In what ways would I like to change my social life?

What are the things I'd like to keep doing? Think of three or more social activities I enjoy doing.

____

____

____

____

What are some things I'd like to stop doing? Can I think of one thing that isn't fun anymore?

____

____

If I had the courage to do *anything* I wish to do, what would I be doing? Name three.

____

____

Who would I be doing it with?

What kind of people do I truly enjoy being around?

Do I thoroughly enjoy the time I spend with my friends now?

Am I feeling the desire to attract some new friends that are more like-minded?

If I could handpick a new friend, what would their personality be like? Describe it.

____

____

What would we be talking about?

____

____

Where would we go or what would we do together? Imagine how it feels to be with them.

Can I see myself venturing out alone to enjoy a movie or dinner? What if that's how I end up meeting someone new?

Am I ready for that? How do I need to feel in order to make it happen? How does it feel to have self-confidence and courage? Can I think of any times I've been brave enough to do something out of my comfort zone?

____

____

How does it feel to love my own company?

What's it like to be so confident and at ease with who I am, that I could go anywhere alone and feel comfortable? If I had this trait, what would it feel like?

What's it like to have the freedom to go out and do whatever I want without having to wait for an available friend to join me?

What does that level of confidence feel like?

Write or think of all the words that describe the way I believe I need to feel in order to achieve the social life I desire. And if I'm perfectly happy with the one I have right now, I can think of everything I enjoy about it.

____

____

____

____

It's time to create a perfect day out for me, where I'm feeling free and fun and have unlimited options. I will take part in activities that light me up, excite me, make me laugh, or delight me in some way.

I walk about this day in a quiet confidence, with a slight smile on my face.

I'm doing whatever I wish with whomever I want.

> How does the day start out?
> How would I describe everything I'm doing in the morning, afternoon, and evening?
> How does the night end?
> How am I feeling afterward?
> Who did I spend my day with, if anyone? Who did I meet?
> What did I love about it?
> Did I let my confidence show?

If I close my eyes right now, I can take myself there and be in the feeling place of it. What does it look and feel like? Reach out and touch something in each of the places I go. Smell the aromas, taste the dinner, feel the warmth of candlelight on my face, and more.

How much fun is it? How good does it feel? What else would be happening? Imagine it now.

How do I want to feel when I wake up tomorrow? How would I like my day to go? If I'm looking for amusement, I'm going to create fun wherever I go. I intend to do this as often as I wish. I'm going to find things to smile and laugh about.

When I spend my day like this, how great do I feel at the end of the day? Wouldn't it be great if others joined in my fun? Does it matter to me if they don't?

I am so good at being in the joy of who I am that I sometimes feel like I'm in my own little world. And that's just fine with me!

Action: Consider putting yourself on the calendar right now for at least one day a month where you re-create your "perfect day." Write a list of all the things you thought you'd like to do, put them in an envelope, and pick one out on your chosen day each month.

Visualize your day the night before and the morning of, and boldly go where you haven't gone before. You can make it happen. Know that the universe is on it, and it will happen when the time is right. Wouldn't it be amazing if you happen to meet someone new by next week that could join you?

Why is it so easy for you to attract what you want now?

When All Else Fails, I Have My Sense of Humor

One can never take themselves too seriously. That's been said, and it sounds about right. What if I could say the same about everything else? One can never take *life* too seriously. Does that sound about right?

What if I could rely on my sense of humor as a coping mechanism for stressful situations? Especially when it comes to something that I just can't seem to let go of or get through without wanting to unravel?

You know, those times in my life when I'm confronted by someone or something on a routine basis that I might call a tyrant in my life? Or it could be a situation that keeps coming up with other people around me, and I'm in the middle. Doesn't it sometimes feel like they just want to make my life harder?

Even though I know that's not the case, aren't there times when it feels nearly impossible to ignore or not let it affect me in some way? At least until my superpowers kick in (and they will!). It could be an ex, colleague or a boss, or relative, but it's usually someone you can't avoid too easily.

So how can I get past it unscathed or without reaching some form of insanity? Well, that wouldn't happen, but what if I used a little tool that might be insane in itself? If it works for me, is it worth a try? Even if it could be considered quite ridiculous?

If it allows me to free my mind of it, stay in a good-feeling place, and stop me from reacting or causing further havoc, then maybe it could work for me.

Basically, if I associate anything with humor, it cannot harm me. When I'm amused by something, or even feel like laughing about it, this allows me to release my resistance to *any* situation. Then I'd be saying, "Stress? What stress? I'm over it."

Of course, it may not work for the sad moments in life, but it's a great tool. It's something I call a wonderful method of madness for great relief. It puts me back in control of my emotions, even under some of the most difficult circumstances. It's really weird, but it works.

When I tap into my creative mind and use a hilarious image for something I find annoying or scary, I end up laughing to myself instead of getting upset like I once did.

How does it feel to be able to let go of the most troubling or frustrating situations in my life?

What's it like to free myself of this *thing* I once let take control of me?

What if I use my brilliant imagination to wash it away, never to bother me again?

So what will I do the next time I encounter something that has me at my "wits' end"?

Action: Ok, ready to try it? Let's call it *My Silly Associations*. Think of someone or something that feels like a "thorn" in your side at times, or something like that. You get the idea.

Now think of a recent incident, and try to imagine the whole scenario in a comical scene. You've heard about speakers seeing the audience in their underwear to get over their fear of public speaking. Well, it's a similar idea, but doesn't include the naked part. That's up to you, of course!

Some ideas, very silly ideas, would be to imagine them as one of your favorite cartoon characters. Even more hilarious is to imagine them with a giant head of hair that surrounds their face and reaches the ceiling. And then add a color to it. Pink? Purple? Yellow or green?

Make it curly or straight or cascading down the hall. You choose. But have fun with it. Maybe add some furry feet or great big eyelashes. It doesn't have to be mean. They can still look cute!

Close your eyes and picture that someone right now, and the last thing you see in your imagination is their little, tiny face surrounded by all that hair.

Told you it was weird. Bizarre. Ridiculous. But did it work for you? Don't give up on the idea if it's something that could clear away your frustration for all of time!

Close your eyes, and try it again now. Really give it a good try, and see if it makes you giggle to yourself. The more you practice visualization, the easier this will be for you. And it has the potential to completely take away any thought or feeling of angst about seeing the person. It really makes you feel in control again when you don't let that person get to you.

You can even try doing this as you're speaking to them, especially if you feel like you're ready to "blow." It can provide immediate relief, truly! This is obviously something that you'll only need to pull out of your tool box if you happen to encounter a really difficult situation.

Another idea that can help you keep someone's negativity from affecting your energy is to try imagining them in a giant pink bubble. And do your best to just listen without commiserating with them or guide the conversation to what they're hopeful about or what you're comfortable with.

As for the comical scene, you can also try it on situations that scare you. Use it for pesky bees or bugs. Are you bothered by ants? Try picturing them wearing blue wigs and riding around on tiny motorcycles. This could work especially well if you ever have an ant invasion in your house one day and feel like you can't fall asleep until you know they're all caught.

Once you start laughing about them, they stop bothering you, even the bees! Remember it's what you focus on that you get more of. Your fear of them brings them around more. Laughing about it appears to make them magically disappear. What's that saying? Don't mock it until you try it.

You can also use this if you have a fear of flying in planes, or when a driver cuts you off. See the plane or the car or person encased in a giant cloud of pink cotton candy. Who could be mad or afraid of pink cotton candy? Especially when you associate that with carnivals and childhood fun?

It keeps getting weirder. But if you can take anything that bothers you even slightly and associate it with something that amuses you, it will never bother you again. It just takes practice remembering to use it when you need it.

Didn't we say this was an outlandish solution? Well if it made you laugh, it did its job. Laughing is truly the very best medicine.

If you're open to it, practice this the next time you have to handle a stressful situation. And if you really must use it on family, be extra nice, and make sure they look cute! Perhaps they're in a tutu?

Use your brilliant imagination to create the joyful life you want to live. In time you'll find that no-one or no-thing has the ability to take you out of your good-feeling place.

Let your creativity and sense of humor free you!

I Love My Life & All It Brings

I am practicing a feeling of appreciation for all that life brings me. I choose to keep this going so I can go through my days feeling happy with effortless ease.

Why is it so easy for me to do this now?

When I'm in this beautiful energy, I only notice what I like. I can see the part that I like about anything. It's easy.

When I have a sincere appreciation for my favorite things, it almost feels like being in love. How does it feel to be in love with everything I see?

How does it feel to have a slight smile on my face all day long as though I have a delicious secret?

When I think of my life, I focus on my appreciation for anything that makes me feel good. Anything I am. Anything I have. Anything that I get to do. I feel so fortunate to be who I am.

Why am I so fortunate to be me? What are the many things I feel fortunate to have or to be doing, and what do I love about myself and how I'm feeling?

____

____

____

What am I appreciating about my typical day from morning to night? Think of how I would describe it and what I love about it.

____

What can I appreciate about the people I see around me?

How does it feel when I'm only noticing the kindness, cooperation, and joy I see in others? Why is that getting so easy for me to do now?

I appreciate what others bring to my life experience, good or bad, for it always guides me to a better-feeling place.

How does it feel to know that wherever I am, I have everything I need with me?

No matter where I am, I take my heart with me. And that's all I need to remind me of who I am. All that I seek is within me. I feel that I have a "home" frequency of joy and abundance.

No matter where I am, I make the most of it and do what I can to enjoy it. In this way I will take that energy with me to the next place I'm at. Whether it's where I live or work or something else.

Wherever I go, I go in the spirit of joy, love, and appreciation. What I experience next, tomorrow, or in the future, is always based on my current thoughts. So, I am now creating a very bright future, as the saying goes!

I love that I'm getting better every day at inviting what I truly desire into my life. As I look ahead, I know things are looking up for me.

Action: Check in with yourself and see how you're feeling about your life. Are you able to accept or appreciate what is happening around you in some way?

If there's anything you're not enjoying, are you finding a solution or something else to focus on that feels good to you?

If desired, set an intention right now to feel differently if something like this comes up again. You're deciding now that you're not willing to let it bother you anymore. Imagine right now that you're in that setting.

You're at ease, and you're choosing love and blissful wellbeing. You have the feeling that anything that bothered you before is no longer active in your energy. It's left you. The desire for blissful wellbeing is stronger. You're so worthy of feeling good, and you know that.

And if other people are involved, you know there's no reason to get annoyed, upset, defensive, or guilty—or any other unwanted emotion—if blame is being put on you.

Because nothing anyone *else* does has the power to change your current state of joy or self-worth. You're not letting it.

You're now feeling more lighthearted about it than anything else. You're wishing them well. You're wishing for them to have more joy in their life and a better relationship with themselves.

And you feel so much better when you're able to coast along through your day like that. Afterward, you're feeling so in control of your emotions. You're empowered for life!

Look forward to loving your life more every day!

I Am in The Joy of Who I Am

Deep down inside, I feel so good about who I am now. I'm mastering my ability to be present, joyful, and in the flow of life. I easily let go of anything that could hinder my good-feeling place. I feel comfortable wherever I am and have no resistance to anything. This is always my powerful intention.

How did I get to this point? I made myself important. I became more mindful of my thoughts and emotions. I started to love being in my own company. Can I think of anything else?

____

Why do I want to feel this way? Because it feels so good and I deserve to feel completely happy in all areas of my life. Do any other thoughts come to mind?

____

When do I feel this good? Every moment of every day, I continue to practice guiding myself to feel the way I wish to feel. How? What am I thinking or saying or doing to feel good throughout my day? What is my focused attention on? Think of this now.

____

____

What does it feel like to be in the joy of who I am? It's become natural for me. And I'm seeing the results of my positive thoughts. I'm loving it, I'm being it, I'm making it mine. Think of as many words as you can to finish this sentence:

My internal joy feels like __________.

How do I guide myself back to a good-feeling place if I start feeling a negative emotion? Think of three or more ways I do this now.

____

____

If I start feeling any physical discomfort, what am I doing to soothe it? Is there a way for me to take my attention off of it and focus on something that makes me smile, laugh, or distracts me long enough for it to clear itself?

What kinds of activities or hobbies can I do that will totally get my mind off the issue? What are they? Can I start doing them more often?

How brave am I feeling about doing activities by myself? What kinds of things do I feel comfortable doing alone? Can I think of any?

What is the next activity I'm ready to try doing, alone or with my significant other or children, that would bring us to a place of utter joy?

What's fun about it? Does it make us giggle like school kids? Perhaps a water park? Paintball? Hula-Hooping? Swing dance lessons? Or share a giant bowl of ice cream with all the toppings? Any other ideas?

What if I picked a day for us to do this right now?

Action: Gently place your hands over your heart center, right palm first, and breathe golden light into your entire chest with your intention and ask "Mind, body, and spirit, show me how it feels to allow pure joy in my heart."

Allow your body some time to respond. Close your eyes, place your attention on your heart center, and silently repeat the words again.

State the following intention or use your own words: I can take this feeling of joy and peace wherever I go. It's forever in my heart and will remain my "home" frequency.

In your daily meditation, begin stating the intention that during the meditation you'd like to double your ease, double your clarity, and double the feeling of love in your heart.

Before coming out of meditation, ask to be shown how it feels to feel blissful or have twice as much ease, clarity, and energy, or whatever you wish for the rest of the day. Keep asking until it becomes your natural state.

Love the pure joy of every moment in your life. Just allow yourself to revel in it. And celebrate how good you feel!

I Am Gentle with Myself

I feel that an overall sense of happiness and personal freedom is becoming a part of who I am. And I can't even explain how good it feels. I'm simply allowing myself to feel good, and it's easy. Now I find myself really looking forward to more self-discovery as I continue to evolve.

And while I'm determined to strive for a *feeling* of blissful wellbeing and believe that it's always within my reach, I also need to remember that it's okay when I'm not there. What's important is that I accept and support myself in whatever way I can and let myself be when I need to.

So even though I'll always do my best to feel as good as I can feel, there may come a time that I feel like I'm trying too hard to "do whatever it takes." Or I could just have a feeling that I'm not feeling as good as I'd like to and can't seem to snap myself out of it. And I'll know when that happens.

Why is it so easy for me now to listen to that guidance that tells me to slow down and rest or stop thinking about something or do whatever my body needs?

If I'm ever overworking myself to get something done or trying to make something happen, wouldn't it be nice if I could stop pushing myself and just let myself be?

How is something achieved in life? Some believe that hard work and long hours are required. They're not. It's whatever a person believes, I suppose. But when I take the pressure off and let things be and have faith that it'll work out for me, it's amazing what I can do.

So again and again I'll remind myself that nothing in life has to be hard. Sometimes "working hard" means that I will give my all to something and make the most of it. I do it because I enjoy doing it that way. And that is such a great reason. So that's a little different.

But hard work is not required to achieve my goals, nor is it required to gain a feeling of self-worth. My self-worth comes from within, and is natural to me. There's nothing I need to do to be worthy of everything I desire. I am worthy.

And if I'm just being hard on myself for not feeling good sometimes, I'd be sending myself in the wrong direction. Being gentle on myself is about not getting mad at myself when I'm falling off the whole happy-cheerful-me train.

I'm going to know it's the wiser part of me getting me to slow down, take a step back, and simply allow myself to relax. I will do my best to stop thinking about whatever it is I may be pushing myself to do. Or whatever is overwhelming me, if anything. Or maybe I just feel blah or tired for a day.

Whatever it is that I'm feeling will pass. It always does. It can be rather quick, or it may take longer for more difficult things. Either way, answers and solutions or ways to get past it always come to me more easily when I'm not thinking about it so much.

And letting myself take it easy sometimes and not being hard on myself about it (ever!) will open me up to all kinds of inspiration and ideas. The pressure's off, and everything suddenly begins to flow.

So *I'm* going with the flow. I'm never being hard on myself. I'm letting myself be when I need to. And I'm okay with wherever I'm at. I completely accept myself and know I'm always doing the best I can. And that always means I'm doing what feels best *to me*. And it's pretty great, actually.

Action: Do something more to nurture yourself in some way this week, and maybe you'll find yourself doing it every week or so! Some ideas would be a bath, massage, self-massage, or self-healing technique or some form of energy work. Or take a swim somewhere or an extra walk, or simply allow yourself to take a nap.

And now, if you're open to it, you can do a basic self-healing technique which is also considered "energy work." Feel free to make up your own affirmations or steps as you go along. You'll be placing your hands over different parts of the body and saying the affirmations.

Begin by rubbing your hands together to warm them up. And then leave your palms together for a moment as you set an intention. Intend to call light to yourself and ask that you bring cleansing and balancing energy to your body at this time and throughout this mini session.

Breathe in naturally, and then focus on the palms of the hands as you slowly *exhale* throughout this exercise, lightly placing both of your hands...

On top of the head: My mind is clear and open for new insights and ideas. I am feeling connected to all that is. Stay here a moment and feel the healing energy. Breathe in, feeling warmth in your palms; exhale slowly, and sense a pulsation in the palms as they radiate energy to your body. Again: breathe in, then exhale very slowly, and sense the pulsation there. And take a couple more breaths here.

Over the forehead (with one hand on the back of the head): I am intuitively guided on my path to more joy. Pause here again, taking two more breaths, and feel the energy.

Over your eyes: I have a clear vision of my perfect future. Imagine you're breathing light into your eyes. Cover the eyes now, and take another few breaths, and feel the energy.

Over the ears: I hear my higher wisdom. Continue taking three or more breaths at *each* position, allowing time to feel the energy.

Cross your hands and place palms on shoulders: I feel supported.

Over the heart center: I am peaceful, happy, and free. It feels safe to follow my heart.

Over the upper abdomen: I am energetic, confident, and successful.

Over the naval area: I am calm and balanced.

Over the lower abdomen: I am flexible and strong, and I am safe.

Over each knee: I am moving forward and upward and easily through life.

Over each foot: I am centered and grounded.

Over the mid to lower back: I allow myself to release any subconscious fears and allow wellbeing and abundance to flow easily and effortlessly into my life.

I allow my back to melt into blissful energy here. I see it as something hard to the touch like ice, and it's melting into water, and now the water is turning into a mist and dissolving completely, as is any discomfort I may have had.

I am now sending what feels like a smiling energy to my kidneys and adrenal glands. I am feeling recharged. And once again, take a few more breaths, and feel the pulsation of the energy in the palms as you slowly exhale.

Feel free to do this again or take more time in each position if you decide to practice it regularly. But just a few minutes of this can give you great results. It may take practice and the more you do, the stronger the pulsating energy will be in your hands. And you may notice your hands getting very warm during the session and it's completely natural.

Also, it's always a good idea to drink a little extra water after any energy work. The energy work can be thought of as a flushing out of stagnant energy, and water will help it clear.

Pay attention to how you're feeling the rest of the day and in the days ahead. Any healing benefits that result from energy work like this are known to continue working or showing results of releasing any blocked energy. Either way, your body will respond in delight when you take the time to nurture yourself in this way.

Until tomorrow! Have a great day!

Happiness Is My Choice

I am so glad that I made the decision to start feeling happier on a daily basis. All day, every day. At times, I have to remind myself, but that's it. I made it so important to me that I won't allow it to be any other way for me.

So I make it my daily goal to feel as happy as I can feel. I may have been doing this for a while now or for all my life, but I'm getting better at it every day. There's no limit to the amount of happiness I can have. It's a feeling that keeps building.

My happiness is based on how I feel and how I view myself and my life, so it's easy for me to feel happy. It's always a choice I can make. And that's what I want for myself. I deserve to feel good! And I keep finding more ways to allow myself to feel even better. I find reasons to smile every day.

So, if happiness is a choice that I make every day, is there anything I can do to ensure it continues?

What am I already doing that I want to continue doing because it makes me happy?

What people, places, activities, special moments, or other things make me happy? What makes me smile, laugh, or get excited?

____

____

____

____

____

____

Is there anything I don't enjoy that is not obligatory and I'm still doing it anyway?

____

____

____

Is there anything in my life I'd like to change that I know would make me happier? Or maybe it's something I never thought of changing, but I'm open to other options I have now that I'm aware of them.

What do I need to stop or start doing that will make me feel more aligned with my desired reality?

____

____

____

How does it feel to do everything that feels good to me and let go of anything that doesn't?

What if I started small and tried doing some things differently if I knew it would make me feel happier? Or discovered that only after I gave it a try?

If watching television is something I enjoy, what if I started watching more comedies and less dramas? Laughter at the end of the day and before I go to sleep has a great influence over the way I'm going to feel when I wake up the next day. And it may even make for great dreams!

How about making my own party in the kitchen by turning on some music and cooking up a storm? What are my favorites? Tasty snacks or a gorgeous dinner? And of course I'll be dancing all the while! What kind of moves can I come up with? What if I tried some funky music and came up with some new moves I didn't even know I had?

I can have a party any time I want. On my own or with company. I just decide that I'm going to do it. I'm going to celebrate. And I decide I'm going to have fun. And then I let my imagination run wild.

It's also been said that a picnic is a state of mind that can be made anywhere. I *love* the simple meaning of that statement. And it's *so* true. So very true. And it's the concept I want to live by!

What about taking myself or my partner or family on a picnic, and letting everyone be involved with preparing our feast?

What else makes me feel happy?

____

____

What if I did something special for myself while I was sitting down on a porch or watching television or some other sedentary activity? Such as massaging my hands or feet, or indulging in a foot bath?

There's so many things that will keep coming to mind for more and more ways to feel more joy in my life. And when I follow my bliss, I am aligning more and more with my true nature and bringing my desires closer.

Why is it so easy for me to feel happy all the time now?

> I'm getting *so* much better at being my best supporter.
> I completely accept myself as I am.
> I'm allowing myself to be more fearless.
> I'm better every day in every way and in every area of my life.
> I am now feeling as happy and free as I was born to be.
> This is my intention, and so it must be.

Action: Gently tilt your head upward, close your eyes, and allow your *whole* face to smile. Feel it in your eyes and feel it spreading to the outer edges of your face. Imagine a golden light shining down on you like a beam of sunshine, or see yourself standing in front of you in this beam of light.

Intend to breathe its light into your face, and feel it wash over you. Take a couple more nice, deep breaths, intending to breathe light into your face. Try doing this now with your eyes closed.

Straightening your posture and allowing a smile to come over your face is an easy way to raise your vibration and lift your mood up. Research studies have been done to suggest that smiling is good for our health and longevity and a natural antidepressant. Just making yourself look up and smile every so often can work wonders for your state of wellbeing.

Here's a bit of a challenge for you, or perhaps you already do this. Begin smiling and saying hello to everyone you see or pass by. That's right, everyone. Try it for seven days and if it feels good, keep doing it. It's a great way to gain more courage, confidence, and friends, and enjoy your day more.

I expect you to find it so enjoyable that you'll never want to stop, especially when you start attracting more friendly people into your life because of the positive energy you're giving out.

Have a happy day!

I Set Myself Free

Freedom is my choice. When I'm feeling free to be me, I'm living my life exactly as I wish it to be. I get up every day and know that I have the freedom to choose how I want to feel. I have a natural air of confidence that I take with me wherever I go. There are no obstacles in my way.

I have my usual obligations, but my lifestyle is of my own choosing, and I embrace every part of it. I make the most of everything and find solutions to any conflicts to maintain the balance I seek. It's easy for me to feel good.

I have an incredible ability to focus and feel energized by anything that inspires me. I know who I am and what I want to do. I love this amazing sense of self-awareness I now have. But it's an easy feeling, not one of self-analysis. I expect things to keep flowing.

This is how I feel when I've practiced any feeling I want to feel until it becomes a part of me. I'm feeling my way into any way I want to live. Any way I want to be. Anything I want to accomplish. And anything I wish to have. I'm creating everything I desire with my magnificent words, thoughts, energy, and actions.

Why does it feel so easy for me to feel happy and free now?

What does my life look like when I'm feeling free to live life the way I intend to? If I close my eyes and take myself there, how does it feel? I can close my eyes right now and play the narrator that describes how I'm feeling as I go from place to place throughout my day of feeling free to be me. Do this now.

How did it feel?

____

____

____

____

____

____

____

____

____

____

How has it changed my life? Can I think of any ways that it's changed me or my life?

____

____

____

____

____

____

____

____

____

Now, just for fun, let's see what a "no rules" life plan looks like:

No rules
Be free
Eat what I want
Do what I love
Do it *when* I want
Enjoy it all

Other than the necessary family obligations, is this possible? Well, I only wrote it jokingly. But sure, it is. Am I already living this way now?

I like to believe I can use these rules for the family obligations as well. It may take a little time to come together, like changing from a job that pays the bills to a job I love to do, if that was even a desire. But it can happen. Anything is possible. Everything is possible!

Action:
Silently read the following questions nice and slow and allow yourself to feel the possibilities that are always available to you:

How does it feel when you allow yourself to feel completely free?
How does it feel to be so free and at ease that everything you desire begins to flow into your life?
How does it feel to free your mind of overwhelm?
How does it feel to allow enough ease to free your body of any discomfort?
How does it feel to be fully aligned with the blissful wellbeing that's natural to you?
How does it feel to confidently say what you mean and mean what you say?
How does it feel to offer your genuine loving spirit when you're in conversation with your partner, family, friends, or acquaintances?
How does it feel to grow closer to your partner?
How does it feel to share your true desires with them?
How does it feel to grow closer to your children or parents?
How does it feel to be as free as your inner spirit?
How does it feel to let your light shine in all areas of your life?
How does it feel to do whatever you want?
How does it feel to be and have and do all that you desire?

How do you feel? Did you let yourself feel the inevitable outcomes that are moving their way toward you?

If you feel inspired to act on any of these, think of a way that you could initiate things and set your intention to follow through with it. What's the obvious next step? Would you like to write it down or set a reminder?

Now, close your eyes, and see an image of yourself walking toward you. You're in a state of blissful wellbeing. You're feeling happy, healthy, and deeply satisfied with your life. You're feeling completely free to be your authentic self at all times. You're on top of the world.

As you get closer, see that smile and sunny glow on your face, and then feel that energy come into yours. This is you in your purest form. Embrace yourself, Beautiful!

Don't forget to close your eyes and see it, feel it, taste it, and touch it! And hold the vision of it, and think of it often. You're already there!

Why do I suddenly feel so lighthearted and carefree?

Appreciation Is the Key

It's time to practice more appreciation. How much more can I appreciate? Can I ever have too much? Not when I know it's the key to more happiness. And it's the key to achieve all my desires. The more I appreciate, the more I put myself in the positive energy that attracts all that I wish for. And it just feels so good.

So I can never appreciate too much, and I can never hear enough reminders to use it. Or to feel it and be in the energy of it. I want to be in a constant state of appreciation.

When I'm in that state more consistently, I'm noticing more good things happening for me. There's nothing like seeing the evidence of my positive thoughts begin to show up.

It's also a great thing to use if I ever feel the need to snap myself out of a funk or anything that feels like that. Who needs to feel blah, stuck, or can't-seem-to-get-myself-out-of-this-mood kind of feeling? Not me! If it ever happens, I try to get out of it as quickly as I can. And appreciation does it for me!

I can start simply by focusing on appreciation for who I am, what I have, or what I believe is working out for me. Or take a rest and appreciate my body for getting me to do that!

But this day is not about using appreciation for just getting myself to feel better.

It's about having a genuine feeling of appreciation for everything. I love thinking of ways to feel appreciation from morning to night. It's becoming natural to me because I've done it so often.

There really does come a time when it's all I think about without even trying. It's just how I feel and it's so natural to me. It's taken over any other kind of thought.

I am even noticing that I often take a breath and feel appreciation for my body in some kind of involuntary way. It's like I'm sending myself a thank you.

I love to appreciate my day, my life, my mind and body, my family and my work, just about my every waking moment that feels good to me.

So, what am I appreciating today?

What am I feeling lucky about? Can I think of the many ways I appreciate my life?

What do I appreciate about my mind or body? My strong immune system? My perfectly functioning body? Anything else? What do I love about my mind and how it works?

What do I appreciate about myself?

What do I appreciate about my life?

What's making me feel proud right now?

What am I really good at?

I am completely free to love and appreciate *everything* about myself and my life. Why is it so easy for me to find a way to embrace it all for making me who I am, and guiding me to where I'm going?

I am always in the right place at the right time and moving forward and upward. I am always on my way to better things.

Action: From the time you wake until the time you rest, what are you appreciating? Write a long list of what you love about your typical day. You can do this in your appreciation journal. Include every detail you can think of from how you're thinking and feeling to what you're doing, who you're with, and where you are. Use one-word answers or short phrases.

As always, keep doing your best to feel more appreciation for things in your life. And when it gets harder on some subjects, think of your favorite thing about the person or situation and focus on that. Or put your attention on something completely different that feels really good to you. Easy, right?

One last intention for you: I am now allowing things to be easier for me. And the people and situations that show up in my experience are transforming to accommodate this desire.

Always include yourself in daily thoughts of appreciation. You're amazing and may need a reminder of that!

I Always Feel the Way I Wish to Feel

How do I want to feel today? I love that I can feel any way I want. Each day upon waking, I pick a feeling I want to focus on. Today it could be a feeling of joy. Tomorrow it could be clarity. Of course I can have both, or a myriad of feelings, but I like to pick one or two to focus on when I'm setting my intentions for the day.

If I set my sights high, all the components of my day will fall under the spell of that one powerful intention, and my day will unfold just so. It helps that I have an expectation for feeling ease with all that goes on. I love feeling at ease with all that is!

I think my favorite one of all is when I decide to focus on fun and amusement. Appreciation is another one, but I'm staying in that mindset nearly all the time now. Of course blissful wellbeing feels pretty great, too.

I can even set my intentions *way* in advance for how I want my week or month or year to go. I find it thrilling to use my creative mind to plan things out like this. It's even better when I see the evidence of my wishes coming to life. But the best part is, it just feels so good. And it's so exciting to imagine what's to come.

So, how do I want to feel today? Think of it now.

____

____

____

How do I want to feel by the end of this week? Am I feeling satisfied about what I've gotten done? Am I feeling happy with myself for making time to relax and have fun? Think of how I'd describe it. How many words or phrases can I come up with?

____

____

____

____

____

How do I want to feel this whole month and the next?

____

____

____

____

What is the goal? What's my desired end result?

____

____

____

____

How does it feel to have achieved it?

____

____

____

____

How do I want to be feeling this coming year? What are my goals this year? What's the desired end result?

____

____

____

____

How does it feel to have achieved all of it?

____

____

____

____

I've set my intentions, and if I can keep this in my thoughts until it *feels* like a part of me and I'm certain it's going to happen, I can achieve it.

Action: Write down a list of words that symbolize the many ways you may wish to feel in the weeks ahead—anything you can think of that will help you achieve your goals or wishes. Do this for home, work, or play. And pick your two favorites for tomorrow.

You could also write "How do I want to feel today?" on a sticky note and put it on your bathroom mirror to remind you to set your intention each day. Or for fun and inspiration, put each word you wrote on your list on a small piece of paper and place them in an envelope, and pick one each day.

If you're ever having a day or moment where you're feeling off-balance, indecisive, or unhappy, remember to ask yourself how you want to feel. Begin to think of the words that would describe it, and soon you'll find that the fog has lifted. In addition, tell your mind and body it's time to feel blissful.

Use this process any time you want to feel better or align with what you want to achieve in any given moment. You can use it to gain energy, clarity, or anything you wish. The more you practice, the quicker you can get yourself there.

Also, a great way to keep your positive momentum going is to ramble on about things you feel good about: how you feel, what you love about how you feel or what's happening in your life, and anything that comes up while you're doing it.

You've already been doing the "rambling" thing quite a bit while reading this book, but here's some more practice for you.

If desired, tap gently on the chest just below the collar bone on either side. This can help instill the words. You may also want to try the under-eye point used in EFT, just below the center of the eye where there's a tiny indent. This point is on the stomach meridian and is known to relieve fear or stress. As you tap, read or say this as slow or fast as you'd like:

How do I want to feel today? Mind, and body, it's time to feel blissful. What can I say that will lift me up higher than I am right now? I want to feel good about where I am. I want to feel really good about how far I've come. I wish to always honor myself with words of encouragement and acknowledge how far I've come, no matter how small my steps have been. I also intend to be more aware that I've come a lot farther than I give myself credit for sometimes. I love that I am certain that I am becoming all that I'm meant to be. *Nice deep breath...*

I love that I'm peeling away the layers, one layer at a time. And I am bit by bit, moment by moment gaining clarity, blissful wellbeing, and feeling happy and free from morning to night. I am attracting every wish I've ever thought of. Every desire I've ever had is happening now. I wish for things and the wishes are now coming true.

And no matter how it seems, I can go from worry-worry-worry to free-free-free. With baby steps or giant leaps, I'm peeling away the layers of any life experiences I've had that ever made me fear anything, doubt myself, or overthink things. I am now in a place where I expect great things to come. And I know I'm always in the right place at the right time and feeling safe. *Nice deep breath...*

I'm feeling aligned with blissful wellbeing. Even when I'm not, I move forward in my practiced state of wellbeing with unwavering purpose. I'm at ease with who I am and all that life brings me. The more I practice it, the easier my life gets. And that's worth every bit of time I spend guiding my thoughts. And I'm doing it until it's *so* instilled in my mind that my subconscious has melded into one with every part of me. *And breathe...*

I love that I have brand new cells being constantly replenished in my body, and every one of them responds to my newfound thoughts. Every one of them is resonating with the love and freedom and lightheartedness of my spirit! I love knowing that the quality of my thoughts are creating the quality of my life, and it's lovely. This can only be the best environment for my body and every cell in my body to maintain the most blissful wellbeing for me. I'm so happy to know what I know and feel what I feel! *Another deep breath...*

At times I may have wondered if it was totally possible, but I'm starting to believe it may be so because my body's showing me evidence. I can feel the changes taking place in my mind and body. I can feel my energy more, and I'm getting better at it every day. I'm celebrating that today! It's also great to see my positive thoughts creating better experiences for me. I've been noticing more kindness and love around me. And it's getting easier to accept or appreciate anything else that's happening. And breathe...

Continue this with your own words right now. What's making you happy today? Go on and on for a minute or more, letting it all out, beginning with I love that I am...

When you're finished, take a few deep breaths as you gently squeeze your wrist. Place your crossed hands over your heart center and intend to call back all your energy. Drink a little extra water, as tapping can get your energy moving and may clear out toxins more quickly.

If you're feeling really good, allow the energy to stay with you for the rest of this day, and wake up feeling even better!

Everything Is Working Out for Me

With all knowing within me, I'm being guided to trust that all is as it should be. For myself and everything else. There's a sense of freedom in allowing this to be my belief. And I like the idea of going with the flow and accepting all that life brings me.

So ideally, I like trusting that all is right with me, all is right for everyone, and all is right with the world. It's exactly as it should be, and things are always working out as they're meant to. Each of our journeys will guide us to what's best for learning who we are and what's needed for our personal growth. No one else can choose that for us.

I hold the same opinion of my family and friends and anyone I know. Nothing is wrong, and they're getting it right. What's right for them is right for them, and *how* they get to where they want to be is just right. I want to put my whole trust in that.

What if I could believe that all that happens, good or bad, creates expansion and inevitably makes things better? If I desire it, I intend to hold that thought as my perception.

What if I released any concerns and decided that there's no need to push against anything, as attention to it invites more of it? When I release any concerns about what's to come, it frees me. As awareness prevails, I'll go with what feels right to *me*.

Can I see myself accepting or embracing all that occurs in the world, knowing that it's in a constant state of change and still becoming what it is?

How does it feel to trust that nature is at work? The universe is at work. And there are individuals, groups, and the masses finding solutions to every issue that arises.

What if I believed that we're all connected to a vast universe of knowledge and have the ability to resolve anything?

What if it was easy to see that the earth's in balance, and new resources are being created to replace what's depleted? To remember that it's not done becoming what it is?

How does it feel to believe that everything is right where it should be, including me? And that I'm always moving forward and upward, becoming clearer, brighter, happier, and more abundant?

Isn't it nice to know that even though it's tempting to feel sorrow for those in need, noticing the wellbeing and prosperity in the world will help create more of it and better serve humanity? Which one feels better to pay attention to?

I also love knowing that *my* feeling good, no matter what's happening with others, puts me in a better position to help them. If I'm focused on their problem, or worry or sorrow for them, I'm unable to help from that standpoint.

It feels so much better to send them well-wishes and expect things to improve for everyone involved. I have much greater influence over any situation when I hold this vision. I'm better for everyone in my state of total wellbeing!

As desired, I intend to send well-wishes where they're needed, yet stay focused on the evolution of things. And I'm able to take time to focus on myself. This is in no way selfish, as I am contributing more to the wellbeing of *all* by living out my life purpose.

I *could* think of that purpose as loving myself, loving my life, and loving *all* that is. If I love to give of myself, I'll give myself at least an equal amount of attention. Although the more I evolve, the more I may be able to give of myself *and* still keep that balance. I'm the only one that knows what makes me happy.

What if I put my whole focus on the great things I expect to work out for the world and for me?

What if I could feel certain, without a single doubt, that *all* is right with me?

Can I trust that the more I think or *say* that everything is working out for me, that I will be shown more evidence of that? I'm deciding right now that I'm going to say it every day, starting now. Everything is always working out for me!

What's been working out for me? Is there anything that I can think of that I've wished for and it came through? If I look back a year or five or ten years, has anything happened that turned out for the best? Take a moment and think of this now.

Have any of my intentions in the last few weeks manifested anything for me? Such as a new feeling or mindset, a better-feeling body, more enjoyable experiences, contact with an old friend, or material things I've desired? What are they?

We all have an inner knowing that guides us to discover what needs to happen for even more wellness, joy, and prosperity to abound. And it's always available to me. All I need to do is be open and receptive to it. I'm doing that right now.

I choose to allow blissful energy to flow *to* me and through me and to all those around me and accept the limitless abundance that's available to all of us.

The more I accept or appreciate what is and have faith that it's all becoming better in time, the more I'll stay in a harmonious place of ease and joy. It's in this place where I fully align with my blissful wellbeing, my freedom, and my every wish.

Action: Continue to be more aware of things that work out for you. Acknowledging and appreciating new positive energy or emotions or anything that shows up for you will bring more of it to you. Thinking of it or writing it down on a daily basis builds a wonderful momentum, and every day is better than the last.

If you haven't already, consider trying to go without hearing or watching the news for seven days. Imagine it now. Does it feel better or worse? If desired, give it a try, and if it feels good, continue going without it for as long as you can.

If you hear of any world events that concern you, intend to send well-wishes, imagine the situation improving, and do your best to allow yourself to let it go.

Also, back in Step 1, you were asked to say "ease, joy, wellbeing" during the first minute or so of your meditation. If you're still doing that and it feels good, great! Now I'd like to suggest that you add to them or replace them with "loving, happy, and free."

So beginning with your next meditation: with your attention on your heart center, smile to yourself, and as you breathe in, think "loving," breathe out and think "happy," and breathe in and think "free." And repeat the words for about a minute or as long as you'd like. Try it now.

During your regular meditation or deep breathing practice, allow it to naturally instill the feeling of what each of these means to you. See how you or your body feel afterward.

Remember, it's just another way to guide your thoughts or train your subconscious mind to think only thoughts of happiness and freedom. Until one day you find yourself completely aligned with everything you've ever desired and are living the dream.

Why is it so easy for you to feel so satisfied all the time? Is it because you know deep down inside that everything you desire is working out for you?

My Life Feels Deeply Satisfying

It's my relationship with things and how satisfied I feel about them that is creating the quality of my life experiences. When I have a sincere appreciation for what I've chosen for myself, whether it's a job, a partner, or something else, I'm putting the kind of positive energy into it that paves the way for a better future.

So even if I'm not feeling quite fulfilled with something, I focus on the parts I like. And this way, I set myself up for the best possible circumstances in the next experience I have. And they will come as I become ready for them. I attract a better relationship, a better job, and better circumstances for all areas of my life.

I love it when I reach that state of mind where everything feels more satisfying to me. And I'm noticing that a lot of things have become easier in my life.

How has my life been feeling easier for me? What parts are feeling easier? How many can I think of?

____

____

In what way has it become easier to be my authentic self?

____

How much easier has it become for me to meet new people?

How much easier is it for me to talk to someone I'm interested in getting to know?

How has my relationship been easier?

____

How have relations with my family become easier?

____

How has my work day become easier?

____

Is there anything in my life that has started feeling more effortless?

———

What other parts of my life would I like to be easier, and what can I do to initiate that change?

———

One at a time, write down or think of all the things that make me feel satisfied about my life. What do I feel good about when I think of:

My family:

My friends:

My personal life:

My workplace and the work I do:

The state I live in:

My hometown and the people in it:

Other:

Be sure to finish this step now before continuing.

If I wasn't feeling particularly thrilled about *any* one of these things before, am I feeling any better about them now?

———

I've reached such a wonderful place in my life that I am now feeling deeply satisfied with my life. This intention is affirming my belief that I am now achieving anything I desire.

Whatever is meant to be will be. Life is good and I am free.

Action: For the next few days or so, think of all the things you like about the people you're with or the places you're at. Do your best to keep that thought going until it's the only thing you think of when you're there. And it will be your practiced thought until you find yourself in a new and better experience, if desired. And if you're deeply satisfied with everything in your life, it's even better to keep that thought going. Well done!

Allow yourself to feel deep satisfaction with any part of your life that feels great to you, and the rest will come along. Have a wonderful day!

I Am in the Qualities & Energy of Happiness & Freedom

There's an inherent source of energy within me that always feels happy and free. Why is it so easy for me to connect with this now? I intend to be in the qualities and characteristics and energy of happiness and freedom from now on.

I easily stay aligned with this energy when I practice feeling appreciation, self-love, autonomy, lightheartedness, clarity, peace, courage, and confidence. Being self-governed and the ability to speak my truth naturally comes along with it.

I have the feeling that I'll always be tuned in like this. It's as if there's no turning back. There's only forward motion for me now. What a *glorious* feeling!

What are the qualities or characteristics that I'm in, or intend to be in, to continue this feeling of happiness and freedom? There's a long list of them. What are they?

____

____

____

____

____

____

What am I choosing to be or have or do from this point forward? Finish the sentences below, giving as many answers as you'd like for each one.

From now on, with the best of my intentions:

I choose to feel _______.

I choose to be more _______.

I choose to have more _______.

I choose to enjoy more _______.

I choose to do more _______.

I will do my best to _______.

I am really good at _______.

I am excited about _______.

I am ready for _______.

I am now achieving _______.

I decided, and it's done.

How does it feel when every part of me is in harmony with my spirit? What words would I use to describe it?

____

____

____

____

____

____

I want to express my appreciation for the support of my mind, body, and spirit, as well as the universe or word of my choosing, for keeping me in harmony.

Mind, thank you for the _______, _______, _______, _______, and _______.

Body, thank you for the _______, _______, _______, _______, and _______.

Spirit, thank you for the _______, _______, _______, _______, and _______.

Action: Do your best to remind yourself daily of the qualities and characteristics that you wish to be in to achieve more joy and personal freedom. Or simply say to yourself: "How does it feel to allow myself to feel happy and free today? Mind, Body, and Spirit, show me how it feels to be in that blissful energy."

In what ways will you allow yourself to feel happy and free today?

I Am Focused & Unstoppable in My Spirit of Joy, Love, & Appreciation

In my invincible spirit of love, I feel a *tremendous* sense of fearlessness and wellbeing. I feel safe and know that wherever I am, I belong there. I'm never out of place.

How does it feel to have the courage to go where I want to go, be who I want to be, and do what I love to do?

Why is it so easy now to allow my heart's desire to guide me there every step of the way?

How does it feel to be so in the flow with life that traffic and weather seem to transform to accommodate me?

When did I start believing that I'll always arrive safely and on time, wherever I go? And *always* have a great parking spot as well! I say this often and it never fails. What else can I say often and make happen?

____

____

____

____

____

____

____

____

How does it feel to always expect good things? And to expect goodness from others?

What's it like when people go out of their way to be kind to me? And to know that the more I notice and appreciate it, the more often it happens?

When did it become so natural for me to share only the most positive thoughts that I'm focused on?

And how does it feel to have so much love in my heart that I see someone else's potential, even if they haven't yet?

Why is it so easy for me to be myself now, without *any* pretense whatsoever, no matter who I'm with?

How does it feel to be in a place in my life where being alone never means feeling lonely?

What's it like to bravely take part in some new venture I never thought I'd try? Do I hear ziplining? Or perhaps kitesurfing? Woohoo! (*Come on, you know you want to...*)

Why am I feeling so certain that everything in my life is becoming better every day in every way?

I am always in the right place at the right time and moving toward a better place. I believe that and feel certain of it. When I carry this feeling with me wherever I go, only the best outcomes can come from that.

With my positive words, thoughts, and energy, I am able to transform or guide any situation I am in to an outcome that will benefit all.

I am now easily and freely moving forward and upward on my wonderful journey of life.

To create the life I wish for, my only work is to feel as good as I can feel. What are ten or more words or phrases that describe me when I'm feeling focused and unstoppable in my spirit of joy, love, and appreciation? Think of them now.

Finish these sentences with something that I've already done or want to accomplish. Give multiple answers for each question, using the most powerful words that I believe will guide me to that feeling place or state of mind:

Why am I starting to feel so _______?

Why do I feel more at ease with _______?

When did I become so good at _______?

Why is it suddenly so easy for me to release _______?

When did I start having more _______?

Why am I now able to be so _______?

When did I start to feel more _______?

I can now see myself doing _______.

Is there anything else I'd like to add?

I love feeling focused and unstoppable in my spirit of joy, love, and appreciation!

Action: How does it feel when you wake up one day and it has happened? You got your biggest wish. What's the first thing that comes to mind when thinking of it? What was your wish? Are you ready to start creating it more purposely in step three?

On another note: just as intending to arrive safely, think of one thing that you could start saying that you believe you can make happen. You can make anything happen and could pick anything, but choose something that you're feeling ready and fairly certain about at this time in your current mindset.

As you see more results, you'll gain more confidence in your ability to make things happen for you. That is, if you haven't gotten there already. Write it down and set up a reminder to say it daily. You'll make it happen! Yay!

Allow yourself to feel empowered. Have a great day!

1–2–3: I Feel Free

As you read this day's intentions, do your best to feel these words are true for you, changing words to those you prefer, if desired. Notice if you have any tension in your body now, and check in afterward to see if it's still there. Now, take your time, smile and breathe deeply, and allow yourself to feel really happy. If desired, do some gentle tapping on the chest or place hands over the heart center.

1-2-3, Mind and Body, it's time to feel free. Show me how it feels.

Inner Being, how does it feel to be set free?

You could say that life is effortless. I am at ease with who I am. I am at ease with all that is. I am lighthearted and carefree. I am energetic and lively, and *full* of vitality.

I am confident, clear-minded, and in the joy of who I am in *this* present moment.

I allow myself to feel good, to feel happy, and be free.

I know who I am and what I want, and my ideas and I continue to expand. I feel certain about the best possible outcomes for my future.

When I want to feel happy and free, how do I guide myself there?

I intend to connect to my heart center by putting my attention there, and think of words that feel like freedom to me. Something like this...

> Now I've been set *free*, and I feel as my inner spirit feels.
> How does it feel to be happy and free, as I was *born* to be?
> The only way to describe it is a feeling of being balanced and whole again.
> Having a clear mind and a soft, comfortable feeling in my body.
> A feeling of complete ease, where there's nothing pulling me in different directions.
> It's brought a tranquility to my life that I'm not sure I've ever known.
> It feels like my mind and body have united and taken on the essence of my inner spirit.
> It feels like I'm living in harmony with all life, as an invincible being of light and love.
> I feel that life is a gift and something to celebrate every day.
> I am relaxed and know that all is well and always works out.
> I expect good things to come to me and those around me with effortless ease.

The energy within me is *pure* and *present* and *joyful,* and spreads beyond *all* boundaries.

I see *all* things through the eyes of love, and it sets me *free!*

I am playful and purposeful, and positive outcomes and opportunities find me.

I am inspired to be the person I was born to be, and do what I love!

I recognize my connection with all that is and this precious earth we call home.

My inner spirit continually guides me to stay aligned with my true nature.

I trust in the power of my words, thoughts, energy, and actions.

I am enjoying the sights and sounds and aromas all around me.

Everything seems to taste better, smell better, sound better, look better and feel better.

The only things that exist for me now are those that please me.

And I feel free to be me.

The part of me that's been waiting to be set free.

I want to live this way because it feels so good, so me, so amazingly free.

My reality is becoming what I wish it to be, what I think it to be, what I imagine it to be, and what I feel it to be.

I am attuning myself to a very high vibration frequency of love and above.

And as I do, I am shining the light for others.

This radiant energy uplifts and inspires.

This is how I choose to live my life.

This is my powerful intention.

Action: Now if you're feeling really good at this moment and you want to lock this feeling in, place your whole left thumb in the palm of your right hand, wrap the fingers around the thumb and gently squeeze it. Now breathe in "1-2-3" and say **"Free"** as you exhale.

Again: 1-2-3 **Free**, and state these intentions or create your own—I feel free. I intend to feel this way throughout the remainder of my day and anytime I choose. When I breathe in and think 1-2-3 **Free**, what that means to me is that in that instant I am allowing my mind to become clear and spacious. All my thoughts have been taken aside. All tension is leaving my body. I feel my entire body soften, beginning with my forehead, eyelids, and shoulders. I am suddenly feeling lighter and freer and have blissful energy flowing through me.

Release the finger if you haven't already. I can bring this feeling back to me any time I wish by breathing in to the count of 1-2-3, and say or think of the word **Free** as I breathe out, or by squeezing the thumb, or both.

You can even picture the word over your heart center; breathe in, 1-2-3, slight pause, exhale, **Free. I feel free.** Now breathe in to your heart center and imagine the word "free" written there, or allow yourself to feel the meaning of it. As you exhale, send out love and light anywhere you wish: to your body or to loved ones.

With practice, you'll be able to see the word written over any area or feel the meaning of it to clear a headache or other discomfort, or just to feel good. You can even try using it to balance your chakras! All you need to do is have the desire for it, the belief and expectation of it working, and a sincere intention. And then remember to use it. If not now, it will work, so keep trying if it feels good.

If you think of it like a decision you're making, you can say "from now on, when I count to three, whatever words I say after that will be." And each time, specify what you want, such as "1-2-3, my mind and body are at ease, my body is full of energy, and I feel blissful." Your body will respond.

Try aiming for the next best feeling from where you are. So if you're feeling great, aim high. If you're feeling a lot of discomfort for any reason, make your intention be simply to feel better. And keep leveling up from there.

Now, if you're open to it, send out appreciation or well-wishes. Say or think of anything you wish, or consider using this powerful visualization: imagine "Thank you; I love you" or "I wish more wellness for you" written on the ground in front of your feet, and watch it float away, multiplying by millions and covering the entire earth.

Feel as though you're giving the earth a great big hug of appreciation, and allowing the high vibration of your words to reach the animal and plant kingdom and all bodies of water, as well as the people. Lastly, see it reaching your family and send them extra words of love. Close your eyes and visualize it for a moment.

Feel the energy you sent out coming back to you now. Expressing this love and appreciation is such a nice way to raise your vibration, and it feels great. So do it as often as you'd like. You're making a difference!

You've made it through Step 2! Well done, My Dear.

How does it feel to be aligned with more happiness and freedom? How does it feel when you allow yourself to be struggle-free?

Why is it so easy for you to keep this going? It's available to you, and it's inevitably becoming a part of who you are, if not already.

Life keeps getting easier for you! It's better every day in *every* way. Be in your pure positive energy and expect it to be this way for you. It's on its way to you now.

Continue to acknowledge and appreciate the good things that are showing up for you, and you'll create more of the same or better. You're setting yourself up for more positive outcomes. And if you enjoyed any of the actions during Step 2, mark the pages somehow, and continue practicing them.

What did you learn and how do you feel after completing this step?

Has anything changed (*your energy, thoughts or feelings about something*), or have you experienced any stress or pain relief? If not now, you will in time; have faith, and keep moving forward! I believe in you!

What's Next

And now you're ready for Step 3...

The next 30 days will be focused on a state of abundance

where all your wishes come true!

Step 3

I Am Creating the Life I Wish For

The purpose of this step is to practice an abundance mindset that allows you to find that feeling place of anything you wish to be, have, or do. A place where all your wishes come true. And they *will*, of course.

Where your attention goes, energy flows. So you have the ability to direct that energy to achieve more success in any area of your life.

So you'll be practicing a feeling of abundance and alignment with your desires until:

> You feel that your desires are a part of who you are.
> Your energy is in the feeling place of having achieved them.
> You believe in your dreams and expect them to happen.
> You trust it's working out in whatever way it's meant to.
> You're in the spirit of prosperity.
> You're at ease with all of it and let it flow into your life.
> You've become energetically aligned with all your desires.
> Your wishes come true.

All you really need to do is feel your love for life and the ease and joy of your present moment as often as you can, and everything you want will naturally fall into place.

But you can use your actions, intentions, and creative thinking to feel that it's already a part of your life and who you are. And doing so can help move your plans along.

If desired, set this intention for the next 30 days, or create your own:

> I choose to do whatever it takes to feel my way into the state of mind that aligns me with anything I wish to achieve.
> I will be in the energy and qualities of my desires.
> I am open and receptive and allowing good things to happen for me.
> I intend to achieve all my goals, wishes, and dreams!

You're on your way. And it's going to be great. But, most importantly, always remember to have fun along the way!

I Know What I Want & Why I Want It

I am now and will always be creating the joyful life I was born to live. I love that I'm being more purposeful about it every day. I know the possibilities, and my potential is limitless and allows me to achieve anything I wish to be, have, or do. If I can imagine it, I can achieve it.

When I have a strong desire and believe in it and expect it will happen, I plant the seeds for my ideal life to unfold perfectly right before my eyes.

I am now becoming energetically aligned with every one of my desires. I intend to feel my way into the energy and mindset I need to be in to achieve them. And I will remain focused on my why. I want what I want because I know it will *feel* amazing.

Most of all, I intend to revel in every moment leading up to the manifestation of my desires. The best part of any of this is the journey I am on and how I feel when I'm living it!

Some of my desires naturally came about as a result of any challenges I've faced. They certainly made me want a better life for myself, and for that I am thankful. But I'm happy to say that I'm better at controlling the kinds of conflict that show up for me. And that's making it easier for me to focus on creating my life with my positive words, thoughts, and actions.

I'm going to write another wish list today, but it's become way bigger than the one I wrote in Step 1. My desires are bigger and stronger and are feeling more achievable the more I align with this blissful wellbeing. And I feel that I've set myself free! It's making me feel bolder about what desires are possible for me.

When creating this wish list, I imagine there's a giant store with all the things I want and more. This "store" includes things to do, places to see, new stuff to buy, courses to learn new skills, and career or lifestyle changes. Anything at all.

I'm going to think big. I can pull out every big and little thing I ever thought of doing, while staying open to the new ideas that I know will come to me. Are there any hidden desires I set aside because I thought they were beyond my reach at one time? If I had a desire for it, it's achievable.

Let's ask some questions to get me thinking about what I want my ideal life to be like.

What is calling me?
What keeps coming to mind that might just be my life purpose or a hint of a new passion that's waiting for me to discover it?
What do I *love* to do?
What do I love to do for work?
What hobby would I love to be doing full-time and get paid really well for it?
What courses would I take or what new things would I love to learn?
How would I like to become a teacher or leader in some way?
Is there anything I want to do in my community or for the world?
What kind of lifestyle do I have?
What would my perfect day be like?
In what ways would I like to spoil myself?
What would I love to do with my family?
Where do I want to travel to? Who would I go with?
Where would I take myself?
What material things do I wish for?
What gifts would I give myself?
What qualities do I want to make my own?
How do I want to look and feel?

What is one thing I really, *really* want more than anything?

____

Is there anything in my life I wish to change or improve upon?

____

____

____

Is there anything I'm still doing that I don't enjoy anymore?

____

____

____

When I'm ready, I intend to trade it in for something that lights me up!

Briefly state or think of what my ideal life would be like in the categories below. Let it be easy and fun or full of intrigue and adventure; whatever I wish it to be.

Home Life:

Love Life:

Social Life:

Career:

Passions and Dreams:

Material Things:

How much money do I want to make next year? And in five years?

____

What does it feel like when I've achieved my desires?

I can close my eyes and take myself there right now and feel it with all my senses. In each area of my life, what do I see and hear? What can I taste or touch, and how do I *feel*? Do this now. How did it feel?

____

And now, I've just met someone new and they'd like to know more about me. I'm telling them all about who I am, what I do, and what my life is like upon achieving my desires. What would I say?

____

____

____

What do I wish to achieve this year? And by the end of next year?

____

Where do I want to be in five years? Ten? Twenty?

____

____

____

I give myself permission to fulfill my every whim. I am now achieving all that I desire!

Action: From now on start writing anything that comes to mind that you wish to achieve in a new journal that you will call your "Wish List" journal. Let your first page be your all-inclusive wish list that you were thinking through just now. Start it now, if possible.

Include answers from today's questions, as well as a description of yourself and how you feel once you've achieved your desires.

Also, write every detail you can think of for *any* desires you find yourself dreaming about. Include how you want to feel, what qualities or skills you'd like to acquire, new ideas for ways to have fun, people you want to meet, places you want to go, or things you want to have. Everything.

Write down a date that you'd like to achieve your bigger goals or desires by. If you get any inspired thoughts on how to make it happen, write it down and consider taking a step in that direction.

Keep the book with you if possible so you can add things as more things come to mind. Consider reading them each night before sleep to keep your vision in mind. At some point, you can look back and see what you've achieved.

Also, choose one to three wishes from your list that you feel really good about when you think of them. Write down on paper or a sticky note: "I am now achieving ___" for each wish in order of priority, and fill in the blank accordingly.

Put it somewhere that you'll see it often, like inside your bathroom cabinet. Every time you open it, say the affirmations out loud and ask yourself how it feels to have it or be doing it. Then think of the words that would describe how it feels once you've achieved it.

Write it a second time on paper or an index card and carry it with you in your wallet or purse. Keep thinking of the end result. Do this until you achieve it. Then pick a few more from your wish list when they start feeling good to you, and do the same process.

The law of attraction governs all things. Anything you see around you was once a thought. Your thoughts are becoming your reality. Always. Know that the quality of your life is equal to the quality of your consistent thoughts. And you're getting it right!

Enjoy making your wish list! This is the really fun part...

My Desired Reality is Ready for Me

Once I have a desire, the energy of it exists.

So, all that I wish for is available to me, and all *I* need to do is feel receptive to it and line up with its energy.

To do so, I need to let go of any limiting beliefs and feel worthy of my desires.

I need to believe in my dreams and expect them to come true.

I need to be open to whatever way that happens.

And for the best possible results, I need to practice a frequent state of joy and appreciation. This allows me to align with *all* my desires more easily.

I'm already living in this energy, but there are many other ways I can help my dreams along. And the better I feel about any particular desire of mine, the closer I am to seeing it come to life.

If I can focus on one or more things in my life that make me feel really happy, I will hold an active vibration that aligns me with *all* my desires, and I will start seeing results.

And no matter what undesirable circumstances I've been in before, it will never have a role in what I'm attracting into my life *now*. All I need to do is take my attention away from it.

I am now putting my energy into all the great things I *want* to experience. And this is how I *always* get to where I want to be.

So, there's really no need to be concerned that anything could *ever* get in the way of my desires or stop me from moving forward.

It's time to allow more abundance to flow into my life, and fully accept it.

It's time to surrender to my dreams and love and nurture them.

It's time for me to create the life I'm meant to be living. Where I live in peace, joy, love, and prosperity.

All good things are coming to me.

How does it feel to be completely receptive to anything I wish for? So much so, that I become magnetic to all that I love, all that I want, and all that I deserve.

In the weeks ahead and always, I will be practicing how it feels, and preparing myself to allow and accept all the great things that I know are manifesting for me.

Action: Reread this day's intentions and allow it to resonate for you in whatever way you can. Ponder it. Let it sit with you. Intend to hold it in your thoughts. Do whatever you need to do to keep it in mind from this point on.

On another note, isn't it nice to have an easy "day" for a change? You're not off the hook yet! You have more "work" to do, but only for a little while longer. Hang in there. You're doing an awesome job! I just know you are. I have faith in you. Do you? I hope so, and if not, it's time you do. Just decide *that,* right now, and say "I have so much faith in me!" And just like *all* your desires, it's *done*.

I Am Creating an Atmosphere for Success

It's time to set myself up for success in living a life I love, without exception.

What I want is ready for me, and my only work is to create a *feeling* and an atmosphere that allows my desires to easily manifest.

To do this, I want to practice working *with* the law of attraction, rather than against it. That means I want to be more consistent in offering a higher vibrational energy.

And I want to offer thoughts that invite the *right* kind of circumstances into my life. Basically, my thoughts are an open invitation or a magnet for what I'm attracting to me.

What do I want to invite into my life?

____

____

____

Whatever it is, I want to become one with it. I want it to be part of me. I want to feel good about it. I want it to be who I am. I want to live it, and breathe it, and be in the energy of it.

How does it feel to be one with my desires?

How would I feel when they're a part of me?

____

____

____

How would I be living?

____

____

____

If it's different than how I'm living *now*, how can I align with it? If I become energetically aligned with it, what I want can manifest rather quickly. It's the lining up part that may take some time. *Or* maybe not!

What changes could I make to my lifestyle that would prepare me to receive my desires?

____

____

Am I looking and feeling the part of a successful person in relation to my particular desires? If not, what can I do to change that?

____

____

What changes could I make to my home or work space to make me feel like I'm getting closer to the next step I'm seeking?

Could I make a place for the people I want in my life?

How can I set things up to be more receptive to what I want?

Am I making room in my life for a partner if that's what I desire?

Am I offering the positive vibe I have when I'm at my place of work so I create a good vibe going into the next job, if applicable?

In the days and weeks ahead, I am taking more steps to help my wishes come true. I am creating the right atmosphere for my desires to manifest. I'm getting comfortable in my role as a successful person, whose only job is to feel joy!

Action: Hopefully you're still doing your deep breathing or meditation practice daily or as often as you can (no pressure intended!).

Before you begin, start asking how it feels to allow yourself to feel twice as much clarity and joy, and ask to double your ability to visualize your perfect future. Then begin the meditation with the intention that this change is taking place during the meditation and the energy will stay with you through the day.

Here's a little visualization exercise to stimulate your kidneys and solar plexus. The solar plexus, just under the rib cage, is felt to be our power center. It's associated with our self-confidence, motivation, will, and destiny. Stimulating the area can improve your success and help you reach your destiny. Just because I said so.

Start by seeing or sensing a golden sphere of light that's shining brightly and beaming like a ray of sunshine just in front of you.

Its energy is reaching your solar plexus and connecting to your core or inner light. Breathe in deeply, and intend for it to fill you with the energy of abundance.

Allow it to energize you and your kidney energy. Let yourself feel it. This light has a magnificent quality to it, and it's providing nourishment to your body and soul and fueling your success in all that you do. The energy in and around your kidneys is becoming lighter and freer.

See or sense this beam of light moving to the top of your head. Breathe in here and feel the energy clear your mind. Now, follow it to your heart center. Breathe in here and feel the energy of unconditional love.

Now intend to take a slow, deep breath into the solar plexus, pulling the golden sphere of light in here, then sense it flowing upward to the crown of your head, and as you exhale, feel it coming back down the front of you and back to the solar plexus. And for you...

> I've tapped into the earth's balancing energy.
> I've tapped into the universe's infinite energy and intelligence.
> I'm connected to my internal source of wisdom.
> Ever increasing as I focus on my solar plexus.
> This is where I connect to my natural self-confidence, my willpower, and my motivation power to achieve my greatest destiny.
> I breathe in the powerful energy that's available to me.
> All around me and always within me.
> As I make this connection and put my attention on it, I cultivate energy that stays with me all day, every day.
> I am breathing it in to every cell in my body.
> From this moment on, I intend to embrace my pure positive energy and allow it to permeate every area of my life.

Skip this next step if you're feeling pretty confident in your ability to achieve success: Now, place one hand over your heart and the other over your abdomen, breathe naturally, and set this intention or reword it to your liking:

> I am deciding right now that I am giving up any fear-based thinking, self-doubt, or second-guessing myself on any subject. I will not allow anything to keep me from my desires. *Nothing* can. I will continue doing what feels right to me and have fun while I'm doing it!

You are naturally successful. Have a great day!

I Am Worthy of All My Desires

I'm becoming that person that has it all. People are wondering what's gotten into me. Why is it so easy for me to feel happy? How did I get to be so confident in myself? Where did that glow come from?

I am feeling worthy of *all* my desires. What am I worthy of?

How does it feel when I allow myself to feel worthy of all my desires?

In what ways do I value myself and know that I am valuable to others? Is there any question about how fortunate someone is to know me, to be with me, or to have me as a family member?

Could there *be* any valid question about my worthiness to be happy or achieve my goals?

Never!

What is my worthiness based on? Isn't it my opinion of myself? What if I took away any learned beliefs that I'm more worthy for being a hard worker, a good friend, or a superhero, or someone that goes above and beyond in general? What am I left with?

At my core, I am all that I need to be. There's no need for me to be anything more than I wish to be. All of the great things I do are worthy of praise. But all I need is me.

When I believe in myself solely because I know I am magnificent as I stand here, just as I am, this is my self-worth. And I am deserving of all my desires. I was born this way!

What's it like to feel worthy of my desires?

What's it like to feel like I'm part of the crowd when I'm among highly successful people?

What if I allowed myself to be at the level they're at in terms of their mindset? I like knowing I can be, and I am when I let it in.

Isn't it nice to know that any self-doubt I've ever had will naturally be transformed by my abundance mindset?

How does it feel to be proud of who I am and what I've achieved, whether it's being a full-time parent or big-time leader?

What's it like to feel worthy of love and know that I'm a cherished friend, child, parent, or partner? And for my love alone to be enough for me?

How does it feel to know that when my loved ones aren't with me, they're secretly praising me?

What if I knew that I'm way more appreciated than some people will ever admit?

How does it feel to know that even when a loved one is a little mad at me, they're loving me, or they wouldn't care enough to get mad?

How does it feel when I appreciate myself for just being me? For my brilliant mind, beautiful body, and amazing strength of character?

And that is the part of me that people are seeing and attracted to. And these are the same qualities of the people *I'm* attracted to. Hey, that means I'm in the character of the person I wish to be!

On another note, am I the kind of person that tends to put in more hours at work than I'm expected to? If so, I will consider this:

Why do I overwork myself?

Am I busying myself to keep my mind off something else or because I was taught that working hard was the key to success or to feel worthy of it?

What if I slowed down long enough to hear inspired ideas on ways to earn a lot of money doing something I love?

What if I don't even realize how much more amazing my life could be if I just started paying more attention to myself? And do more of what I love to do.

When I find a way to enjoy the work I do, or choose to do something I love to do, I never really "work" a day in my life.

I can make my life experience any way I wish it to be. I'm in control of it all.

If it doesn't feel like that now, it will as I empower myself with thoughts of abundance. There are limitless possibilities.

I will know this when I begin to see my thoughts turning to things. Maybe I've already had a taste of it, but there's so much more to come!

Action: Decide that things don't happen to you. They may happen to someone else but they don't happen to you. Your life is in balance. You always arrive safely. You never get a cold. You always get picked for the job. There's no lack here.

You are abundant in nature. You are whole, you are perfect, you are strong, and you are healthy, happy, and harmonious. You can be and have and do anything you set out to do!

If you could think of one action or intention or affirmation that would inspire you to feel your true self-worth, what would it be? Choose something now and practice it as often as you can. You can do it. You can do anything. You've made it this far in this crazy-ass long book, haven't you?

You're paying attention to yourself and sticking to the plan, and you're doing an awesome job! Allow yourself to continue to grow in your adoration of your precious self.

That's what you're doing now, isn't it? Hooray, I say!

I Am Open & Receptive to Unlimited Abundance

I'm ready to allow more abundance into my life. I want more for myself. To feel better, to live better, and to love better. I want to be more, do more, and have more.

So I'm feeling really open to more joy and adventure and doing more of what I love to do.

And I'm giving up excuses. There's nothing keeping me from what I want. I decide. I choose. I make the rules for myself and my life. I'm making it happen.

I am now, more than ever, open and receptive to the unlimited abundance that's available to me. I *love* knowing that abundance is a choice, just like happiness.

I am all in. I'm all in for my wellbeing. I'm all in for more freedom. I'm all in for abundance and way more fun.

My energy is aligning with my desires. I'm becoming a vibrational match to every bit of it.

How do I allow the abundance to start flowing?

What if I knew, without a doubt, that I could have it all? Every *single* thing I've ever wanted comes to me. It finds me. All things are set in motion. The answers come to me. The next step becomes obvious.

Synchronicities are occurring left and right. Each desire is playing out in front of me. Showing up on my doorstep. And all at the perfect time.

And it's all happening because of this effortless process of allowing.

What can I do to get myself into a state of allowing and stay there?

How does it feel to know the ideas and insights on how to achieve my desires are flowing to me?

What if I could just tune in to myself frequently during meditation or on a walk and hear these insights?

What if an idea of a lifetime came to me while doing something that made me feel so relaxed that I allowed it in? An idea that will change everything!

What if it happens while I'm in the shower? Isn't this one of those places where amazing ideas or epiphanies can come through? As it has for so many? This is how easily it can happen, and I'm open to it. I'm open and receptive to anything that's beneficial to me.

Why is it so easy for me to do this now?

Action: How does it feel to be open and receptive and allow abundance to flow in your life? Similar to how you've been feeling, it can feel like this...

Silently read the words below, *very* slowly. Start by slowing your breath.

Mind, it's time to be at ease. With attention on forehead: breathing in, 1-2-3, breathe out, **E-A-S-E**. I allow my mind to be clear and feel spacious. Mind, how does it feel when I allow myself to release all resistance? Release *all* resistance. How does it feel to *allow* myself to feel blissful? Breathe in, 1-2-3 **Blissful**. Breathe in and out, repeating the word: blissful, blissful, blissful.

Body, it's time to feel free. With attention on the heart center: breathing in, 1-2-3, breathe out **F-R-E-E**. I allow my body to feel *blissfully* free. Body, how does it feel to *allow* myself to release all resistance? Release *all* resistance. *All* resistance is leaving me.

Feeling softer. Even softer. I am lighter and freer. How does it feel to allow myself to feel blissful? 1-2-3 **Blissful**. So very blissful. Body, thank you for the wellbeing.

To *allow* is to find ease. It's the absence of resistance. To allow is to follow your bliss and feel as good as you can feel. You're guiding your thoughts and transforming any negative emotions to positive thoughts and emotions.

All of this is allowing your desires to manifest. Let go of the need to know when or how something will come about. Just expect it *will* and be open to whatever way that is.

And when you least expect it, amazing ideas on ways to achieve your goals will come to you. The more at ease you are and the more you focus on what is working well in your life, the more the ideas will flow.

See the abundance all around you as you enjoy your day!

I Believe in My Dreams

I wished. I dreamed. And I am now believing my vision is achievable. I believe in it so much that it has no choice but to materialize.

I really enjoy dreaming about my desired outcome with faith and trust and expectation it will come. My consistent thoughts will bring it into my reality.

I am not wanting it or yearning for it because I know with certainty it will come. It will come when I'm ready. I feel that it's mine. It's a part of me and who I am. It's my own creation that's unfolding perfectly before my eyes. This is my powerful intention.

So, what do I believe I can achieve? Do I believe in all my wishes, dreams, plans, or goals?

Is there anything that I think I need to do or change about myself before I can achieve them?

I am deciding right now that no matter what I know, or don't think I know, I am capable of doing everything I desire. I have unique talents and gifts and the natural ability to accomplish anything I decide to do. What I seek is already within me and the answers will come.

How does it feel to believe in myself? To know that I can do anything I decide to do?

How does it feel to believe in my dreams?

How does it feel to think about my ideas playing out? To daydream until it becomes a clear vision and then a plan...

How does it feel when I think of my dream life? And imagine how I feel when it's mine?

How does it feel to love it and appreciate it?

How does it feel to be excited about what's to come for me?

What's it like when I trust that it will?

How does it feel to be certain that I'm going to know what to do and how to do it when the time is right?

How does it feel when all my words, thoughts, and actions are in keeping with the energy of the successful and joyful person I intend to be?

How does it feel to know that the plans I have are all getting done?

Action: The law of attraction is always responding to your vibration and your consistent thoughts. If you're not already, start getting yourself to that feeling place that you wish to be in every single day. You're telling the story of who you choose to be on a continuous basis, and lack or limitation does *not* exist.

Here are some affirmations to get you started, and some you can make up yourself. The more you say things like this to yourself, the more your brain is being retrained with new thought patterns and washing away any old limiting beliefs that weren't yours to begin with.

As you recite the intentions, *very* gently tap in a clockwise motion on your solar plexus, just below the rib cage. Stop if it's uncomfortable.

I love being me. I love being in this body. I love living this life. I wouldn't want to be anyone else. I believe in myself. I feel the value of getting to be who I am. I love the way I think and feel. I love knowing what I know. I love that I cherish my thoughts and ideas. I love when I let myself revel in the spirit of fun. I love knowing that I can do anything.

I can choose how I want to feel. I can choose what I want to do. I get to choose what I believe and what I invite into my life. I can create any feeling and any reality I want to exist in. I am using my creative mind to be what I want to be. I can see it, feel it, taste it, and touch it, and it's mine.

I am now achieving blissful wellbeing. I am now feeling happy and free. I am now achieving all that I wish for. I love that I gave myself permission to have as much fun as I can have and to know that is all I need to do to get to the point of inspired action and achieve my dreams!

My consistent thoughts are creating my reality.
So I focus on the spectacular things around me.
I am in the present joy that surrounds me.
And that's the key to attracting what I want.
Why is it so easy for me to do this now?
Why is it so easy for me to believe in my dreams now?

To be successful in anything in life, you must love and accept yourself. You are now matching the vibration of the reality you wish to achieve. You are a magnificent creator, and you are worthy.

What you want is working its way toward you. It's inevitably becoming yours. You are holding a mental conception of yourself in the highest level of joy, wellbeing, and abundant prosperity. You are practicing it until it's all you know. All that you know to be true for you.

You believe in your dreams now more than ever, and life is becoming way more fun!

Day 67

I Always Expect Good Things to Happen

I always expect good things to come to me and those around me with effortless ease. And I get what I expect.

I fully expect my dreams to come true. What would a dream be without my faith and trust in that?

And I love knowing that focusing on what I love in my life and expecting more of it will always keep that energy coming back to me.

Where my attention goes, energy flows. This is not only so in my body, but also applies to my desires. It gives me the ability to direct my attention and energy in a deliberate way to create my ideal future. And whatever quality of energy I put into it will come out of it.

As I focus on one or more of my desires that feel achievable and good to think about, I'm offering no resistance and remain in a state of allowing. I'll soon be expecting all of them to manifest.

That is how I know all my desires are achievable. Always. It's up to me and the quality of my thoughts, intentions, beliefs, and expectations.

What do I expect?

What do I expect my life to be like?

____

What do I expect from my body?

____

What do I expect for my family life?

____

What do I expect to work out for my career?

____

What do I expect to achieve?

____

What kind of success am I expecting?

____

How much wellbeing, joy, laughter, love, and abundance am I expecting?

____

How much more fun am I expecting to have in my life? What are some fun things I expect to happen?

____

How good do I feel about the quality of my thoughts and intentions? Are my expectations high enough? How much higher can I go?

When feeling inspired, how much easier is it for me to take the necessary steps to follow my dreams?

How exciting is it to move forward with faith and purpose?

Isn't it nice to know that all I need to be doing in the meantime is allowing myself to be at ease and focused on whatever brings me joy?

Why is it so easy for me to expect that all my dreams are coming true now?

Action: In your wish list journal, make a list of everything you expect to come to you in your lifetime: goals, dreams, things, people, relationships, fun, success, and more. Begin the page with something like "I expect all good things to come to me, beginning with:" and use the categories mentioned for an outline, or create your own.

Have fun and enjoy how good it feels when you're writing them out. Let it inspire you!

Make a point to daydream about any part of it that feels good to you. Envision your desired outcome, and expect that all your desires will start to feel this good.

You are now becoming a masterful creator!

I Am Constantly Expanding

When I think of how much I've been evolving and know there's more self-discovery to come, an eagerness comes over me, and I feel empowered. I'm constantly expanding in all areas of my life and becoming more of who I truly am!

And I know that means *I am now becoming fully aligned with all my desires.* Once again, I had to sneak that one in there. I could say it all day and it wouldn't be too much!

However, I never want to downplay how amazing my life is just the way it is, or ever feel that I'm only thinking of tomorrow. I'm actually really good at being in my present joy and totally appreciating all the great things that are happening in my life.

I also know that every step of the way toward meeting any *one* of my desires is too good to pass up. The journey that leads up to it is the best part of all. I love this time in my life! And I also love thinking about how far I've come.

What's life like when I'm in the midst of my ever-expanding life? Doesn't it seem to keep getting better? Through any ups and downs, I always come out of that with a stronger desire, a clearer knowing, and more determination to be living in joy and effortless ease.

With my free will, I have a choice in how much expansion I allow. I can choose to open myself up to more expansion in *any* area of my life.

How does my life change when I intentionally decide to allow myself to expand more?

Can I see myself stepping out of my comfort zone, if need be?

What new things will I dip into?

____

____

____

____

____

Isn't it nice to know that I'm going to keep growing into who I am, even if I don't consciously decide to? But which feels better? Having control over what comes to me and seeing it happen sooner than later, or sitting back and taking what comes?

Does it make sense for me to stay where I am in certain parts of my life? Does it feel better to allow change to happen or stay where I am?

Whichever feels better is my answer. There's no wrong answer. I choose. I decide. I make the rules. My expansion comes from within, and I am right where I'm meant to be.

How do I feel *now*, when I know I'm constantly expanding my level of wellbeing, clarity, and joy? I am *always* aligning my thoughts with the life I want to live.

Can I see how well I'm doing? Do I feel how much I've grown? Why is it so easy for me to feel a sense of personal freedom now? I'm constantly expanding my awareness. And I love that my desires are also changing and expanding with me.

Why is it so easy for me to follow my emotional guidance now? How I feel has become my compass for making excellent choices for myself.

I'm learning more of what I want and don't want, and it's helping me decide what path to take the next time similar choices come up. And I like that I'm feeling encouraged to embrace new interests and experiences.

And if I'm ever bored with my life, or feeling "stuck" in any way, I do something about it. If I change even one thing, there's the potential for everything to change. Every move I make creates a wave that's set in motion.

Am I feeling stuck or bored in any area of my life? What is one thing I can do differently that will get a different result for each situation? Write or think of them now.

How does it feel to know these little changes will help keep my positive momentum going?

What if I believed that even the act of *physical* movement increases my positive momentum and success?

The most important expansion and changes come from within, and are shown to me in how I perceive things. How has my perception changed? Are there any topics that have come up in the past year or so that I have a new outlook on? Can I think of one or two?

____

____

____

____

____

I love when I realize that my life has become easier just by changing my way of thinking about something. Even a slight change can create a ripple effect that has the potential to transform my entire life.

Each time I step out the door, meet someone new, or go a different route, I could be led to a whole new life experience. Anything is possible.

When I hold a sense of wonder in my heart that feels something like a childlike abandon, something amazing could happen at any given moment. Isn't it fun to go through life this way?

Action: During your meditation practice, start asking your inner guidance to provide more positive opportunities for you to expand.

And during this coming week, choose three changes you can make in your routine that may cause that ripple effect. Examples would be to take a different route on your walk or drive to work, try a new type of cuisine (I dare you!), go to a different coffee shop or restaurant, or sign up for a fun dance class or kickboxing, golf, or whatever you like.

Can you think of an adventure you're ready for? If not, are you willing to do it anyway? Come on, you know you want to...

Allow yourself to be in the energy of a person who's having the time of their lives. That's you, Darling! Your life is what you make it.

I Am Practicing an Abundance Mindset

I choose to be in the qualities and characteristics of my abundant nature. A feeling of abundance is simply feeling good. The better I feel, the more abundance will flow. I am living a life I love more every day. I'm opening myself up to *all* possibility.

I am so happy with where I am in my life right now, but I'm always ready and eager for what's to come. Yet I never feel the need to chase it. I know my desires are all happening. There's no rush. I'm just feeling satisfied right here and now.

I love knowing this is the best feeling place for me to be to continue inviting the flow of abundance that's all coming to me.

How does it feel to have an unstoppable mindset of abundance? All that means is that I'm frequently feeling appreciation and blissful happiness must ensue. To appreciate is to receive. And that means that good things must come. My life is unfolding perfectly.

How does it feel to allow my life to be as wonderful as I wish it to be? And to know with certainty that more great things are coming? All the pieces are laid out for me. My work is only to allow it to flow, and that's what I intend to do.

What if I knew that feeling more appreciation for the abundance I see around me would create more of it in all forms? How much better can I get at noticing the evidence of abundance in my life?

Can I decide to pay more attention and feel more pleased by the gifts I receive in the form of kindness, gifts, services, or other things given to me?

The gift of nature is a great form of abundance that I witness every day. *Feeling* more abundant is also evidence of my positive thoughts.

What signs of abundance have I been noticing recently?

____

____

____

____

What if I made a point to notice the signs of abundance that I enjoy seeing in others? So if I'm happy for happy couples, I will notice their wonderful connection or affection for each other.

If I like to look at nice cars and want to see myself having one, I'll appreciate their shine, their color, and feel happy for the person driving it.

And remember, the more I appreciate things, the more of it I will see. If I find myself surrounded by happy couples or my favorite vehicles, or anything else I want, it's evidence I'm attracting the same circumstances for me. Have I noticed anything like this showing up for me?

What if my appreciation of all of this creates way more joy, fun, money, vacations, or anything I wish?

As I focus on the areas of my life that are joyful or successful, the rest will come along.

What else can I do to practice a state of unlimited abundance?

To begin with, I am focusing on anything and everything that brings me joy.

I think of being happy, healthy, and wealthy as my lifestyle. It's something I do all day, every day. I practice my way into the feeling of blissful wellbeing and limitless abundance, and I attract everything I wish for.

Wellbeing is a part of me, and abundance comes naturally to me. No doubt enters my mind on this subject or any other.

I also love to pose fun questions that get me thinking about what I would love to be, have, or do without limitation. This is not about wanting more money. This is about how much more fun I'll be having when I get what I wish for.

Of course, I'd *love* more money, and *I can* and *will* have more money. But the reason I am now intending to have it is more about how it allows me to have endless choices and more opportunity for self-discovery.

It's really joyful living that I'm wanting. And that will be my focus in this exercise, and always. So let's begin...

If I had an extra $100 dollars a day and I had to spend it before the end of the day, what would I spend it on?

If I had an extra $100,000 dollars right now and had to spend it within three months, what would I spend it on?

If I had an extra $1,000,000 million dollars and had to spend it within three years, what would I spend it on?

If I had another million dollars every three years after that, what would I be spending it on?

This is just a great way to help me know what I want, without limits. And it's also kind of great to know all of it is possible. I can expect to wake up one day with an amazing idea that will give me the ability to create this reality.

Remember, it can show up in various forms from various sources. It can also be a priceless amount of joy that is equivalent to that amount of money. It's up to me.

Why is it so easy for me to be in the energy of abundance now?

Action: Just for fun and to help your wishes manifest, as it has for others: occasionally imagine something falling out of the sky that represents abundance to you. It could be flowers, gifts, plane tickets, money, checks, photographs of you feeling really good, or a symbol of an end result of a project you're working on.

Let it shower over you, landing at your feet or all around you. See it filling your mailbox, purse, car, or house. If it feels good, do it often.

Visualization, along with feeling the emotion of having your desire now, is one of the most powerful tools you can use to manifest. If it hasn't already, it will get easier with practice. And it's much better when you let yourself have fun with it, even to the point of giddiness when you think of your dreams.

That's how you'd feel when you've achieved them, right? If you knew they'd come tomorrow, you'd easily feel that emotion. So think of it that way as much as possible. Because any one of your desires—or all of them!—could happen tomorrow. Absolutely!

Consider letting go of any preconceived notion that wanting or having more money is greedy. Money is just another form of energy that's plentiful. And in this case you're just using it as a symbol of limitless abundance.

The only reason anyone wants money is to allow them to do more, expand more, and have more choices. Allow yourself to embrace it. It's available to all of us, and there's absolutely no limit to it.

If you're looking to create more abundance today and every day, remember to enjoy the abundance that you see wherever you go. Notice how good it makes you feel.

Allow yourself to feel happy for others who are doing something you would like to be doing or who have something you would like. The universe wants you to have it too!

I Am So Very Fortunate

I am truly happy right now and feel very fortunate when I think of my life. No matter where I am, I can look around and notice things that make me believe that more every day.

When I look around when I'm driving or taking a walk, what am I noticing?

____

____

What are some things that make me feel fortunate when I think of my life?

____

____

What are some things that make me feel fortunate about my family life?

____

____

What are some things that make me feel fortunate when I look around my home?

____

____

What are some things that make me feel fortunate about the work I do?

____

____

What are some things that make me feel fortunate about my hobbies or social life?

____

____

When I'm in nature, near trees and perhaps water or mountains, what are the words that describe how I feel when I notice its beauty?

____

____

What words describe how fortunate I am to be in my body?

____

____

Think of three things that make me feel fortunate to be who I am.

____

____

When I'm in a wonderful mood and feeling very fortunate, it's the best time to think about my wishes and dreams. With some real enthusiasm, finish these sentences in relation to my goals or dreams:

I *love* how good it feels to know that I can accomplish _______.

I love when I feel like celebrating about my progress on _______.

It feels so good to know that I'm going to _______.

It feels so good to be doing better at _______.

When I am _______, I feel so fortunate.

What are the words that describe how fortunate I feel when I think of my future?

____

____

If I can close my eyes right now, I can envision my future and be in the feeling place of it. How would I describe what it looks and feels like? Imagine it now.

What's my favorite part about it?

____

____

____

I am now tapping into the fortune that's waiting for me.

I find the feeling place of having anything I want, and I make it mine.

I am deciding right now that I am *forever* rich.

And this fortune I have is whatever I believe will make me even happier than I am now.

It may include a part of life that I haven't experienced yet.

Or perhaps I haven't had as much of something as I'd like.

I'm ready to bring it to me now, and I know it's going to be so much fun!

Action: Make a point to notice anything that makes you feel fortunate to be you, no matter where you are, whether you're at home, work, socializing, driving, waiting in line somewhere, or anywhere.

If you don't like something enough to enjoy it in some way, find a solution. Add some color. Add a picture or other decor that you can focus on, or whatever works for you. Someday you'll find that you're feeling fortunate all the time, without even trying.

If you're feeling dissatisfied with your job in any way, but unable to leave it at this time, consider scheduling a half hour every couple weeks or so to check out other options. Think about what you enjoy doing most, and if there's a way you could do that for work or teach others what you know.

You may be surprised at how many people are getting paid well to do what they love. It could change the rest of your life and make it so much more enjoyable. You can look back some day and say, "Oh, wow, I'm so glad I set aside some time to research that!"

Here's another goofy game for you. Or should we make it a challenge for the next 30 days, or longer if you'd like?

Gold and red are colors of fortune. Play a game while you're driving that every time you see a gold or red car, imagine you've just achieved one of your dreams. Think of which one it is, and imagine that you and a friend are taking a sip of champagne in celebration. Feel the sweetness of your success in that moment.

Yeah, it keeps getting weirder, I know. But isn't it fun? And if this action brings you results, wouldn't that be *marvelous*, Darling?

You're forever rich in whatever way you wish to be! Have the kind of day that makes you feel so very fortunate to be you!

I Circulate the Wealth in My Life

Where my thoughts or attention go, energy flows. This gives me the ability to create my future. I can nourish and fuel my desires with my positive energy, but I can also hinder the best outcomes by offering resistance. There are times that I don't even realize I'm having these mixed emotions, but there's an easy solution.

I need to be more at ease and have a gentler focus on my desires. Sometimes it's best to decide that it's okay to let it be and let it come to me. And I need to feel more confident in my ability to achieve my goals.

And in the absence of doubt, there's no resistance. In the absence of resistance, my wishes manifest when I least expect them.

Another way to clear any possible resistance to my success, is to make sure I have a favorable relationship with wealth.

To cultivate my wealth consciousness, I need to feel open and receptive to prosperity, have a generosity of spirit, and feel genuine happiness for others' success as well. This will better prepare me for the ideal life that I am now achieving.

What does having wealth mean to me? To have more joy, love, happy relationships, time with my family, more adventure, or more things that I want? It can include anything and everything I want. My ability to achieve it is boundless.

What forms of wealth would I like to have in my life?

Do I limit myself a little or a lot? Have I learned to be practical with all my choices? Do I worry myself about money or things that go to waste?

What if my fears could slow down the level of abundance I seek?

What if I could start over and practice a state of abundance without limitation?

What if I decided right now to release any limiting words from what is often called a "programmed" thought pattern? Words like "lack" or "limitation" and thoughts like "I can't afford it," or something similar to that.

And instead say:

> We're not going to buy that right now.
> There's always more where that came from.
> I love money and money loves me.
> I always make more than I spend and get more back than I give out.

What if I only focused on the plus amount I receive in my paycheck or elsewhere whenever negative amounts or deductions are involved?

What if I only thought of the advantage of spending money on something? Such as calling it an "investment" I'm making in myself. Or what if I focus on feeling thankful for the privilege of driving when gas prices go up?

What if I decided that there's no such thing as scarcity? It's only the beliefs that I hold that will limit *or* empower me to create the circumstances of my life.

How does it feel to allow the wealth to flow in and around my life? I'm not only wealthy in money; I am wealthy in all the many forms of wealth that are flowing into my life.

How does it feel when I'm completely comfortable with the idea of wealth and prosperity in my life and in the lives of others? How comfortable am I? Do I enjoy spending money on myself?

And while there are many forms of wealth, why is money the cause of so much fuss?

How does it feel to know that money is just another form of energy, and I'm entitled to have as much as I want? There's no limit.

What if I decided to take the emphasis off of the *need* for money and saw it flow into my life more readily?

Can I imagine how it feels to have a really great relationship with money, if not already?

Before I can get to the point of relaxing about money and thinking it's just another thing that flows in and out of my life, I need to practice getting really comfortable with it.

When I really want to get comfortable with it, I do what I can to cultivate my wealth consciousness. I find words that guide me there. I practice it until the thoughts become natural to me. When I practice it, it might sound something like this…

What if today was the first day of my life, and I never heard a word about the fear of spending too much money, but instead heard words like this:

By nature, you know how to keep the wealth circulating in your life.
You're a naturally successful person and everything always works out for you.
You're rich in abundance that easily flows to you.
Your life's full of whatever brings you joy. Some things will cost money but you'll always have plenty to create the life you want.

I've heard this so often it's ingrained in my being. And I believe it with all that I am. And I know that my thoughts are creating my reality.

Guess how my life's going to go? How does it feel when this is the only belief I've ever learned? Isn't it nice to know that I'm in charge of my own beliefs and guiding my thoughts to be who *I* want to be? And that it's never too late!

How do I feel about the money that's flowing to me? The thought of not enough money never enters my mind. There will always be enough. More than enough.

I notice that:

The more I spend, the more I make.
And the more at ease I am with spending, and the more I enjoy what I buy with it, the more easily it flows to me.
It's nice to know the more I wish prosperity for others, the more I attract to me.
But, it's not about money, is it?
It's really about having the freedom to do more of what I love to do, and how good that feels.
And when I follow what calls me, and do work that I love to do, and spend time doing anything that gives me joy, even more good things flow to me.
I will never be without.
All that I am seeking is within me.
I feel free and limitless.
The more I practice these thoughts, the more I notice it's true.
It's showing itself to me.
It's become true for me.
My life is going my way.
And my way is always just right.

What if I could circulate more wealth in my life by staying open to giving and receiving gifts of caring, affection, compliments, appreciation, or things?

What if I could offer gifts in the form of wishes for prosperity and knew that it would help keep the abundance flowing in my life and in the world?

When I can believe in my success and genuinely feel happy for the success of others, I know that I am aligned with my natural state of abundance, and all forms of wealth can flow.

Action: To get more comfortable with money, decide to love it. Money has always been flowing in your life, and it's going to continue flowing into your life. It's increasing in volume as you embrace the idea of money without any thought of the lack of it.

For any small items you'd like to purchase, be mindful of any cost-conscious thoughts, and practice redirecting them with an affirmation like "There's more where that came from," or you can even use "Every time I spend a dollar, it comes back to me tenfold," or it can be a thousandfold.

When possible, try buying things based on whether or not you will love it rather than the cost of it. Imagine having it, using it, or wearing it, and decide if you *can't* see yourself without it. The more you allow yourself the freedom to enjoy things, the more will come to you.

Hasn't money always been there when you needed it? You of course know what's best for you, so follow your own judgment. Think baby steps.

Also, try to allow balance between what you give and receive and let it be a more equal exchange. For instance, it's wonderful to give out compliments, but always do your best to graciously receive them as well. If you're just saying thank you, perfect; if you tend to brush it away, intend to let that habit go and start enjoying the compliments.

The same goes for gifts or money. And if someone wants to return a favor or pay you for something, consider letting them, because it may feel good to them and keep things flowing. If you're always giving things out and never accepting anything in return, by natural law, wealth is not as likely to keep circulating. The flow of abundance becomes hindered.

On a positive note, there are people who've been told they were going to be successful or a millionaire from the time they were born who made it happen. Their belief created their reality. And you can do it too, with any area of your life!

The worthier you allow yourself to feel, the easier receiving will be for you.

I Am Inspired to Be the Person I Was Born to Be

It's time to live my dream. I'm inspired to be the person I was born to be, doing what I love. I live my life on purpose and always follow my heart's desire.

Why is it so easy for me to do this now?

When did I start trusting my instincts and doing what's best for me?

How does it feel to be free of any guilt I once had for choosing to do what makes me happy?

What's it like to know my inner being is always calling me toward the many ways I can realize my dreams?

What if I knew that every inspired thought or impulse I have is guiding me to an experience I find so satisfying that I wouldn't be the same without it?

What's it like when I'm *so* tuned in to my intuition that I find myself where I need to be at the exact moment I need to be there for a life-changing event?

How easy are my life's decisions when I only need to choose what feels better or hold off when I know the choice isn't blatantly obvious to me? I find ease, and the answer will come.

When I'm feeling inspired to be the person I was born to be, what kinds of things am I thinking? It might sound something like this…

> I continue to evolve and get better in every way.
> I'm at ease with myself and with who I am and feel comfortable in my own skin.
> I speak from the heart, and I know exactly what I want to say the moment I want to say it, no matter who I'm speaking to.
> I am abundant in nature and have unlimited potential.
> I easily allow wellbeing and prosperity to flow.
> I am feeling so full of joy that nothing can stop the abundance from flowing.
> I can be and have and do all that I desire.
> I am being the person I was born to be.
> I am living the life I was born to live.
> I am following my heart's desire and doing what I love to do.
> I am mastering my alignment with all that I wish for.

And all the while I will bask in every moment, appreciating both the ups and the downs.
For I know what may feel like a misfortune is sure to lead me to something better or something more to adore.
I feel absolutely no resistance to anything I've set out to do.
I can feel it in the air,
I can feel it in my bones,
I can feel it in my heart.
And with the power of my words, thoughts, energy, and actions, I am unstoppable in my quest.
As I practice these powerful intentions now and always, I am purposely creating my life.

I love that I'm allowing everything that's meant to be to take its place.

And I love that I'm *not* allowing myself to have any excuses.

If I ever need to conquer a fear of doing something, I imagine myself doing it with confidence. Can I think of something I've been trying to muster the courage to do? Is there something that keeps getting pushed back? Perhaps a skill I'd like to learn or project I want to do?

I can close my eyes right now and see myself doing it with ease. If athletes can use visualization to achieve Olympic gold medals or put more baskets in, I can certainly find a way to make it work for me also.

How does it feel? How do I feel after I've accomplished it? Take a moment to imagine it.

I love that keeping myself inspired to be the person I was born to be makes me even more determined to stay in a good-feeling place. And I'm not allowing anyone or anything to change that.

That's because no matter what I'm doing or who I'm with, I make it a rule to spend more of my precious time finding reasons to smile and laugh, and it's happening all the time now. I'm unwilling to feel anything less than fabulous!

Action: When we're inspired to live more purposely, we're generally more aware of impulses to take inspired actions.

The idea behind an inspired action is to wait until you're feeling really good about a particular desire you have, and take the obvious next step when you're feeling inspired to.

You might have a strong urge to jump into something, but do your best to wait until it feels so good that you can't resist. It's feeling right. You're feeling ready. You're feeling really good about that desire. You can see the end result, and it feels good to think about it.

As you become more aligned with the energy of your desire, the ideas and answers on what to do will come easily. If you did nothing and kept enjoying your life to the fullest, your desires will still come, and may even fall right in your lap. So you can just relax and allow inspiration to flow.

We'll revisit this topic from Step 1 in case it's helpful now; if there's ever a big decision you're needing help with like whether to move, buy a house, take a new job, or anything that comes up:

Think of all your options, or write them down in columns. For example, 1) buying the new house, 2) staying where you are, 3) staying until you find another house.

Close your eyes and imagine taking each route. See yourself there, feel how you'd feel afterward if you were living it, and reflect back on what you left behind.

Do the same with all choices. Which one felt better? Which one gave you relief?

Or which one *doesn't* make you want to overthink it? Which one feels like you're trying to convince yourself of it?

Did your body or heart energy give you any sign of which felt better? Which one is a big no? Do any of them feel like a definite yes?

Any time a decision causes overthinking or confusion, it's not a good time to decide. If it doesn't require an immediate decision, consider taking a step back, relax, and let the answer come.

Without resistance or pressure, the answer will come to you in minutes, hours, or days. Do something else, take your mind off it, and focus on what feels good. But you know that!

It can feel like a decision is only hard because you know you're used to being practical or for some other reason, but if a choice is right for you, there will be no doubt in your mind that it's a definite *yes*. It will feel irresistible.

You are now being the person you were born to be. Why are you suddenly so confident about achieving and living your soul's purpose?

Day 73

I Am Unconditionally Happy

What's it like to feel deeply satisfied when I look within or look around me?

What kind of place am I in when I can rely solely on myself to feel happy?

When did it become so easy for me to feel this good without something needing to be in place?

I *love* that nothing special needs to be happening in order for me to feel happy. Even though I love to have music on, friends to talk to, or something of interest to keep me busy, I no longer require any particular circumstance for me to feel really, really good.

How does it feel to be so in charge of how I feel? I easily guide myself to where I want to be.

Why is it so easy for me to do this now? And to feel free of constraints, dependency, or insecurity?

How does it feel to be set free like this?

How great is my life when I'm feeling so good that I don't need *any* particular thing to be happening in order for me to be happy?

Can I see how easy my life is when I'm not reliant on anything to satisfy me? It's like all I need is within me. I'm enjoying my own company. I'm feeling connected to my inner guidance and never feel alone. Practicing this is making it so. It feels amazing!

What would I do if I ever found myself waiting for something to be in place before I would allow myself to feel happy or satisfied?

What if I chose to do everything I *could* to focus exclusively on the parts of my life that make me happy? I'm really good at that, but I'm always open to more practice.

I expect unconditional happiness to be my way of life. It just keeps getting better.

Action: Have you had enough fun and games yet? Well, try this one. Make up your very own theme song. Actually, it'll be more like a jingle. Are you envisioning yourself singing in the shower yet?

276

Well, the idea is to have one or more affirmation phrases that you think of often enough that it's instilled in your mind. What better way to do this than with a jingle that gets stuck in your head? Except this time, you want it to be one that you love!

So make it simple, yet specific to your desires. Make up one or two sentences for now, and you can add to it once you get the hang of it. You can use this one and fill it in with different answers:

I am now achieving ________.

If you can't think of any, try:

I am now achieving all that I desire.
Everything is always working out for me.
I am now achieving total abundance in an easy, relaxed manner.

You can get more specific if you'd like. For example, if you're wanting to attract an ideal mate, try "I am now achieving love from my one true love."

Now think of what your tune will be and practice it. Sing it in your head, in the car, in the shower, as you're getting ready to leave the house, or whenever you can. But give it a shot. If it feels good, it raises your vibrational energy and creates the right environment for your desires to manifest. You're a magnet, and you know it!

Another idea is to change a word or two of a song you're singing along to and make it apply to you and your wishes. Once you get started, you may never want to stop. Consider that a warning to those of you who are willing to try it.

Can you let your hair down and be silly for a few minutes out of your day? It might surprise you how much this helps you break out of your shell. And what if it helps you align with the energy of your desires? What if it increases your chances of manifesting the very ones you're singing about? Woohoo!

When did it become so easy for you to feel so happy all the time?

My Vision Is Clear

It's time to use more of my brilliant mind to achieve my goals. My imagination is one of the most powerful tools I can use to bring my plans to fruition. I have the ability to create my dream life, and I intend to see it through. It's no longer a dream, but a vision. And I have a plan.

I'm keeping an image of my vision imprinted in my mind. I think of it often, and it holds all the key points of my desires. It symbolizes the end result of what I see as my ideal life.

Although it's *not* necessary to do this to get what I want, it helps me feel energetically connected to it, rather than it being some far off destiny. And the more I practice my ability to visualize my desires and feel that I'm there, the sooner they may come.

I only do my visualizing when I'm feeling really good. And I never feel like I'm comparing what I have with what I want. I'm feeling genuinely satisfied with my life and just having fun thinking of what's to come. This ensures the best outcomes.

Let's start thinking about what my vision is for my ideal life, and what image would best symbolize it:

What is my desired end result of everything I want at this time?

What does my house or place of business look like?

What color is it?

What's in the driveway?

What's in the front and backyard?

How does it feel to walk inside the house?

What does each room have in it?

What's hanging on the wall in my office?

What's extra special about my house?

What do I see when I look out the windows?

What's in the refrigerator?

How do I look and feel?

Who am I with?

Who or what else do I want there with me?

What would we be doing?

Do I hear the sound of laughter?

Who's coming to visit?

What's for dinner?

The image I use can be of me standing in front of the ideal house I envision for myself. I can see my partner, family, or pets standing with me. We are all smiles, of course.

Details make it more real, so I notice our style of clothing and perhaps I'm wearing a watch or ring. I can see the cars, boats, or toys in the driveway.

Behind the house I can see the yard, garden, patio, water, or mountains or anything I want to include. I see the plant life that surrounds us. I can feel the sunshine and smell pine in the air.

Inside the house I imagine there being an office or room for me to work in, fitness equipment if I'd like, a large kitchen, Jacuzzi tub, big, cozy bed, walk-in closet (and I see my clothes in it), a great room with a fireplace, and a guest room for family to visit.

I see myself lounging on a cozy couch or sitting at the table or on the patio, sipping on wine or lemonade, and dining on delicious food.

I can see or hear that there's laughing and clanging glasses among friends or with a partner, and taste the food and drink and how it feels to be there.

This can take all of a minute, or I can bask in it for a while if it feels good to me. With a little practice, the entire experience is embedded in my mind and I call the image back to me in an instant.

And all my senses are recalling it with me. If my vision changes over time, I make the adjustments.

I allow myself to feel exhilarated when I think of the image of this ideal life. As I keep it in my thoughts, I'm calling it to me. And the energy *I'm* in and the energy of my desires are one and the same.

Action: Take a moment now to close your eyes and see the image of your ideal life. Choose where it takes place: your home, in front of a business, or places you want to travel. Anything you wish.

Think of all the details and anyone you want there with you. After you've looked at everything you want to see, look at the front of it one last time and notice there's a beam of sun lighting the entire face of the image. The front of the house and your face is glowing in this light. Imagine it now.

This will become your symbol to call back to you as often as you wish. See the whole image as though it's on a canvas or movie screen in front of you, slightly above you, and make it quite large. Always put yourself in the picture, in the house, or in the car.

Another way you can use this image is to draw it toward you. With eyes still closed, see it in front of you slightly above you at a distance. Imagine there's a line or cord of light coming from your core and reaching out to the image of your ideal life. See it wrap around the image and pull it toward you.

See it getting closer and closer to you. And then watch as it plants itself right in front of you. Use the key in your hand to walk in the front door and feel your feet on the floor as you check out all the rooms.

Soak in the Jacuzzi tub. Walk around outside. Pick something from the garden. Get in the car and drive away. Feel the steering wheel beneath your hands.

Think of all the great details you'd like for yourself, and imagine someone with you, if desired. Do your very best to get your senses involved and *feel* each experience in all of the scenes. And touch something in each scene: Jacuzzi water, a person, the couch, etc.

If it feels good, start doing this daily or as often as you'd like. It's a great thing to do while lying in bed before falling asleep. You're getting that image into your subconscious and could also end up dreaming about it.

Maybe a sticky note on your nightstand will help? What should it say? How about: "I see my perfect future, and I deserve it!"

You could also consider creating a movie or a vision board that has all the images of things you wish to achieve. Or try using a picture or painting that's hanging somewhere in your house where you spend a lot of time.

Either of these will serve as a reminder to think of your vision more often. But for the painting, just imagine your ideal scene on it just as you visualized it before, but choose a place to put all the pieces into the picture, and always include yourself.

In time you will find that you start adding things to it or imagine it coming to life. If you decide to buy a picture or painting, find one that makes you feel really good when you look at it. One that has a sky, flowers, trees, and a path on it works very well. You can imagine yourself walking on that path, surrounded by all that you've achieved and all that you love.

All of the pieces are falling into place. It will happen for you, and it could be today. Each day as you wake up, try to have the feeling that something wonderful is about to happen.

If you can visualize your kitchen, you can visualize anything, and it gets easier with practice. Many people have found themselves in the exact home or situation or relationship they imagined, or better.

Have a happy day and enjoy creating your vision!

It's Time for My Lifelong Pep Talk

One of the things I find very comforting is that I'm always able to have a fresh start on something if I wish to. There's always a way to set new intentions and take myself in a different direction.

And if my day ever seems to spiral and I can't seem to get myself back on track, I actually get to start over with a new beginning *every* single day.

And for those occasional days that feel even slightly disappointing, I like to have a ready-made pep talk that instantly lifts me up. It's written or spoken in such a way that I cannot deny its irresistible spell.

That's because it's generated from a feeling place of sheer bliss. I create my best work when I'm feeling empowered and overjoyed with happiness.

If I could have the perfect handbook for a happy life, what words would I love hearing?

What words would provide the life skills for immeasurable joy and success?

What words would inspire the courage to conquer anything I want in life?

What words will make me believe in my potential and ability to achieve limitless abundance?

What do I already believe is true for me?

Action: It's time to write your pep talk. Write out sentences that would inspire and empower you or ignite your passions. Write them in your wish list journal, and write anything that comes to mind that's personally uplifting for you.

Think of it like your lifelong pep talk. What do you want to hear in the months ahead that will help you instill thoughts you'd like to believe for the rest of your life? The words you want to hear will change as you evolve, but go by what you need to hear now.

Think of words that will give you more value than you may have given yourself in the past. Think of how you want it to make you feel. Perhaps you'd like it to evoke the feeling of being loved and cherished and self-empowered.

You can write it from a first person or second person point of view, whichever one feels better. Do you want to be saying affirmations that say how you feel, or tell yourself how to feel? Which one feels better: *I* am strong or *you* are strong?

Let it sound like it's coming from you, your best friend, and allow it to inspire you to be in the joy of who you are. It's giving you permission to feel happy and free and be in your natural state of blissful wellbeing and limitless abundance.

Let each step of it go up a level, so that you can take yourself from where you are to where you want to be, to build yourself up higher and higher, better and better.

It can start with something like: I'm in charge of how I feel, and I can always feel better. And then a list of what you choose, or "I can," "I will," and then shift to what "I am now achieving __________."

Another way to do this is just start writing at the time that you want to uplift yourself and just write out how you're feeling, how you want to feel, or how you want a situation to be, and the words will naturally come that guide your mindset to a better-feeling state.

It will hopefully guide you from a so-so place to a really good-feeling place any time you may need it.

Have fun creating your little handbook for life!

I Am Celebrating

What if I could think of every day being my special day?

You know, like that feeling I get when I wake up on my birthday, feeling excited to have a reason to treat myself better than usual. But shouldn't it always be like that? Can't I choose to feel this way every day?

What would it feel like to live that way?

How would it feel to celebrate every day like my life has just begun? To give myself permission to spoil myself with thoughts of love, appreciation, and adoration.

How would it feel to walk around every day with an extra spring in my step and a big smile on my face? The kind of radiant smile that I feel in my heart and uplifts everyone I come in contact with.

How does it feel to be less inhibited and more lighthearted and friendly wherever I go?

I feel like I'm on holiday every day and someone just gave me free rein to have more fun.

And how does it feel when I don't hesitate to treat myself to something that's just for my personal enjoyment? It's so much fun, I can't stop!

What special things do I do for myself on my birthday? If I don't do this, I need to start now.

____

____

____

____

____

____

Don't I feel a little bit lighter or extra special on my birthday? What can I do to feel that way every day?

What would I do if the "slate" was clean and I was starting over? What would I be doing on a daily basis if I were inspired to feel any way I wish? Like on top of the world?

____

____

____

____

What's it like to be in the habit of looking for the many delights that can be found in my everyday routine? In fact, I'm in that habit now, aren't I?

Can I start feeling that extra special feeling now? And imagine every morning when I wake up that it's my special day? Like that feeling I get right after someone gives me a bouquet of flowers or I booked a vacation?

I love knowing that I have a choice to feel this way *every* day! After all, I have so many things to feel fortunate about. And someday there *will* be another bouquet of flowers or another vacation and so much more. I choose to celebrate that now. My "someday" *is* now!

Does any of this resonate with me? How about this...

I love my ability to allow wellbeing.

I love my ability to live the life I wish for.

I love my ability to guide myself there.

I love my ability to train my mind to think the way I want to think, and believe what I want to believe, and make my life exactly the way I wish it to be.

I love my ability to allow *anything* and everything I desire to take place.

New life experiences, happier and healthier relationships, and *all* my wishes and dreams.

And I love my ability to contribute to the wellbeing all around me and in the world. My abilities stretch far and wide, and I celebrate that.

I love that every day has the potential for something really magical to happen. Every day has the potential of being a day that I get an opportunity. Make a new wonderful friend. Meet my soulmate. Or have a breakthrough in my current relationship. *Anything* is possible.

And every day I feel that possibility. That certainty that great things are coming for me. And the more I expect it, the more likely it will.

Action: Are you up for a challenge? For the next seven days, ask yourself, "So, what am I celebrating today? What's there to celebrate?" And with a lot of enthusiasm and a little bit of your heart and soul, say what you're wanting to celebrate.

Write it down, or better yet, say it out loud while you're driving (again with the driving!). Every time you get in the car to head out each morning for the next seven days, I'm giving you permission to talk to yourself. Yes, it may feel silly, but let it be fun. Think of anything and everything you can think of that you appreciate and feel like celebrating.

Start with "I love ____" or "I love that I ____."

The words could be about your life, your body, your mind, your wellbeing, your family or friends, your progress or changes you've made to your life, things you've let go of, your past or current accomplishments, new desires or projects, or anything that's lighting you up these days.

Go on as long as you can. Make your last statement be about how great your day's going to go. Then say thank you for all that you're celebrating.

If it feels good to you, do it another seven days, and another seven days. It only takes a few weeks to form a habit, and these thoughts will become your beliefs. You're headed for way more fun.

Try it now, beginning with:

I'm celebrating that I am ____.

I love being ____.

I love having time to ____.

I love that I've started ____.

I love that I've let go of ____.

I love that I can ____.

I love that I am ____.

Keep going and going and going.

I intend to celebrate all the days of my life. Even if I don't remember to say it every day, I am thinking it, feeling it, and owning it.

Happy Special Day, every day!

I Am Practicing the State I Wish to Be In

In order to achieve what I want in life, I need to already be in the qualities and characteristics of the person I wish to become. So I'm practicing the feeling place of any state I wish to be in. I'm choosing to be in the energy of the quality I seek for a specific purpose.

I can practice being in the qualities that are needed for the career I want. I can be in the energy of the happy relationships I want. I can be in the feeling place of *any* quality or skill I wish to develop.

I am mastering my ability to create the life I wish for. I am doing whatever I need to do to align with what I want. I am feeling how I'll feel when I've achieved my desires. I am in the spirit of it right now.

It's like I'm playing the part. I'm already there. I'm feeling it. I'm living and breathing it. I'm being it. And I'm doing it easily and effortlessly, and having fun all the while.

I'm feeling the success of what I set out to achieve. I relate to others who are successful and feel that I'm on the same playing field they're in. And when I'm feeling genuinely happy for them, I'm also feeling happy for myself, as though I'm just like them. That's how successful I feel. I'm already there.

I can see and feel the abundance flowing in my life. I'm seeing happy couples and families everywhere. I'm seeing a lot of successful people. I'm noticing signs of prosperity like this everywhere I go.

Isn't it exciting to know that when I start seeing a lot more of something, it means I'm aligned with that energy and the success is coming for me too?

How does it feel to be in control of how my life goes?

Why is it so easy for me to put myself in whatever state of mind I need to be in to create the life I wish for now?

How does it feel to practice a state of blissful wellbeing and feel myself aligning with it? I am the happiest person I know!

How does it feel to practice the feeling of abundance and allow more good things into my life? I can feel that I'm aligning with all my desires now. It's so exciting!

How does it feel to be in charge of my destiny?

How does it feel to be in the qualities and characteristics and energy of my success? The energy of prosperity! Yes, yes, yes. I accept!

If it's simply a happier home I want, I'm leading my family in the spirit of peace and love and practicing what it would feel like. How does it feel to be with my family now? How do I think they feel when they're with me?

____

____

____

____

____

If there's something specific I want to achieve, I can think of things like this...

(Take some time to think of each answer before going to the next question)

What do I want to accomplish?
When I imagine myself being in that role, what qualities do I exhibit?
What does success look and feel like? Do I look and feel confident, successful, and happy?
For anything I want to achieve, can I imagine myself doing it? My focus upon it can help me gain insight on how to go about it.
If I was living my ideal life right now, how would I feel?
What would I be doing? What is my life's work?
What things would I like to learn? What classes would I choose to take, if any?
Where would I like to travel? What other adventures would I like to try?
What am I spending time on?
Who would I be with?
How do I want to feel?
If I want to be healthier, do I envision myself that way and take steps in that direction? Have I been doing anything that supports my goal?

When I have an upcoming event, I can improve the outcome by practicing how I want it to go. I can focus on the feeling that I need for each situation.

For instance, before a job interview, I can imagine being there and see it going well, and hearing them offer the salary and other benefits I'd like, or imagine seeing it in writing on a document. Then imagine receiving the email or phone call giving me the good news!

I can use the same process to visualize any scene like this. Such as my first bid on a house being accepted, getting a really high test score, achieving the desired end result of a project, or getting the phone call I was hoping for, or anything at all.

This is working really well for others, and I'm going to try it when I'm in a really good-feeling place. I can conquer any challenge I wish!

To help things along, I can:

Keep the end result in mind.
Pay attention to ideas, impulses, or guidance I receive on where to step next.
Find ease and allow the answers to come.
Focus on what's working well in my life.
If something doesn't work out, trust that the situation wasn't the best thing for me. It leaves me open for better things to come.
Stay in the role of a confident, successful person or whatever qualities I'm wishing to be in and carry myself that way.
The more I practice, the faster I can get myself there.
Only tell the most supportive people about my dreams. I want to keep the energy around me and my desires very positive.

Action: Imagine telling someone about your success. It could be someone you know or someone you just met.

They're sitting in front of you. You've achieved all your desires. Tell them all about it. See their reaction, feel proud. Put something in their hand that symbolizes a part of it. It could be a photograph of you receiving an award, or the finished product of what you've been working on.

Close your eyes and think of it now. Allow yourself to be in that feeling of elation upon completing your deepest desire.

Now, close your eyes and see an image of yourself walking toward you. You're in a state of blissful wellbeing. You're feeling happy, healthy, and deeply satisfied with your life. You're feeling completely free to be your authentic self at all times. You're on top of the world.

As you get closer, see that smile and sunny glow on your face, and then feel that energy come into yours. This is you in your purest form. Embrace yourself, Beautiful!

Don't forget to close your eyes and see it, feel it, taste it, and touch it!

Wishing you success!

How does it feel to be in charge of your destiny?

I Am Playful & Purposeful

I love to be in the spirit of fun as I purposely create my life.

I've chosen to live my life by design rather than by default, but it's not meant to feel like work. If I'm ever *too* serious about it, I could be shutting myself off to what I want and certainly wouldn't fully enjoy myself in the process.

And there's *always* an easier way to do things. Right? What I *perceive* as easy, *is* easy. And I choose to make life easy for myself.

Even though I'm putting some effort into mindfully guiding my thoughts and practicing the feeling place of what I want in a more deliberate way, it doesn't mean I can't have fun while I'm doing it. Actually, that's exactly what I need to be doing.

So, I do what I can to practice creating my life more playfully. How do I go about it? There are endless ways!

To begin with, how does it feel when I decide to stop taking myself or anything else too seriously?

What if I decided to be more playful in how I live my life in general?

Or more playful in how I *think* of my life, and how I think of myself?

I love finding ways to amuse myself throughout my day in whatever way I can.

What if I could enjoy feeling amused about most topics?

How does it feel to be more playful in my interactions with others?

What would my family think if I started (kindly) teasing them more often? Especially when they're about to break down in a tantrum or try to start an argument?

Would it at least be more fun for *me*? Isn't it better than joining them in their frustration? And what if it turned out to be an icebreaker that made it all better?

How does it feel to be more carefree and trust that things are working out?

And what if I could actually be *more* productive at work when I go about it in a lighthearted way? This is always possible, even for those seemingly grueling tasks that I thought required serious contemplation.

Anything's possible! I get to make it the way I want it to be.

One of the most playful ways I have found to purposely create my life is in my daydreaming. I can get very creative in my daydreaming. And I love what I can do with it.

What if I could daydream my ideal life into reality?

What's it like to use visualization to imagine my wishes have come true?

It's all about practicing the feeling of the reality I wish to achieve and bringing it to life. It's a very powerful tool that helps me feel good about the plans I've made and make them happen!

I'm attracting my ideal life as I imagine being in it. Again, I do this in the spirit of fun. So, if it makes me think about how I don't have it yet, or doesn't feel good for any reason, I don't do it until that changes.

Isn't it nice to know that getting myself into a happy state of mind before I begin something is all I really need to do to be successful at anything I do in life? I'm just following my heart's desire. I'm following my bliss and taking the path of joy. It's easy. It's simple. It's fun. And it's done.

And haven't I noticed that the more mindful and happy I feel in the moment I set an intention for my plans ahead, the more perfectly it unfolds, or even better than I imagined?

So, what dreams do I daydream about? And what can I do to bring it to life?

How does it feel to be playing the role at my new place of work? I can imagine sitting at my home or company office, or standing in front of an audience. I can go as far as acting out a speech if one of my desires is to be a teacher, leader, or speaker.

How does it feel to be my own boss? How does it feel to make double the salary and work less hours?

How does it feel to be vacationing more often, and spending more time relaxing now that I have more free time? Can I see myself lounging on the beach or in my Jacuzzi? Can I taste that champagne I'm sipping on?

What if I saw the ideal car or house as I drove up to my house? How does that steering wheel feel beneath my hands? How does it feel to walk inside the house?

What if I imagine my partner with me? What's it like to see them around the house? How does it feel to dance with them in the kitchen?

What if I thought about what they love about me or I love about them? How does it feel to wear that ring I've been hoping for?

How does it feel to have my best friend sitting next to me? What are we talking about?

You could say that it's more than a bit odd to think like this. But if it settles into my imagination and carries over to my subconscious thoughts, and those thoughts turn into things, as all our thoughts do, wouldn't that be nice?

I am living the life I love. I am practicing how it feels to live it and love it, and make it a part of me and who I am, and how I expect to be living.

And it keeps getting better. The more I see the results of my purposeful thoughts, the more thrilling it is. It lets me know that my thoughts *really* are creating my reality.

How does it feel to be that person who's achieved everything they wanted?

Isn't it nice to know that being in this energy is creating what I want or better? Acting as if I have it is a very powerful invitation that calls upon my *every* wish.

And the best part is, I'm having so much fun!

What's it like when I choose to make my life feel as happy as I wish it to be?

How does it feel to know what success feels like?

How exciting is it when I start to see evidence that my focus is creating amazing results?

Am I feeling completely empowered by how I've taken charge of my life?

I am now achieving total alignment with all of my desires.

Right now, my life is unfolding perfectly and everything I want is now moving toward me in a wave of positive momentum.

And it's coming to me at the perfect time.

There is nothing I need to do but enjoy my life.

I'm always in the right place at exactly the right time.

And I do what I feel guided to do for the sake of feeling more joy.

What I consistently think of is attracting its vibrational match.

My thoughts are always on what I love to be, love to have, and love to do, so I'll be inviting more of that into my life.

I'm receiving guidance to go places that have potential opportunities.

I'm meeting the people I am meant to meet.

I'm feeling inspired when I need to take a step toward my goals.

What if I gave myself permission to not try too hard at anything? What if I knew all my dreams are happening, whether or not I put any effort into it, just because I'm feeling happy?

I am in a place of allowing ease and joy, and more love and abundance is coming into my life. I am preparing right now to receive all of it. I am aligning my energy with all that I want out of life.

Action: Start practicing playful and purposeful daydreaming. Think of something now that you'd like to bring to life in your daydreams. Choose something that feels achievable and have fun with it.

You can also try imagining the various things you'll be doing in your ideal life. Get creative. Think of things you've always wanted but thought they were too silly or frivolous at the time. Now, hopefully, you know you can have anything you want, and more than ever!

If you wish to feel more pampered or have funds to do whatever you want, daydream about the many things you would be doing: imagine you're getting a massage or sitting in a Jacuzzi. Feel the results in the ease and warmth of your muscles from head to toe. Your imagination can create the same results if you take your time and fully get into it. And oh, what a nice way to fall asleep, by the way!

If it feels good to daydream like this, keep practicing. Let your imagination run wild and free. There's no limit to what you can create with your powerful thoughts, intentions, and imagination!

If you start to feel like you're trying too hard and lose focus on the simple joys in your life, take a different approach or allow yourself to sit back and wait for inspiration.

Do your best to choose what your heart's calling you to do. Leave out practicality, at least for some of it. Ask yourself what you want to be, have, or do that makes your heart sing. What would thrill and excite you? And then imagine doing it.

I may not know you but as I write this, I am feeling so happy for you! Because I know great things are coming for you. I really hope you're allowing yourself to feel happy and excited about where you are and for what's to come.

How does it feel to allow yourself to have fun every day?

I Am Inspired to Take Action

I can spend time working hard on my goals, or I can wait for the inspiration and ideas that allow it to come with effortless ease. The kind of ideas I wait for are those that feel so exciting that I can't wait to take action on them. When I get that feeling of elation and an urgency to get it done, that's my sign that it's meant to be.

By the way it feels, I know the idea was sparked by a desire. It's an answer to a wish. I love romanticizing my life, don't I? Ah, but it's my life, and I see it the way I want to. And the best part is, it's all becoming so very real.

Without a doubt in my mind, I know anything I act on that came from an inspired thought is an idea that will turn into success. It's almost as though it's primed and ready for me. And I know how important it is to act on it right away.

This is a crucial point where I want to stay the course and allow it to flow without introducing any opposing thoughts. And I'm getting better every day at dismissing indecision and uncertainty. I decided that nothing's in the way of getting what I want, including me. It's all getting done.

I am confident the idea will turn out well or turn into something even better.

And with passion and a sense of faith and purpose, I then take an inspired *action*. On all naturally inspired ideas, the next step will be obvious to me. But I always make sure I get myself into a good-feeling place before I take that step.

What's it like to allow myself the ease of simply moving forward on a goal when I get an impulse to do so? What if I just let myself feel free to go with the flow and let momentum build?

Isn't it good to know I don't need to force anything? I don't need to know all the details. I just stay focused on how I want things to turn out, and stay open to whatever way it happens. And when the time is right, I'll be provided with insights and information and just the right guidance to see it through.

What if I knew a simple impulse to make a phone call would turn into something big? This is why I always take action on my impulses if I'm feeling good when it happens. It's my intuition speaking loud and clear. That's how *great* things can get started.

And if I put my focus on one thing at a time, I can swiftly move forward and make the most of my time and progress toward my goal. Focusing on the obvious next step each moment that I spend time on it moves me forward to the next moment and the next moment. And more progress is made than if I tried to tackle the entire goal all at once.

Why is it so easy for me now to put my heart into every part of it, allowing me to move forward with ease?

Can I decide that anything I spend on my goals or dreams is money well spent that I'm happy to invest in myself?

How does it feel when I expect to get back way more value than I put in? And to know that if I was guided to take an action, it will undoubtedly be so.

What frame of mind am I usually in before a truly inspired thought comes to me? I'm feeling that:

> I'm tuned in to my inner guidance and feeling inspired by what calls me.
> I appreciate my emotions for letting me know the right choices for me.
> My actions are more in alignment with my true nature.
> I follow the impulses or nudges I'm getting with ease.
> I trust all that I need to know, to get me where I want to be, is coming to me.
> I'm attracting it by imagining it.
> I've got the talent and skills necessary to achieve what I want.
> The connections and opportunities are coming.
> I'll always be in the right place at the right time for it to happen.
> It may show up in various forms, but it will show up.
> And I'm open and receptive to whatever way it presents itself.
> I am now achieving it as I align my energy with it.

Action: If you have an inspired idea now, or when you do, here are some ways you can keep it going so it won't fizzle out. That can happen if there's no action taken soon after you get a great idea, but it can always be rekindled later. If it's meant to be, it *will* be.

Get yourself in a good-feeling place, and grab a pen and your wish list journal to write in, and start with this:

> What's the idea? Write it down at the top of the page.
> What's the desired end result? Write it down on the bottom of the page.
> What's the plan of action? What feels like the obvious next step toward your goal?
> It helps to decide this by thinking about the desired result; what needs to happen for this to be achieved?

What research do you need to do, if any?

What skills do you need to acquire, if any? What needs to change or stop happening for this to be achieved?

Write a step-by-step plan of action that includes any necessary steps to get you there, including answers from the above questions.

Begin listing the steps in order of how they'll be done, or do it in reverse order, beginning with the end result. One may be easier than the other.

What date do you wish to complete it by?

Fill in all the details and then decide what step you will start with.

When and where and at what time will you spend time on it?

What else can you do to prepare for it? What needs to happen to prepare you or your life for it? How can you prepare yourself or your life to better receive it?

If you feel inspired to make a move on one of your goals but don't feel you have the time to put into it, consider setting aside a half hour or an hour once or twice a month or more. If desired, schedule a reminder now.

You can use the time to research your idea, make phone calls, or do anything that will get the ball rolling. You might be surprised at what little actions are required to show you a whole avenue of simple ways to make things better and easier for you.

There are many times when people feel too busy to search for a more fulfilling job and discover years later, it only took a phone call or a moment to see a post or advertisement about something they've always wanted to do but never thought it would be that easy or pay enough salary.

Why is it so easy for you to know what your next step is in creating the ideal life you are now achieving?

I Get Things Done

This is the most amazing part of my life, and this is the time for me. For me to focus. For me to feel inspired. And get things done. With diligence and determination, I can get things done, but I know the biggest and best outcomes come with inspired action.

The more inspired I feel, the more effortless things are. It even feels good to do the things I *need* to do. And when I decide to get something done, I find the easiest way possible. I like things to be easy.

The best place for me to start anything is from a good-feeling place. Whatever energy I have going into a task or project is what I'm going to get out of it. For anything I don't particularly like to do but have to do, I find something to like about it. And before I act on it, I get myself in the mood for it. I'm always happy about something.

How does it feel to know that I'll always accomplish anything I set out to do? Some things will get done quickly, and others may take time. But they're all getting done.

When it comes to big dreams, what if I could easily accomplish them by breaking down my goals or plans in small steps? How could I ever feel overwhelmed or confused on what to do next if I follow a simple plan? How much more achievable does it feel when I focus on one little part at a time?

And how much faster do things get done when I keep going like this? Boom! Done, done, done. The list is getting shorter and shorter. Check, check, check. And thank you! All my goals are done before I know it. Hooray!

It helps me see myself getting closer to its completion and inspires me to keep going. I make fast progress as I focus on one goal or project at a time and conquer all my need-to-do tasks better this way also. I proceed with all of this, and as I hold my vision in my mind, it's all getting done.

And isn't it nice to know that even when I'm *not* getting things done or they're going slowly, I won't get mad at myself? Slow and steady often brings the best outcomes. And taking a break might be exactly what I need to stay in the flow and allow things to take their natural course.

Things can really start happening when I allow myself to relax and take my mind off what I'm working toward. I'm always moving forward, and it's always getting done.

And the law of attraction is always at work and bringing it to me as I align with the energy of abundance and success.

How does it feel to have so much energy, clarity, and determination that I know everything I want to do is getting done with effortless ease?

If I could put it into words, how good does it feel to accomplish all the goals I set out to do each day, each week, and each year? Every one of them!

____

____

____

____

____

The more I get done, the better I feel, and now I can't stop! I allow myself to feel this now.

I'm getting it all done because I have this wonderful positive energy flowing to me and through me and around me. I am feeling so in the zone that I just can't wait to get to the next thing. What's next? Life is *full* of surprises but it all feels natural to me.

It kind of feels like this...

I know who I am and what I want to get done.
I love being productive; I always have.
It feels really, really good when I get things done.
I decide to do something that's important to me, and I know I'll get it done.
I always know the next obvious step to achieve it.
This is the most exciting time of my life. I am living out my passions and dreams.
And when I get that undeniable inspiration, I say now is the time to act.
Since I know the amazing feats I'm capable of, I believe in myself.
I succeed at everything I do.
I follow my three d's of success: decisive, determined, and diligent.
And then I always add fun and spontaneity.
I am now initiating an effortless flow of creativity and productivity in my life.
I do this just by thinking of it. And whatever way I decide to get it done is right for me. I don't have to force anything. The inspiration and ideas just flow.
And all the while I feel the energy of the total financial abundance that I am now achieving. And it feels amazing!

Just doing what I love is bringing more opportunities for bigger and better things.

I decided...
I am the type of person that gets things done.
I am decisive, determined, and diligent.
I am focused and unstoppable in my spirit of abundance.
And most of all I'm having fun!
I always have fun doing something that excites me. And I find a way to let all my tasks excite me in some way.
I am clear-minded and organized and energetic all day, every day.
I always have enough energy to get all the things done that I want to get done.
I love making a game of it: what can I finish today? I challenge myself...

Why is it so easy for me to be "self-disciplined" when I need to be? Wait! I don't think I like those words. What if I decided that I don't need self-discipline?

What if I decided that I'm the kind of person who gets things done with little or no motivation required? It's just something I do naturally and easily when I'm doing what interests me. I love it! And I'm letting this powerful intention carry me through the next thing I want to get done. And the next.

Why is it so easy for me to get my projects done now? When did it become so easy for me to know what I want to do? And have the inclination to do what I need to do to make it happen?

Isn't it wonderful how much better I am at receiving guidance for lucrative ideas, as well as the path to achieve them?

How does it feel when I know my dreams are coming to life?

What if I knew there's never a need to overthink it? What if I knew that in the moment an inspired thought comes in, more ideas follow that tell me how to get things done.

What if I could trust that those insights will come to help me achieve my goals more easily? Can I see myself sitting back and letting it come to me without the need for action until it does?

And when I start to feel *really* good about any one of my goals, it means they're likely happening *soon*. I only need to stay open to them and allow the wondrous things that will come of it.

Isn't it great to know that as I work on one goal or project that I'm excited about, the rest will flow along with it sooner or later?

Why do things start to flow when I feel good about just that one? How aligned do I feel with unlimited abundance? Joy? Wellbeing? Appreciation for myself and all that is?

All of these are aligning me with total success in every area of my life. The quality of my thoughts are creating a lovely quality of life for me.

Although there's a lot of emphasis put on the importance of making a plan for the best success in starting a business or in achieving our goals, there may be no need for any set plan at all. This is something I need to decide for myself, but there's a natural course I could take:

> I get an inspired idea.
> I follow my heart or guidance in the direction of what's calling me.
> There's no pushing or resisting.
> The right steps come to me when I'm at ease and in the flow of things.
> It all unfolds naturally and perfectly.
> It's easy. It's effortless. It's fun. And it's how I truly like things to be.

If I like to stay busy, I'm busy doing what I need to do and love to do. I'm just going to go with it. It's getting done when it gets done and with effortless ease. I just know it. I feel it. It's already done in my mind. And I'm in no rush.

Being in a place of ease will bring things about. More so than if I were trying to make something happen. It's like when you're trying really hard to find something that's misplaced. And when you stop trying, it comes to you. And sometimes it's right where you were looking. You just couldn't see it until you stepped back and took your time.

It's the same when I'm trying to make dreams come true. It's the same for the outcomes and opportunities that are manifesting for me. They're coming. I'm patiently waiting. And I'm so happy right here where I am.

If something I'm working on is taking longer than expected, I remember that it's my thing and I'm doing it my way. There's no timetable to follow when I'm doing it the way I want to do it.

And there's never a reason to compare myself to others or follow their criteria. Some of the most brilliant works have been done over a period of years.

That being said, if being more productive is what feels right to me, I'll find a way to get things done.

Action: Think of a creative project that you would like to do and haven't started yet, or use what you came up with yesterday on Day 79.

Get out a piece of paper and do a mind map of what you want to do. This will just be an outpouring of thoughts on your idea or goal.

Write the end goal in the center or top of the paper and form two or more columns under it or to each side of it.

Write as many different things you can think of that work toward completing the goal.

Then circle what could be considered main categories and draw lines to connect subheadings that are similar to the main categories.

Then make an outline from it. It doesn't need to be perfect. The order you're doing things in will likely change. You can revise as you go.

Take the next obvious step: what's the first thing on your outline?

If it's more than a quick step, break it down into small steps on another outline. Then do the first step on it, or pick a day and time when you would like to do it.

This is a great way to get ideas flowing on how to achieve your goal.

Just commit to five minutes; sit down and get started. Once you get started, more ideas begin to flow. And soon you'll realize you're still at it a half hour later. This is a great way to get past any procrastination.

Consider trying it now, or tomorrow, or on the weekend.

Keep your vision in mind, and it will get done. Before you get started each time, remember to get yourself in a good-feeling place. Ask your mind, body, and spirit to show you how it feels when you allow crystal clear clarity and blissful energy to flow in and around you and into anything you're working on.

When you're in the zone with that energy and excited about what you're working on, time seems to stand still. Soon you may find yourself whizzing along with your plan and not realize until afterward how easy it was to get it done. You and the creative force within you are getting it done!

Know you're capable of doing anything you set out to do, and encouraging yourself in this way will bring out your best work. Brilliant work. By you!!

Now imagine how good it feels to have done it. How great it feels to get that done and be so proud of how well you did it!

Always allow yourself to feel that you're creating brilliant work, even for the smallest of details. And do your best to have fun doing it.

I Have a Positive Momentum Going

I feel energy moving. I feel clarity flowing. I feel that I'm in my element. All forces are moving in order to bring me every desire, and I'm ready. I am in the energy of all the qualities that are necessary for my alignment with every wish, every dream, every plan, every whim.

That's what I sound like when I'm getting excited about my plans moving along or feel like they're about to. It's easy to feel passionate about my wishes and dreams. And sometimes I just coax myself into that feeling place because it feels good. The better I feel in general, and the better I feel about my plans, the more positive momentum I build.

When I feel inspired about any one of my desires, I get really excited and start getting ideas about actions I can take. And as I act on inspired ideas, I experience the absolute best kind of momentum. Words cannot describe it. It has to be experienced.

But when I'm in it, I feel it flowing. There's an influx of brilliant ideas. I get impulses to make a call, look something up, or go somewhere that results in an invitation and leads to another great opportunity. When I act on my ideas or impulses, I can feel the brilliance at work.

And during all of this, I'm feeling guided. I'm feeling more authentically me. I'm excited and anticipating success. I am certain the actions I'm taking are going to result in only the most positive outcomes for me.

The ideal manifestation is what happens when I allow things to keep flowing like this. Without a doubt in my mind that it will indeed manifest, I am in the most advanced stage of allowing.

How does it feel when I've stopped doubting my abilities?

Why is it easy for me to have so much more confidence now?

How does it feel to allow good things to happen for me?

What are the words that I would use to describe the excitement when I start noticing my positive momentum? I can think of ten of them right now. What are they?

Isn't it thrilling to see the results of my consistent thoughts of appreciation?

How does it feel when I start seeing signs that one or more of my desires is lining up for me?

What's it like when there's evidence of my dreams coming true? The *feeling* that it's coming is the first sign.

Think of one sign that would show me evidence of my favorite wish starting to manifest. What is the first thing that comes to mind? What's the sign? Can I feel it, touch it, or see myself having it?

____

How does it feel to be living it? Who do I want to share my news with?

____

I can close my eyes right now, see it all happening, and imagine telling someone about it and their excited response, and lock in the feeling of it. I'll recall this scene as often as I wish, until it becomes my reality.

In the meantime, how does it feel to give myself permission to have fun? And to have faith that everything I want is coming?

What if I wholeheartedly believed that the law of attraction is always creating a way for what I believe in, and consistently think of, to come true for me?

The more I acknowledge and appreciate any evidence I see or progress I make, the sooner I may actualize my dreams.

Action: Even when you're not feeling naturally in the flow with a positive momentum, you can create it yourself. You've already been doing so while reading this book, and before that, I'm sure.

So, if there's a project or activity you're wanting to do that you'd like to kick-start some positive momentum for, just start with something general and build up to the feeling you're wanting that will help you conquer the task at hand.

As previously mentioned, getting yourself into a good-feeling place before taking an action for *any* reason will always bring about a better outcome.

You can use the fill-in questions below to get you started with a positive momentum for your life in general, or come up with your own that are specific to the action you're taking. Just think of whatever comes to mind first, and give multiple answers on each of them when more come to mind:

It's time to build positive momentum for what I'm about to do. How does it feel to allow myself to have confidence, eagerness, and passion about my life, as well as this subject or project?

I am in charge of __________.

I feel empowered to __________.

I'm programming my mind to think positive thoughts about myself and my life, as well as this task, so that I can be __________, and have __________, and achieve __________.

I love that I can __________.

And I love that I am __________.

I have the ability to feel __________ and __________ in my mind and heart, no matter what is happening around me.

I have the ability to __________, and maintain my __________.

I have set myself free from __________, __________, and __________.

I feel happier every day about __________.

I am living a life of abundance. I have an abundance of __________, __________, and __________.

When I'm in the flow of this abundant energy, this matter and everything else I'm doing gets done with effortless ease.

I have a soft focus on it rather than a high-pressured urgency about it, and that makes everything about it better and easier.

I continue to practice this and I'm loving it! What else am I feeling good about?

If you ever feel overwhelmed or exhausted while thinking of a desire or thinking of acting on it, you may be putting too much effort into making something happen.

Consider taking a break from it and focus on something in your life that's going really well, and then everything will fall into place. Be patient, have faith, and the ideas and answers will come!

Don't forget to make the most of your day!

Positive Outcomes & Opportunities Find Me

I've been purposely creating my life by putting my wishes out there and doing everything I could to stay in a good-feeling place. I set things in motion with some very powerful intentions. I'm taking inspired action and I've built up a lot of positive momentum. And this is when things start to happen and get really exciting.

All the excitement I'm feeling is due to the forward direction of my desire. Doesn't it feel amazing to think of it? And this positive energy I'm giving out is pouring into whatever phase of the plan I'm on.

No matter what part I'm focusing on, every detail feels handed to me. And whatever I'm putting into it, is coming out of it. And I love knowing that never means that hard work is required.

Before I know it, all kinds of signs and synchronicities are happening for me. This is evidence that there's energy moving to make things happen for me. This is what my positive momentum brings. This is what happens when I believe in my dreams and expect good things to come. Yes, thank you! I accept.

A continuous flow of ideas, opportunities and synchronicities are coming into my life experience. They present themselves in a multitude of ways, each one more delicious than the last.

It's as though the universe is shifting things around to accommodate my wishes. There's nothing for me to do but stay out of the way. All that I seek is seeking me, and what's meant to be will be.

I love seeing the results of my good-feeling thoughts! Whether my dreams are big or small, they can happen quickly or may take longer. But I get to see them come together piece by piece. And as I've said before, it's the very best part of it all.

So I intend to enjoy every bit of it. I'm living it, breathing it, loving it, and making it all mine. It's done.

I am thrilled every time I see a little piece of it come around.

How does it feel to know my wishes are coming true?

How does it feel to know my only "job" is to relax and let it come?

How does it feel when things start happening?

Can I imagine each part of what I've been visualizing suddenly showing up as I imagined it or better?

What's it like to be in the right place at the right time and meet someone who offers me an opportunity I was hoping for?

How does it feel to get the salary I expected?

How does it feel when my first offer is accepted for the house I want to buy?

What are the words that describe how I feel when all my desires begin to manifest? Can I think of ten or more words that describe that feeling of elation?

____

____

Isn't it nice to know that a feeling of elation is available to me now? And that's because I get to be directly involved in creating my life. I have creative control. I have the authority to decide how I want my life to unfold. And I love it!

Why does it feel so natural to me once I've achieved my desire? How can it be so exciting and feel very natural to me at the same time?

Could it be that *having* what I desired was the obvious next step? And didn't I expect it before it came?

Could it be because I practiced being in the energy of my desire long enough for it to become a part of me before it manifested? And wasn't that part of the plan?

When did I get so good at aligning my energy with my desires? And in such a way that allowed for the manifestation to come so easily and effortlessly and not surprisingly?

So after the manifestation comes, I realize it wasn't exactly new for me. I felt it was mine all along and fully expected it. And my energy and excitement is always heightened while I'm molding it into existence.

Afterward, I love knowing I'm ready for my next adventure, and the next, and the next.

Feeling good about any or all of my desires is the first sign that I'm becoming aligned with them. When the evidence begins to show itself, I feel even more certain that *all* my wishes are coming true. At this point, my only "job" is to simply allow myself to be in the moment and feel how very fortunate I am.

Isn't it great to see the manifestation process through to the end and see how it works?

Why is it so easy for me to allow my desires to manifest now?

Action: Are you letting things in? Here are some reminders or things you can consider doing that will help you "stay out of the way" and let positive outcomes and opportunities find you:

Think and speak of what you *want*, and leave out anything else.

Practice being in a constant or frequent state of joy and appreciation.

Find ease as often as you can, and practice the feeling state you wish to be in.

Keep asking how it feels to allow yourself to be blissful.

Practice meditation; go within and you will naturally and easily build confidence and a feeling of worthiness.

Any time you start to second-guess or doubt your abilities, do whatever it takes to redirect your thoughts. You're a completely capable, worthy, and powerful creator.

Only share your plans or dreams with supportive people, or not at all.

Keep the vision in mind; wish it, dream of it, believe in it, and expect it to come. Have patience and faith, and let go of the "how."

Focus on the desires that feel good and trust that those that don't will soon follow.

If you find yourself anxious when thinking of a desire, detach yourself from it long enough to let the answers come. Overthinking it can stop your momentum and keep it out of reach; find the balance in it.

Once you come back to it, decide to get creative and have more fun playing with the idea. You may get a whole new idea about it. A goal or project can start one way and often turn into something completely unexpected.

Always be open and appreciative of anyone that shows up in your experience. It could lead to a whole slew of opportunities for you, such as a new job, a way to achieve one of your goals, or getting introduced to someone through them who becomes your best friend or happens to be your soulmate.

So always be open to insights or invitations that could turn into something else. If it feels iffy, consider letting it go. If you feel curious or excited about what you're hearing, follow the impulse.

Why is it so easy for you to expect positive outcomes and opportunities to manifest for you?

I See Any Challenge As an Opportunity

I am so steady and strong in my spirit of love and appreciation that I welcome anything that life brings my way. I am no longer fazed by things that could appear to be a setback. I have an appreciation for anything that's part of my experience. If things don't seem to be going my way, I know that means there's something better to come.

How does it feel to know that I'm available for the right relationship, job, or opportunity to come along because that other one didn't work out?

What if I could trust that something better always comes out of any challenge, no matter how bad it seems at the time?

What's it like to feel relieved when plans fall through, once I find out there's another route I preferred to take?

When did I start noticing the benefit of extra time when something doesn't happen as fast as I'd like? Perhaps it's giving me time to learn something I didn't know that's needed to accomplish it.

Isn't it nice when I gain clarity on a slow-going project that helps me discover another direction to go in? What if it feels like more of what I want and turns out even better than the original plan? Doesn't it seem that it was meant to be?

And what about how amazing it feels to have grown through it all? I know so much more about who I am and what I want with every turn.

All that being said, I love knowing that I can control the contrast or challenges I experience by continuing to focus on what I *do* want, and I let go of any contradictory thoughts.

If I'm so good at taking charge like this, what else can I influence in my life?

____

____

____

____

____

____

____

____

____

____

____

____

____

Have I noticed how much better I am at controlling my emotions?

Do I see how far I've come when it comes to guiding my thoughts?

How does it feel to know that I am now mastering alignment with all my desires?

I have to add this one thing: Yay! Bravo. *Woohoo*!

Oh, sorry. I'm back in control now.

Oh *wait*...those are not the emotions I want to control. I am wild and free and living the dream! Does wild belong in there? Hmmm. Well, we'll see. I'm always evolving, so you never know. Time will tell.

Action: Are there any challenges in your life right now? Is there a way to see it as an opportunity? What if you knew that after it's over, everything becomes clear to you? A weight has lifted. You and everyone involved are better for having experienced it.

Your life has changed. You've made the most life-changing transformation. You're stronger. You're more determined. You're wiser. You're better. You feel more love in your heart than ever before.

Can you decide right now to expect good things to come out of anything that occurs in your life, and believe they will?

Keep saying "All good things are coming to me."

I Am Successful at Everything I Do

My reality is becoming what I wish it to be, what I think it to be, what I imagine it to be, and what I feel it to be. In essence, it will always be what I expect or believe it to be.

I see my future as unlimited potential. I believe that I can be, have, and do anything I wish. I deserve success, and I know that I'm achieving my desires. I'm not concerned with how I'll get there. I just know I will. I always do.

So while I'm excited about my dreams, I'm so confident they're happening that I'm somewhat disengaged from them. Just enough to allow them to come. I just keep an image in my mind of the desired end result.

Anything I want to make possible for me, I just start saying that it's possible. And my faith in myself and my strong desire will always persevere. I'm not fazed by any bumps along the way. I never fear failure because the concept of failure doesn't exist in my world.

All my life experiences are a success when I know they're moving me forward and leading me to the next step on my path. I only feel more determined. I do everything in a successful way. I do it with heart. I do it with faith and purpose. When something doesn't work out, it only means the universe has better ideas in store for me.

And I like to remember that I am not a statistic. I'm not like anyone else. When I want to achieve something, my results are based on the energy I put into it. When I apply for a job, I'm going to be the one they hire. My service or products are the preferred choice. Things are always working out for me.

And there's never a need to concern myself with any "competitors" in terms of business or career. So, nothing is a competition. I'm truly happy for others' success and know there's enough to go around again and again.

And I have a successful day every day when I do my tasks with faith and purpose. And when I enjoy the work I'm doing, it'll never feel like work. And no matter how little I've done or how much time I've spent on the smallest of details, if it's done well in *my* estimation, I've had a successful day.

How does it feel to look at it this way, and to know that I'm becoming more successful as I think of it?

What's it like when I'm aligned with my inevitable success:

> I am in sync with my vision.
> I believe I have the know-how to achieve my goals.
> I keep my vision in mind as I take inspired action.
> I have complete faith that I will reach my full potential, whether that's becoming successful in business or enjoying more time with my family.
> I make the most of anything I'm doing *now*, and ensure only the best outcomes for my future.
> I put my heart into my work.
> I put my heart into my relationships.
> I truly appreciate the parts I like about everything I do.
> I stay open to new and improved circumstances.
> And know that I deserve them.

Now is the powerful moment where I, once again, use my focused attention to create what I want to attract. I am now achieving success in anything I set out to do.

How does it feel to have everything I do turn into a success?

Why is it suddenly so easy for me to live fearlessly, courageously, happily, wholeheartedly, and powerfully?

How does it feel to think and feel and act like the person I was born to be?

> It means I'm being genuine. I'm being passionate.
> I'm living my life with purpose. It means I'm being me.
> The raw and unadulterated me. The invincible, successful, freedom-seeking, doesn't-know-the-word-failure me.

How does it feel when I get a new idea and believe it's so brilliant that I can't wait to take action on it?

When did I start knowing exactly what to do the moment I decide that I want to get something done?

Why is it so easy for me to succeed in anything I do?

My desires are a part of who I am now. My thoughts are turning into things. The stronger my belief and the more consistent my positive emotions, the quicker my wishes come true.

All forces are in motion to make things happen for me, and I'm doing my part to line up with it. The details of my desired outcomes are already set up for me. I bring it closer as I match up with it. And I'm keeping a place for it in my life.

And as always, my real success is based on how much joy I have in my life and how wonderful I feel!

Action: If desired, recite these final intentions aloud with a great big smile on your face (or do it your way):

Everything I do, I do as though I'm a pro. Because I really am. I know what I know, and I'm really good at it. Everything I do turns into a success. Everything I do, I do efficiently. This is not a high-pressure thing. It's about doing each step my way with care and with heart.

And I never compare myself to anyone else. I'm like no one else. And I know that everything I do, I do uniquely my own way. And it's always in a great way. And everything I do is nothing like anyone else has done. And this is not my ego. This is me being me and cherishing myself as it's meant to be. And I'm loving everything I choose to do.

I'm the one person who knows what makes my life the best possible life. I am striving to always be the best version of myself and continue to evolve. I am just right as I stand here now. And I am more amazing every day!

How does it *feel* to be successful in accomplishing your goals? Grab your wish list journal or a piece of paper for a writing exercise. You've done something similar to this on other days, but it's never too much to practice the feeling state of success or any other feeling you wish to have.

Write one sentence that sums up your desired end result for the overall picture of your ideal life. Write it at the top of the page.

Then quickly write the first thing that comes to mind. Write dozens of words or short phrases that describe it: how, when, why, and what it feels like to achieve it.

What's your favorite part about having it? Think of an image that symbolizes how that feels.

Include the new symbol in the mental vision you created on Day 74 if you haven't already.

How does it feel to allow yourself to be successful?

I Am Magnetic to All My Desires

Everything I think and say and do and feel is creating my experiences, my day, and my life. So if I want to be magnetic to all my desires, what am I thinking?

To be magnetic to my desires is to be in a feeling state of limitless abundance. It's about carrying myself in a way that shows the ease I feel in my body, the comfort I feel in any environment, the security of my confidence, and the certainty of my success in anything I do.

As I walk about my day, I do so with my head held high and a smile on my face, with that little-known secret I cherish that all is well with *me*. I exude all of these qualities and never arrive anywhere without them. When I show up, there's no pretense. I'm so good at letting my authenticity show that I am virtually transparent.

What if I decided that *anything I touch will be a guaranteed success*? And then believed it so much so that I make it true? What if I was told *that* since I was born? How likely do you think it would come true, then? I can decide to start telling myself that right now.

How does it feel to be so magnetic to my desires, that I'm getting what I want? I am magnetic to my desires because:

____

____

____

____

How does it feel to be so good at focusing on what I want that my every wish is bringing about some very specific details that are matching up? What are they? Or what do I expect them to be?

____

____

____

____

How does it feel to be so good at feeling like my dream is a part of me, that it can't help but become so?

What has my focus been on? What am I thinking about consistently? Is there anything that's making me feel like it's being summoned to me in some way? Like it's inevitably finding its way toward me? What is it?

____

____

____

____

What else do I want to attract to me?

____

____

____

____

What if I knew, without any doubt whatsoever, that every thought I frequently *had* was inviting that exact thing or something like it into my life?

And what if I knew that my thoughts turned into my desire right then and there and was delivered to me immediately?

What kinds of things would I choose to think about?

____

____

____

Isn't it great to know that this is actually quite possible? But I like knowing that things come to me when I'm ready for them and when the timing is right. Quite possibly during the moments that I'm doing nothing but reveling in the glory of being who I am.

When I'm magnetic to all my desires, I am in that same energy. I'm energetically aligned with my ideal partner or a happier relationship, like-minded friendships, and all my wishes and dreams.

What am I feeling magnetic to now?

____

____

____

What am I consistently paying attention to or thinking about?

____

____

____

What am I expecting?

____

____

____

When I'm out socializing, how do I feel when I'm being magnetic to situations I wish to attract? When I close my eyes and imagine walking into my favorite place to go, how do I feel? What kind of energy am I giving out? Do I feel radiant? What kinds of people or situations do I notice or feel being drawn to me?

____

____

____

When I look back on my life in five-to-ten years, what do I want to know that I accomplished? Write or think of three or more things now, including how I want to feel. When I think of this, I can easily determine how important things are to me and what I'd like to make a priority in my life right *now*.

____

____

What am I willing to do to get there? How much time am I willing to set aside for it? Or maybe it won't take any time at all if I just keep believing and aligning my energy with it. Done.

I feel completely in charge of creating my life. I am the master of my thoughts. I am in control of my emotions. I am mastering my ability to work with the universal law of attraction. I am mastering my alignment with all that I desire, and it feels so good.

Action: For the next few days, try to pay attention to how you're feeling when you go out of the house. Before you leave, set an intention to be magnetic to your desires as you go about your day.

And if desired, smile to yourself and set a more specific intention before entering a room or place, such as: I am magnetic to _____. Choose what you're wanting in that moment such as happy people, your soulmate, or amazing opportunities.

If it feels good, start doing it every day as soon as you arrive somewhere.

And now, think of ten or more sentences that begin with "I am" and say what you want to be thinking and attracting and inviting into your life.

Think about what you want for your home life, career, social life, or personal time. And be thinking of the energy you want to exude as you think of it or say it aloud. If desired, write this in your wish list journal.

And now take a few minutes to finish the question "Why is it so easy for me to ________?" with all of your desires. Anything you can think of that you've been wishing to have manifest for you—for your mind or body or for your life or success.

Think of it or say it out loud. The question itself is very naturally uplifting because it has that tone of possibility or certainty that you are now manifesting these things. It gets your subconscious on board with everything you're doing. Get really into it and allow yourself to get excited as you think this through.

Consider doing this every morning as you wake up. It's a great way to start your day. You can say all the things that you want to get done that day or list your desires. Either way, it's a great way to increase your magnetism to all your desires.

Try it now: "Why is it so easy for me to ________?"

You're doing a great job being playful and purposeful in everything you do and have a wonderfully vibrant energy. You're giving out a pure signal that's attracting the results you want. And it's way more fun to attract what you want and leave out what you don't want. Well done!

How does it feel when I allow myself to believe that anything I touch will be a guaranteed success?

Why is it suddenly so easy for me to magnetically attract all that I wish for?

My Wishes Come True

The process of creating my life is *amazing* to me. I decide what I want. I hold a vision of it. I allow it to come. And I do this by having faith and trust that it *will*, as I stay in the feeling place of joy and appreciation.

And I love how it feels when I put myself in the life I'm creating. I'm really good at aligning my energies to anything I want. I just practice how it feels when it's a part of my life.

How does it feel to have all my wishes come true?

What if today was the first day of my life and all I knew was that I would be happy, healthy, and successful? It's the only thing I ever heard, and it's the only thing I ever tell myself. I believe it wholeheartedly, and there's nothing opposing it.

How do I think my life would go? Would it feel like I'm being the person I was born to be? I can do my best to feel how it feels to be me, as I step into that reality now, where all my wishes have come true.

Only they're not just wishes. I've sorted through my life experiences and discovered what I truly want out of life. I've spent much of my time contemplating the manifested version of my desires, and I hold a vision of it in my mind. I'm in the feeling place of it, and it's become a part of who I am. And I'm ready to bring it to life.

So let's say it's about a year from now, and I've manifested all that I desire. How does it feel to be living it? If I could be in the feeling place of a day in this life, what would it feel like?

____

____

____

____

____

How does it feel to have what I would call my perfect kind of day after all my desires have manifested?

Words can't do it justice, but I can say that I feel like I'm in such a blissful state of wellbeing and abundance. The only thing I know how to experience is joy. Everything in my life is easy. I have so much appreciation for the ability to live this life and be who I am.

I found a way to see everything in my life as easy, joyful, and prosperous. Things started to happen and before I knew it, I was living my dream. It happened more quickly than I expected. I expected a lot of good things, but thought it would take more time.

I attracted the house I wanted, the healthy relationships I wanted, the career success I hoped for, and all the big and little things in between. *And it keeps getting better!*

I feel able to do *whatever* I wish, *whenever* I want, with *whomever* I choose.

I feel a *tremendous* sense of freedom. I'm *quite* literally high on life.

My day starts and ends in the most *glorious* way, and my day is *filled* with activities that please me. Life keeps getting more interesting and exciting. And the opportunities for growth and more fun are *ongoing*.

Step into my life the way *I* see it. I'm in the *same* energy of my desires and I'm feeling the way I do when I *have* all of it. What does it *look* like? What does it *feel* like? I'm going to say it all right now.

A year from now...

> *My lifestyle is:*
> *The best part about it is:*
> *I feel __________ all the time.*
> *My ideal partner is:*
> *The best part about them is:*
> *I feel __________ when I'm with them.*
> *They feel __________ when they're with me.*
> *My family is really happy about:*
> *I would describe my house as:*
> *I've made changes to:*
> *I hired help to:*
> *My career is:*
> *I can see myself at work and I am:*
> *I accomplished all of these goals:*
> *I even learned to:*
> *I have way more freedom to:*
> *I have the time and money to:*
> *The car I'm driving is a:*
> *I love driving it because:*
> *My new hobbies are:*
> *My favorite thing to spend money on is:*
> *I'm most excited about my new:*
> *My favorite thing to touch in my house is:*
> *The best aroma coming from the new kitchen is:*
> *The best-tasting dish I frequently have at my favorite restaurant is:*
> *I wanted all of this because:*
> *I love thinking about all that I am now achieving, and it makes me feel:*

One of the ways I believe I created this life is by seeing it in front of me, as though my life was a blank canvas and I had artistic control as its creator.

I would picture it and be thinking: I am walking toward me right now. I notice the look on my face and how I feel. I have an air of confidence about me. I'm always smiling as though I hold the secret to true happiness. And I really feel that I do. It appears to me and those I meet that I am happy and free. And I'm just being myself.

And in this vision I would see myself surrounded by all that I desired. And now I have it.

In my vision, I always look like I'm on top of the world. Why do I look this way?

> *Because I'm loving myself and loving the life I'm living.*
> *I diligently sought my ideal life by doing whatever I could do to stay in a constant state of appreciation, joy, and abundance.*
> *I let myself be at ease often enough to allow wellbeing and abundance to flow. This, along with finding the feeling place where my desires became a part of me, invited this reality to me. And I couldn't be more thrilled.*

And I am now in the qualities and energy of a happy, healthy, and successful person.

So many people have used this to create their ideal life, and I'm doing it just as well or better. I'm going to keep doing it for every new desire I have. But only when it feels fun. My desires are happening either way.

How does it feel when I wake up one day and it has happened? I got my wish!

How does it feel to be where I want to be?
To feel the way I want to feel?
To be with who I want to be with?
To be doing what I set out to do?
To be successful in anything I do?
How does it feel to have created the life I dreamed of?
How do I feel when it's a part of me?

If I close my eyes right now I can take myself there and be in the feeling place of it. What does it look and feel like? Reach out and touch something in each of the places I go. Smell the aromas, taste the dinner, feel the breeze on my face, or the ocean water touching my toes, and more. What else would be happening? Think of it now.

I feel deeply satisfied right now. I'm in pure joy in every moment of this life I'm designing. And it never ends. I keep adding to its magnificence. When I'm in this magical place, everything I wish for comes true. Only, it's not really magical, it's just me being me.

It's natural for me to get what I want. And it feels so natural to me when it arrives because I am in the energy of it now. I knew it would come. I patiently waited for it in delightful anticipation. And I enjoyed every moment that led up to it!

Action: Now or before you go to bed (when you're in a great mood), write a letter from your future self. This process has been used by many people to help their desires manifest successfully. Handwrite the letter with pen and paper.

In this letter, tell yourself how amazing your life is and everything that's happening. Imagine you're telling a close friend if it helps. Describe anything you want in your life in detail. Take yourself there and feel what it's like to be living it. Allow yourself to feel really happy about it.

Write a date on the letter. Three-to-six months is a good time frame if you feel it's achievable by then, a year being the max. It's all possible, no matter how big your dreams are.

Once it works for you, it gets easier to write the letters with a stronger belief in it. Try to write one every few months or so. Put them into a special box and read them after a while to celebrate anything that's come true. You can also write a second copy and keep it in your pocket or wallet until you've achieved it.

Also, consider recording yourself on your phone or another device; describe how it feels to be and have and do all that you wish for. Do your best to describe how it feels in detail. At the end, describe what your perfect day would look and feel like from morning to night.

Include all your senses as you give details. Finish the recording with something like: "How does it feel when I allow myself to attract all of this into my life? I am now achieving all that I desire, and it feels so good."

Each time you listen to it or say it along with the recording, it can really connect you to the feeling place of being there and take on a life of its own. This is a very powerful manifesting tool!

Try listening to it as you wake up or as you fall asleep.

Sweet dreams, Lovely!

You are now achieving blissful wellbeing, freedom, and abundance in an easy, relaxed manner. You are living a life you love with happiness and freedom. Your wishes are coming true! You're getting everything you want, or better than that. How certain of it are you? If not now, you will be. Just let it in. You're ready!

How does it feel to allow your wishes to come true?
How does it feel to wake up one day and realize that they've all come true?
How does it feel to be you and be happy and free and living in abundance?

Day 87

I Am in the Qualities & Energy of Unlimited Abundance

I am practicing the feeling of anything I wish to achieve until I make it mine.

I know who I am and what I want more clearly every day. I see every day as a fresh start with newly defined desires and acquired skills and qualities.

I decided that I am now in the qualities of the person I was born to be. I'm taking the path to my greatest joy and wellbeing. And I deserve it!

The energy within me is pure and present and joyful, and spreads beyond boundaries.

Why am I suddenly so decisive, determined, and diligent in my quest for more joy, love, and prosperity in my life?

When did I start feeling so worthy and deserving of everything I could ever want?

And how am I able to just sit back, relax, and enjoy the whole journey along the way?

How did I learn to be so good at being deliberate about my intentions?

Why am I feeling so certain that everything in my life is becoming better every day in every way?

How did I become so brave and adventurous?

____

____

____

Why do I feel so free to be myself now?

____

____

____

____

When did I start feeling so satisfied with everything in my life?

I love how wonderful, rich, and alive I feel.
I love how invincible I feel.
I am in the qualities of my blissful wellbeing.
I am in the qualities of a person who has a happy family.
I've created a happier family by being in the qualities of the joyful person I wish for them to be.
I am calm and in control of how I react to every situation.
And I always come home in the spirit of peace, love, joy, and wellbeing.
I practiced it, and it became natural to me.
I see everyone doing well and love to see how happy they are when they're in the house or visiting.
I am in the qualities of someone who's often amused and having fun.
I smile and laugh more.
I am a person who has everything I need and my desires are my reality.
I celebrate who I am every day.
I know I am so very fortunate and thankful.
And I'm always getting the equivalent of the vibration I'm offering.
I have the qualities of those I wish to invite into my life.
I am in the qualities of being in love.
I am in the character of a lover of life with a generous heart.
I'm in the qualities of someone who's intuitive and decisive.
I am in the qualities of my ease with all that is.
I am in the qualities of my confidence and success, and most of all, joy.

What am I choosing to be or have or do from this point forward? Finish the sentences below, giving several answers for each one.

From now on, with the best of my intentions:

I *choose* to feel ______.

I choose to be more ______.

I choose to have more ______.

I choose to enjoy more ______.

I choose to do more ______.

I will do my best to ______.

I am really good at ______.

I am excited about ______.

I am ready for ______.

I am now achieving ______.

I decided, and it's done.

Action: During the first minute or so of your meditation, begin to use "abundant, confident, successful" for your mantra words.

Put your attention on your solar plexus just beneath your rib cage, smile to yourself, and then breathe in, think "abundant," breathe out, think "confident," breathe in, think "successful." Keep your attention on your solar plexus, and repeat for as long as it feels good.

Allow it to instill the feeling of what each of these means to you. Just hearing the words will do this, so there's no need to think about it. See how you or your body feels afterward.

And if desired, toward the end of your meditation session: put your attention on your crown chakra at the top of your head as you breathe in and out. Imagine a violet light shining there, or see it spiraling if you wish—clockwise for women, counterclockwise for men.

Allow yourself to feel open and connected to the universe, or universal life-force energy, and feel the harmony in it. If desired, try it now.

Have the best day you can have!

I Am Focused & Unstoppable in My Spirit of Abundance

My desires want me as much as I want them. I *am* my desires. My desires are a part of me. What are the most powerful words I'm using to guide me there?

What words describe me when I'm feeling focused and unstoppable in the spirit of abundance? How does it feel?

> I feel empowered, as I am consistently in a state of wellbeing, joy, and abundance.
> I'm feeling happy and free, and every day's a wonderful day because I choose it to be.
> I'm getting better every day in every way.
> I feel like celebrating every day just for being alive.
> Nothing takes me out of my good-feeling place.
> I make my own fun wherever I go.
> I feel unstoppable in doing anything I wish to do.
> I feel unstoppable in anything I want to be.
> I feel unstoppable in anything I want to achieve.
> And I'm never finished becoming who I am.
> My desires change or expand as I evolve.
> I have an ever-present knowing within me that keeps me moving forward.
> I move forward in a state of belief and faith that my ability to allow my desires to manifest everything I want is real. *So* very real.
> I have the amazing ability to align with anything I wish to manifest. Anything at all!
> And it's incredible.

If there are any qualities or talents that I don't yet possess, I just intend to practice being in the feeling of what that would be like and I easily create it for myself. The ideas and steps to take to get there come to me in the days to follow. I am a very powerful creator.

How does it feel to know that I am now achieving anything I want? I love knowing that just the thought and intention of this is raising my vibration and leaving me wide open to the most magnificent life experiences.

Can I feel how close I am to aligning with amazing opportunities, new healthy friendships, an easy, fun relationship with my partner, or meeting someone new, or anything that is meant to be for me? I say *yay* to this. Bring more of it to me. I'm ready!

Why is it now so easy for me to believe that I can feel my way into *any* reality I desire; a desire I *wish* for, *dream* of, *plan* for, *believe* in, and expect?

How good does it feel to acknowledge that I *want* what I want because I know it will bring me more joy? And as I anticipate its arrival, it will thrill and excite me to think of it and plan for it.

I am now achieving everything I desire. How close am I? Isn't it nice to know that *every* little thing I do is moving me closer to it? And everything I do, I do with heart. By nature, I don't know any other way.

And I love that my plan continues to evolve. It's becoming clearer and better. All the details are being worked out. And I always keep an image of the best possible outcome impressed upon my mind. I love all of this. It's so exciting!

Finish these sentences with multiple answers on how I'm feeling right now. How well do I know myself, and how far will I go to inspire myself? What can I say here that will fill me up with the energy of limitless abundance I have available to me? I start with a smile, and then go...

    I am an example of ______.
    I feel ______.
    I am attracting ______.
    I invite ______ into my life.
    I am in the joy of who I am because ______.
    There isn't anything better than ______.
    Why is it so easy for me to do ______ now?
    I have so much ______.
    I am so glad to be doing ______.
    I am really interested in ______.
    I am most entertained by ______.
    I am so happy that I am ______.
    I am so happy to have more ______.
    I have a lot of fun when I ______.
    ______ makes me laugh.
    The one thing that always gets me to smile is ______.
    Before I go to sleep I intend to ______.
    When I get up every morning I intend to be ______ all day.
    I am making time for ______.
    I feel more ______ every day.
    I am now discovering that I can ______.

I am now achieving _______.
I believe _______.
I expect _______ to show up for me.
I will continue to choose _______.
Going forward, I wish to be more _______.
I choose to release and let go of _______.
I'm getting better every day at _______.
It's time for me to _______.
I intend to always _______.
Right now I am deciding to _______.
I know I will be _______.
I am on my way to _______.
I started being way more adventurous when I decided to _______.
I am feeling great about _______.
I know how to _______.
I feel fortunate to be _______.
I love _______ about my family.
I love _______ about the world.
Most importantly, I love _______ about myself.
And I love and accept myself because _______.

And last but not least, I am *now* focused and unstoppable in achieving ___________.

Action: Take a couple nice, slow, deep breaths and then close your eyes. Say to yourself: "How does it feel when I'm focused and unstoppable in my spirit of abundance? Show me how it feels when I allow this to happen."

Notice if your energy changes or your breathing becomes deeper. Perhaps the energy around your heart feels lighter? Just take a moment to be in this energy now.

If you're not feeling it, think of the words "I am focused and unstoppable" repeatedly until you hopefully feel something. Do your best to allow it to flow.

Allow yourself to be high on life today!

Thank You in Advance

I know that everything I say and think and do is creating my life. I'm a magnet for love, joy, prosperity, and all that I wish to attract. I also know that appreciation is one of the most effective and loveliest ways to attract what I'm wishing for.

That being so, I think it's time to use a great new habit that embodies the full meaning of the word "appreciation." It shows that I am beyond appreciation for the great things happening for me. The idea is to feel thankful *in advance* for all the wonderful things that are coming into my life.

So, what can I be thankful for if they haven't happened yet?

What if I decided to be thankful for *every* day and how well it goes? And *every* week. *Every* month, and *every* year. There are more good things coming for me, and I am so very thankful.

What if I felt beyond thankful for how perfectly my life was unfolding?

What if I knew that being thankful in advance for any particular thing would ensure that I'd get more of the same or better?

What if I was thankful for each and every desire manifesting right before my eyes?

What if I felt *so* thankful for simply having a particular desire because it felt so good to think about it, that I could infuse myself and that desire with energy that matches us up? Ta-da!

And what if I was thankful for it happening by a specific date and made that happen as well? Shazam!

Too much? No, never! Anything is possible, and I am powerful. It's been done, and I can do it too. How much do I believe it? What I *believe*, I will achieve!

This is another great way to make it feel like it's already happened. When I say thank you it means that I believe in my desire. It means that I believe it's coming, I believe I deserve it, and I believe it's meant to be.

And the reason I'm saying thank you in advance is because I expect it to come. It's a certainty. One that has my complete trust. It means that I'm in the energy of it and already feel it's a part of me. And as I know, this is the greatest mastery of *allowing* the fulfillment of my desires.

Besides all the things that are working out for me, *who* am I thanking, if anyone?

First and foremost, I am thanking *myself* for being me, for being true to myself and my desires, and for allowing my heart to lead me.

I am thanking my wise inner being for the continual guidance and support on my path to more joy, wellbeing, and abundance.

I am thanking the universe for shifting things *all* around and into place for the purpose of accommodating my wishes and desires.

I am thanking the law of attraction for always responding to my vibrational energy and bringing me what I'm giving out, as well as showing me evidence of my beliefs. Because of you, my thoughts are turning to things, and showing me when I'm in or out of alignment with my true desires.

Last but not least, I'm thankful for any troubles that arise which show me the path I most desire, and cause me to wish for more.

My intention will always be to go wherever I go in the spirit of peace. I am so thankful when I stay in this blissful energy and radiate wellbeing, joy, and abundance to all. I choose to go wherever I go with love and appreciation in my heart.

And because I value my time, don't I find myself wanting to spend every minute of it being in the energy of my true nature?

Do I find myself, more and more, *only* wanting to speak of what I love or appreciate? What kinds of things?

____

____

____

____

Isn't it comforting to know that I am now, better than ever, feeling how I want to feel and seeing myself in the most positive light? I do everything in a great way, and I am so very fortunate to be me. How do I see myself now?

____

____

____

How does it feel to be me? How much joy and love and abundance am I willing to *allow* myself to enjoy?

____

____

____

____

____

That's all it is: a choice that I choose. And I say *absolutely, yes!*

Why is it so easy for me to let go and let it all in now?

____

____

____

____

____

Why is it so easy for me to believe that I am forever rich in every way?

____

____

____

____

____

I am the master of my mind. I am the master of my life. I am an extraordinary human being, and I choose to live life to the fullest in my pure positive energy.

Why am I so excited?

> I am totally open and receptive to the unlimited abundance life has to offer me.
> I am the master of my thoughts and beliefs.
> Blissful wellbeing is a part of me now.
> Feeling happy and free is a part of who I am.
> Abundance is within me and all around me.

It's always been a part of me, and I now believe it so, more and more.
I see it in others and love how easily it's coming to me now.
I love knowing that I am now wholeheartedly achieving all my wishes and dreams and deepest desires.
I am in complete harmony with who I am.
Thank you, thank you, thank you.
I thank you, my mind, body, and spirit for the inspiration, guidance, and love that allow me to be who I am and be one with all that is.

I love how I have embraced every part of me, every part of my life, everything I see, and all that is.
I know how blessed I am each and every day.
I am invincible in this state of mind.
I am an example of love, peace, and ever-present joy.
This is my powerful intention. This is my truth, as I choose it to be.

I've opened the gates to my abundant life of blissful wellbeing, joy, prosperity, and everything I want.

It's flowing.
It's effortless.
It's achievable.
It's inevitable.
It feels easy.
It's fantastic.
It's for me.
And it feels really, really good.

Action: Take a moment to say thank you for any gifts or blessings you've received and anything you wish to obtain or achieve today, tomorrow, this week, this month, or this year and in the years ahead.

Consider thanking the earth for its energy and strength and for continually replenishing its resources. And look up and thank the universe or deity of your choosing, if desired.

Thank your intelligent body and powerful mind.

And anything else you wish.

Take your time and do this now.

Thank you for being you! Hope you're having the best day!

1-2-3: My Wishes Come True

As you read this day's intentions, do your best to feel these words are true for you. Take your time, breathe deeply, and allow yourself to feel limitless.

1-2-3, Mind and Body, it's time to feel the flow of limitless abundance in my life. Show me how it feels.

Inner Being, if I were to fully embody my abundant nature, how would I feel?

You would be saying that life is quite magical. You would feel that life appears to be overflowing with bountiful beauty and wonder.

And you're there. You *are* this *now*. Your intention to be so has put you on the path to an endless abundance of joy, love, freedom, and prosperity. It's all you see. It's all you know. It's all that's on your mind. So that's what you're getting more of. Amazing life experiences that are meant for you are ready and waiting for you.

You're using your words, thoughts, and intentions to inspire self-healing and spiritual harmony. And in this place you might call your inner sanctum, all your wishes come to life.

This *consistent, active, positive* vibration you're offering right now is always followed by positive outcomes. And you're always focused on the areas of your life that feel really good to you, and everything else begins to fall into place.

It's such a wonderful thing to be putting more energy into the things you care about. You're doing your best to focus on the people and activities, or dreams and projects that are truly important to you. And you're doing it as well as you can right now. It's so good to give yourself credit for that.

You're living your life with passion and purpose, and you have the faith and courage to keep moving forward until your plans become your reality. You especially enjoy the moments leading up to that. It feels like a part of you, and you know it's coming.

The best part of your abundant nature is having that energy stay with you. You're connected to it right now, and it feels like a pure vibrational alignment with your desires.

There's more than a bit of elation about the gift of freedom that comes with it. You're giving yourself the freedom to choose how you live your life. And you feel a deep appreciation for every bit of it.

In your state of abundance, you love honoring yourself and your life by following whatever's calling you: your wishes and dreams, your intuition and impulses—whatever your heart desires.

You're being shown how to align with your highest path, and you're doing it. Nothing is blocking you from it, and you have no resistance to anything. Your positive emotions and decision to let it go are deactivating anything that's left of it. You expect this to happen and go about your merry way.

You're in the flow with the greatest version of you and living the most magnificent life you can live. And it keeps getting better. And *nothing* can stop you now. You're reaching your highest potential and purpose in the light of love.

Continue to believe that you *are* already *who you wish to be*. You're being your authentic self. You're achieving anything you wish to. You can see it, and feel it, and made it a part of you. You've decided that *you're now the one* that can be, have, and do anything you desire. And so it shall be.

Breathe in: 1-2-3 **Wish**...

Action: *Place your right hand over your heart center with the left hand over it, tap your fingertips if desired, and read or say the following intentions or change the wording as you wish:*

I love that being in an abundance mindset feels so natural to me now, and it's cleared away any previous doubts. It's like I turned a switch, and I'm suddenly feeling rich and brave and fearlessly bold about how I live my life.

I'm ready for anything and open to all possibility. I've stepped into this life of abundance, and there's no turning back. It feels a little like heaven on earth to me. I feel lighter and brighter and so at ease with being myself.

I've never felt so empowered and appreciative of my qualities and talents. I'm becoming more and more open to sharing myself and my expertise with anyone I choose to. I'm very special and I do things in a very special way. No matter how small an act, I'm making a difference.

I have been doing this so well, and I'm doing it right now. I'm living my life abundantly. When this is my practiced vibration, it can be no other way. I am now in charge of my destiny and creating all that I wish for.

I have such a strong desire for my ideal lifestyle, yet I love who I am and where I am right now. It's *all* a part of who I am. And I have patience, faith, and trust that it's all working out in whatever way is best for me.

I am now mastering my alignment with all that I desire. I am prepared to receive all of it. All the love, success, joy, and wellbeing I can take.

Now, keeping your hands over your chest if it's still comfortable, put your attention on the heart center, close your eyes, and very slowly ask: "Mind, Body, and Spirit, show me how it feels when you're in harmony with one another. How does it feel when I allow blissful clarity, wellbeing, and abundance to flow?"

Repeat it one or two more times, and if you're feeling any resistance, ask how it feels to release all that resistance.

Then slowly repeat the word "blissful" with attention on your head, then your throat, your heart, your solar plexus and just under the navel.

Now repeat that going back up: from below the navel, solar plexus, heart, throat, and back to the center of your head. If it feels good, continue seeing the word or feeling the energy of the word "blissful." Then try "thank you." See if one feels better than the other.

And here's another intention for you:

In a moment I'm going to count to three and say the word **"Wish."** In doing so, I am anchoring my belief that I am now achieving all that I wish for. They are working their way toward me, and I am getting ready for them.

Any time I think of 1-2-3 Wish, it means that I decided I am at ease, I am blissfully well, I am free, and I am abundant. Most importantly, it's a reminder that my wishes *are* coming true.

The moment I think of it, I allow it to shift my energy to the frequency of blissful abundance. In that instant, all the energy within me and around me becomes lighter and freer, and I allow it to be. My head and heart even feel lighter.

Now, if you're feeling really good, breathe in and think 1-2-3 **Wish.** Again, breathe in: 1-2-3, breathe out **Wish: my wishes come true.** Feel the energy of abundance flowing to you and through you.

Call back this energy any time you wish by thinking 1-2-3 **Wish**.

You can also see "wish" written over your head, heart, and solar plexus any time you need to feel uplifted. Or feel the meaning of the word washing over you. To you this means that your mind, body, spirit, and the universe are all working in harmony with one another to bring you all that you desire.

How does it feel to be aligning with all that I wish for? Why is it so easy for me to keep this going now?

Congratulations on finishing Step 3! Happy manifesting!

What did you learn about yourself during this step?

Has anything changed (*your energy, thoughts, or feelings about any area of your life*)?

Have you noticed any synchronicities?

From the time you started Day 1 until now, have you noticed any positive changes in the way you feel or anything else?

Do you feel more in charge of how you feel?

How empowered do you feel on a scale of 1–10 to be able to help yourself feel better when you need to or when you're feeling stuck?

Has your life improved in any particular area?

Have you seen an improvement in how you feel about yourself?

Have you noticed an improvement in your relationships?

Do you feel healthier, happier, freer, or more abundant?

Are you experiencing less stress or more resilience to it?

What are three or more things you appreciate about your life or where you are now?

Congratulations on finishing all three steps!

10 More Days to Go!

What's Next

Can you believe you're almost done? Up next are Days 91 through 100, which will be a review of Steps 1, 2, and 3, as well as some reminders for strategies for long-term success in feeling healthy, happy, and getting what you wish for!

3 Steps in Review

I Bring Harmony to My Mind, Body, and Spirit

The purpose of these last ten days is to review the key concepts of Steps 1, 2, and 3. Day 100 and the pages to follow include suggestions for long-term success in achieving your wishes and dreams.

It's also intended as a quick review that you can keep on hand as a form of success kit to help you achieve your desires.

You can also consider marking your favorite "days" or favorite "actions" to continue the practice.

I hope you're feeling proud of yourself for taking the time to do this whole process. It required a lot of time and attention on yourself, and it was meant to be! And if you've made it this far, you're doing great!

Enjoy your last ten days!

My Actions and Intentions Are Creating a Life I Love

Days 91–93 are a review of Step 1:Days 1–30.

I wish for blissful wellbeing to be a part of me, and my actions and intentions are creating this for me. I am keeping my promise to myself to do whatever it takes to align with my highest level of wellbeing. I am doing my best to:

Feel that blissful wellbeing is a part of me.
Acknowledge and release any worries, fears, or limiting beliefs.
Practice connecting with my body and my breath.
Find ease and feel as good as I can feel as often as I can.
Be my own best friend and support myself unconditionally.
Nurture my body in whatever way feels right to me.
Create an environment for inner peace and positive change.
Use self-healing techniques as desired or anything I feel guided to try.
Maintain and protect my energy with intention and exercise I enjoy.
Focus on what I want and leave out what I don't want.
Continually guide my thoughts to a good-feeling place.
Be in charge of how I feel and how I react to things.
Allow my heart to lead me on a path to all that I desire.
Always have fun along the way!

What specific intentions would I like to add to this list for achieving blissful wellbeing?

Wellbeing is natural to me, and my body has the ability to heal anything that needs to be healed. I'm connected to my natural inner healer. All I need to do is practice the feeling of wellbeing until it feels like a part of me and it's who I am.

My body responds to my consistent thoughts of wellbeing, and when I notice how much better I'm feeling, my belief gets stronger. I feel empowered in my ability to feel any way I wish to feel.

I begin to feel invincible. As I practice my alignment with wellbeing, there's no other way for me to be. Nothing but the thought of wellbeing will ever come to mind. I'm feeling well and feel certain that I always will.

With faith and purpose, I think it, feel it, and believe in it and make it mine. It must become my reality. This is how powerful I am. I can create anything I wish.

The quality of my intentions and my unwavering belief in *myself and* in my dreams is creating an amazing life for myself. The joyful life I'm meant to be living.

And I intend to live this life in my natural state of blissful wellbeing. I am meant to feel good all day, every day. And that is what I intend to do.

All I need to do is practice. And as I practice guiding my thoughts to feel more ease, joy, and clarity more consistently, I align my energy with my desires. And any thought or belief that isn't aligned with my higher vibrational energy is naturally falling away, without any further effort on my part.

Action: Choose any one of your favorite "action" steps from Days 1 through 10 and try it again now. I suggest Days 3 or 9.

I Practice a State of Ease & Wellbeing

I am practicing the feeling of anything I wish to achieve until I make it mine. I'm taking the path to my greatest joy and wellbeing. And I know I deserve it!

I am completely in charge of how I feel, and I can guide my thoughts to align with all my desires. And the more I practice my belief and expectation in achieving my highest level of wellbeing, the more I draw it to me.

So I practice my belief and expectation that my body will respond to my thoughts and guidance and feel how I ask it to. And I am practicing my belief and expectation that *I am now achieving alignment with blissful wellbeing.*

Asking myself questions is a great way to guide myself to find the feeling place of anything I wish to achieve. I like how it gets me to feel so open to the possibilities that are available to me. And I love knowing that it puts the very thing it's asking about into motion for the manifestation I desire.

And so, once again I will ask...

Why am I feeling so certain that everything in my life is becoming better every day in every way?

Why is it so easy for me to feel good now?

Why do I feel more at ease in my body now?

What is making me feel lighter and brighter?

When did I become so clear-minded?

Why is it suddenly so easy for me to release unwanted thoughts and beliefs?

Why am I able to be so mindful and present in nearly every moment now?

How did I get to have so much more energy?

How does it feel to allow myself to feel good *all* the time?

When did I become so focused and unstoppable in my spirit of peace and wellbeing?

I am on a magnificent life-changing journey that's ongoing. I will never be the same. I am moving forward and upward. It can only get better.

My thoughts have energy and power to change everything, and I am now allowing myself to be who I wish to be. I am becoming the way I see myself. And what I believe I can be, I can be.

And if I speak of myself, I only share the thoughts of wellbeing that I'm focused on.

When I am feeling focused and unstoppable in my spirit of peace and wellbeing:

> All that I desire is flowing to me as I transform my thoughts.
> All that I desire is flowing to me as I believe in me.
> All that I desire is flowing to me as I believe in my wellbeing.
> All that I desire is flowing to me as I make it a part of me.
> This blissful feeling of wellness is a part of who I am.
> I feel it flowing to me, and I expect it to keep flowing to me.
> I made peace with myself and anything I ever allowed to cause me worry.
> I only associate myself with words of wellness now.
> I'm focused on blissful wellbeing and feeling fully aligned with it.
> I'm an example of joy and wellbeing to others.
> And when I decide to achieve any goal and practice the feeling of what I want as though it's mine right now, it becomes so.

Each day I guide myself to find the feeling place I wish to have. All I need to do is:

> Ask: How do I want to feel? What do I need to do to get there?

> What words will describe the feeling of having it?

When I want to redirect my thoughts to feel better, all I need to do is:

> Ask: What is my focused attention on? What is my favorite thing about this day, this person, or this situation?

> What is the solution? What would love do?

> How does my inner being feel about it?

And then I remind myself that I am the master of my mind. I am the master of my day. And the master of my life. And I'm going to practice the state of mind that I wish to be in to align with whatever desire I'm wanting to be a vibrational match to in that moment.

And the more I feel it, the more natural it is for me and the less willing I am to be feeling anything less than what I wish to feel.

There is no turning back. I get better at it every single day.

As I evolve, I trust more and more in the intelligence of my mind and body and feel the harmony of my inner being.

> Mind, Body, and Spirit, thank you for the wellbeing.
> With every breath I take, I breathe in light and love.
> With every breath I take, I feel more peaceful.
> With every breath I take, I feel more blissful.

Every moment of every day I am choosing to practice living my life in a state of blissful wellbeing and allow the abundance flowing to me.

Action: Choose any one of your favorite "action" steps from Days 11 through 20 and try it again now. I suggest Days 16 or 18.

Day 93

I Am Now Achieving Blissful Wellbeing

Blissful wellbeing is a part of me. I am committed to being in the qualities and energy of blissful wellbeing, and it's the only way I know how to be. It's who I am now. And nothing ever comes to mind that contradicts this.

How did I get here?

I started purposely living a life I love.
I decided to be in charge of how I feel and made my powerful intentions known.
I continually make peace with any worries or fears or anything that comes up that I consider a problem.
I am guiding my thoughts to a blissful place as often as I can, and it allows my wellbeing to flow.
I am letting my emotions guide me and make choices that feel right to me.

I practiced being in a state of complete wellbeing until it felt like a part of me.
I knew it was simply a choice I could make.
And instead of looking for things that could be wrong, I started noticing and appreciating what was going well for me.

While I frequently stay focused in a good-feeling place, my body and everything in my life is transforming to accommodate my wishes.

I am now designing a life I love. The ideal life I'm meant to be living. Things always work out for me, and everything's falling into place. As I hold my vision of blissful wellbeing, I am now allowing a remarkable transformation to take place anywhere it's needed or desired.

How does it feel when I am now living a life of blissful wellbeing?

You could say I've reached a nonresistant place of peace in my mind and body. I am feeling completely at ease in my body, and my mind is clear. Life is becoming incredibly easy.

I easily make choices that are aligned with my desire for blissful wellbeing. I follow my heart's desire and feel more joyful than anything else.

And it keeps getting better. I truly feel energetically aligned with such a blissful feeling that I'm not even sure I can describe it. If I had to come up with some words, it would go something like this:

343

I am feeling so much more at ease with myself and the way things are, it makes me want more of it. As I find more ease, I am gaining greater focus, and that is turning into great clarity.

Now I'm experiencing so much clarity that I have made room for more positive energy and brilliant ideas to flow.

I am now creating a clear knowing of all that I desire, and it's growing. I am feeling so good that I know I'll never settle for anything less. And I'm so happy about that. I am finally allowing my life to become all that it's meant to be.

I am now choosing to always feel the way I was intended to feel when I came into this world. I hold a vision of myself in the state I wish to always be in. It's a part of me now. I live it and breathe it.

And the results of my positive thoughts are being shown to me by the way my body feels and the way that I easily and freely move through life. It's as though my path has been cleared or laid out for me, and all I have to do is simply *allow* good things to happen for me.

Every day in every way I am more. More aligned with blissful wellbeing. More aligned with my true nature. More passionate. More loving. More energetic. More courageous. More at peace. And more connected and in tune with who I am.

I am now more aware of my body's energy and feel a deeper connection to my higher self. This is my direct route to a life of abundant joy and prosperity.

And every day in every way I'm better at allowing myself to be in the blissful energy that is aligned with my true nature and all that I desire.

Action: Choose any one of your favorite "action" steps from Days 21 through 30 and try it again now. I suggest Days 24 or 28.

Day 94

I Choose to Be Happy

Days 94–96 are a review of Step 2: Days 31–60.

It's time to be in the joy of who I am and feel free to be my true self. It's my birthright, and I want to feel happier all the time. I wish for my mind, body, and spirit to be in harmony with one another and guide me through life. And the happier and freer I feel, the easier life gets. And I love things to be easy.

I intend to be in the qualities and characteristics of my most confident, loving, self-respecting, joyful, radiant self from now on. When this is a part of who I am, I am magnetic to all my desires. And life just keeps getting better.

I can easily achieve this by choosing to see through the eyes of love. This is the true secret to setting myself free. And it's my one answer to all of life's questions. It simplifies *everything*.

When I'm looking through the eyes of love, I feel a loving appreciation for anything I pay attention to, including myself. It also gives me the ability to see a solution for every problem or situation, and helps me understand or appreciate what's really happening.

As I change my perception to a more positive view, *the world around me changes with it*. I can already feel how this is transforming my life into anything I wish it to be.

This love guides me when I can't decide. It provides me with the right answers every time. And I always feel better when I follow my heart.

When I follow my heart, I'll always choose to feel happy and free. And there's no limit whatsoever to the level of happiness I can feel.

And I'll always choose to have a wonderful relationship with myself. I'll always care enough to do what feels right for me. I'm setting the tone for how all of my relationships will go. And now that I'm treating myself so well, others are following my lead.

It's also my relationship with things and how satisfied I feel about them that is creating the quality of my life experiences. When I have a sincere appreciation for what I've chosen for myself, whether it's a job, a partner, or something else, I'm putting the kind of positive energy into it that paves the way for a better future.

So I always focus on the parts I like about everything in my life. And this way, I set myself up for the best possible circumstances in the next experience I have. I attract a better relationship, a better job, and better circumstances for all areas of my life.

And I love knowing that I'm in a constant state of change and always becoming who I am. I am exactly where I'm meant to be in my life right now, and I'm better every day in every way.

Action: Choose any one of your favorite "action" steps from Days 31 through 40 and try it again now. I suggest Days 32 or 37.

I Practice Love & Appreciation

It's time to consistently and purposely choose my words and thoughts to create the most wonderful life for me. What words would I say right now if I knew it would result in an immediate change for the better? What is my wish? How do I wish to feel right now? What do I wish to achieve at this time in my life?

The more I practice my belief and expectation in achieving more joy and personal freedom, the more I draw it to me. So, I practice my belief and expectation that I am happy and free and more so every day.

I am creating miraculous leaps and bounds in my life simply because I am now choosing to wholeheartedly love and accept myself. And the more I'm able to accept or appreciate all that is in some way, the easier my life is becoming.

Everything I've ever desired is falling into place in this positive mindset.

How good does it feel to have a sincere appreciation for *everything* around me?

How does it feel to know it's leading me to the freedom I desire?

How does it feel to be led to the right decision every time?

What's it like when I embrace the love in my heart and let it guide me in all areas of my life?

How does it feel to have the courage to go where I want to go, be who I want to be, and do what I love to do?

Why is it suddenly so easy for me to allow my heart's desire to guide me there every step of the way?

What's it like to bravely go where my heart leads me and take part in some new venture I never thought I'd try?

How does it feel to be so in the flow with life, that all circumstances seem to transform just to accommodate me?

When did I start expecting only good things to happen? As well as expecting goodness from others?

How does it feel to have so much love in my heart that I see someone else's potential, even if they haven't, yet?

What's it like when people go out of their way to be kind to me? And to know that the more I notice and appreciate it, the more often it happens.

Why is it so easy for me to be myself now, without *any* pretense whatsoever, no matter who I'm with?

How does it feel to confidently say what I mean, and mean what I say?

And when did it become so natural for me to share only the most positive thoughts that I'm focused on?

Isn't it nice to know that with my positive words, thoughts, and energy, I'm able to transform or guide any situation I'm in to an outcome that will benefit all?

Why am I feeling so certain that everything in my life is becoming better every day in every way?

I always seem to be in the right place at the right time and moving closer and closer to my desires. I have the feeling they're making their way to me right now. I am certain of it. When I carry this feeling with me wherever I go, only the best outcomes can come from that.

To create the life I wish for, my only work is to feel as good as I can feel.

How does it feel to be so free and at ease that everything I desire begins to flow into my life?

I am now easily and freely moving forward and upward on my wonderful journey of life.

How does it feel to be as free as my inner spirit?

How does it feel to let myself shine in all areas of my life?

And what's it like to *do* what I love and love everything I do?

Why is it getting so much easier for me to do that now?

My love for myself and appreciation for all that's in my life is bringing out the best in me. I know that I am more successful in all areas of my life because of it. And I like believing that love and acceptance brings out the best in everyone.

Action: Choose any one of your favorite "action" steps from Days 41 through 50 and try it again now. I suggest Days 45 or 50.

I Feel Free

It's time to stay connected to my pure positive energy. There's an inherent source of energy within me that always feels happy and free. When I make a habit of connecting to this natural-born energy, the wisest part of me, I feel connected to everything.

In my invincible spirit of love, I feel a tremendous sense of fearlessness and wellbeing. I feel safe wherever I am and have this all-knowing, undeniable trust in things working out for me.

Why is it so easy for me to stay connected to this now? I easily stay aligned with this energy when I practice feeling appreciation, self-love, autonomy, lightheartedness, clarity, peace, courage and confidence. Or just by following my heart. And having a sense of personal freedom and ability to live authentically naturally comes along with it.

When I'm in this energy, I feel the harmony of my mind and body and feel in love with the world and everything I see. That's how good it feels to be loving and accepting or appreciating who I am and all that is. I am simply seeing through the eyes of my wisest self and it knows how amazing I am. And it loves when I'm feeling it too.

I love knowing that happiness is always available to me. There's nothing to wait for. No situation has to change in order for me to be happy. I'm focusing on feeling happy and free and letting it be.

I turn my attention away from things I don't like, and focus on what I *am* happy about, and all my desires are falling into place because of that. And it's all happening right before my eyes.

The more consistently I feel this way, the better my life becomes. The moment I decided to feel good from morning to night is when it all began.

I love it when I reach that state of mind where everything feels more satisfying to me. And I'm noticing that a lot of things have become easier in my life.

How does it feel to think and feel and act like the person I was born to be?

It means I'm being genuine. I'm being passionate. I'm living my life with purpose. It means I'm being me. The raw and unadulterated me. The invincible, successful, freedom-seeking, doesn't-know-the-word failure me.

I have the feeling that I'll always be tuned in to this energy that allows me to always feel happy and free. I know there's no turning back for me. There's only forward motion for me now. What a glorious time in my life!

Action: Choose any one of your favorite "action" steps from Days 51 through 60 and try it again now. I suggest Day 51 or 52.

Day 97

I Wish ~ I Dream ~ I Believe

Days 97–99 are a review of Step 3: Days 61–90.

It's time to set myself up for success in living a life I love, without exception. I believe in all my wishes, dreams, plans, and goals. They are all active within me and I feel more energetically aligned with them every day.

What I want is ready for me, and my only work is to create a *feeling* and an atmosphere that allows my desires to easily manifest. So I always expect good things to come to me and I fully expect my dreams to come true. And I get what I expect.

And I love knowing that focusing on what I love in my life, and expecting more of it, will always bring more of it *to* me. Where my attention goes, energy flows. And directing my attention and energy in this deliberate way is creating my ideal future. And whatever quality of energy I put into it will come back to me tenfold. A thousandfold. A millionfold? Yes, I accept!

No matter what I know, or don't think I know, I'm capable of doing everything I desire. I have unique talents and gifts and a natural ability to accomplish anything I decide to do. What I seek is already within me and the answers are coming.

I am using my brilliant mind to achieve my goals. My imagination is one of the most powerful tools I can use to bring my plans to fruition. I have the ability to create my dream life, and I intend to see it through. It's no longer a dream, but a vision. And I have a plan.

I'm keeping an image of my vision imprinted in my mind. I think of it often and it holds all the key points of my desires. It symbolizes the end result of what I see as my ideal life.

My reality is becoming what I wish it to be, what I think it to be, what I imagine it to be, and what I feel it's becoming. In essence, it will always be what I expect or believe it to be. So I always see my future as unlimited potential.

I'll always believe that I can be, and have, and do anything I wish. I deserve success and I know that I'm achieving my desires. I'm not concerned with how I'll get there. I just know I will. I always do. So while I'm excited about my dreams, I'm also detached enough from them to allow them to come. I just keep an image in my mind of the desired end result.

351

Anything I want to make possible for me, I just start saying that it's possible. And my faith in myself and my strong desire will always persevere. I'm not fazed by any bumps along the way. I never fear failure because the concept of failure doesn't exist to me.

All my life experiences are a success when I know they're moving me forward and leading me to the next step on my path. I only feel more determined. I do everything in a successful way. I do it with heart. I do it with faith and purpose. When something doesn't work out, it only means the universe has better ideas in store for me.

And I like to remember that I am not a statistic. I'm not like anyone else. When I want to achieve something, my results are based on the energy I put into it. When I apply for a job, I'm going to be the one they hire. My service or products are the preferred choice. Things are always working out for me.

I have a successful day every day when I do my tasks with faith and purpose. And when I enjoy the work I'm doing, it'll never feel like work. And no matter how much time I spend on the smallest of details, if it's done well in my estimation, I've had a successful day.

How does it feel to look at it this way and to know that I'm becoming more successful as I think of it? It is my intention to always look at things this way when it comes to my goals, wishes and desires.

How does it feel to believe in myself and believe and expect my dreams are coming true? To know that I can do anything I decide to do.

It's up to me and the quality of my thoughts, intentions, beliefs and expectations.

I am now aligning with my inevitable success. I am in sync with my vision. I believe I have the know-how to achieve my goals. I keep my vision in mind as I take inspired action.

I have complete faith that I will reach my full potential whether that's becoming successful in business or enjoying more time with my family.

I make the most of anything I'm doing now, and ensure the best outcomes for my future.
I put my heart into my work.
I put my heart into my relationships.
I truly appreciate the parts I like about everything I do.
I stay open to new and improved circumstances.
And know that I deserve them.

Action: Choose any one of your favorite "action" steps from Days 61 through 70 and try it again now. I suggest Days 65 or 67. Also, if desired change up your meditation mantra words to "wish, believe, allow." Or alternate the words you've been using to fit your desire in that moment.

I Have an Abundance Mindset

I am mastering my ability to create the life I wish for. I'm doing whatever I need to do to align with the energy of what I want. I'm feeling my way into the energy and mindset that matches my desires.

If I can feel how I'll feel when I've achieved them, my desires become a part of me, and I become a part of them. I just need to decide that I'm *letting* it be a part of me, and it will be. I am in the spirit of it right now.

It's like I'm playing the part. I'm already there. I'm feeling it. I'm living and breathing it. I'm being it. I'm practicing the feeling of it until I make it mine. And I'm feeling the success of what I set out to achieve. I can even see myself cracking open a bottle of champagne to celebrate each win, big or small.

The more I practice my belief and expectation in achieving my desires, the more I draw them to me. If I can find a general feeling of abundance, I can align with *all* my desires. Having a nice gentle focus on things is a great way to allow them to manifest. Either way, I'm doing it easily and effortlessly, and having fun all the while.

As I become more aware of how naturally abundant I am, I'm feeling limitless and able to achieve anything I want. And the better I feel the more abundance flows to me in all forms. So, I practice being in the qualities and characteristics of my abundant nature as often as I can.

How does it feel to have an unstoppable mindset of abundance?

How does it feel to allow my life to be as wonderful as I wish it to be? And to know with certainty that more great things are coming? All the pieces are laid out for me. My work is only to allow it to flow, and that's what I intend to do.

What if I knew that feeling more appreciation for the abundance I see around me would create more of it in every area of my life?

Isn't it great to know that appreciation is one of the most effective and loveliest ways to attract what I'm wishing for? How much better can I get at noticing the evidence of abundance in my life?

What if my appreciation of it creates way more joy, fun, money, vacations, or more of anything I wish?

I love knowing that when I focus on the areas of my life that are joyful or successful, the rest will come along.

What else can I do to practice a state of abundance?

To begin with, I am focusing on anything and everything that brings me joy.

I think of being happy, healthy, and wealthy as my lifestyle. It's something I do all day, every day. I practice my way into the feeling of blissful wellbeing and limitless abundance and I attract everything I wish for.

Blissful wellbeing, more happiness and freedom and abundance is all a part of me now. And it all comes naturally to me. I wished. I dreamed. And I am now believing my vision is achievable. I believe in it *so* much that it has no choice but to materialize.

I really enjoy dreaming about my desired outcome with faith and trust and the expectation that it will come. My consistent thoughts will bring it into my reality.

I am not wanting it or yearning for it because I know with certainty it will come. It will come when I'm ready. I feel that it's mine. It's a part of me and who I am. It's my own creation that's unfolding perfectly right before my eyes. This is my powerful intention.

How does it feel to think about my ideal life playing out in my mind?

How does it feel when I'm living my dream life?

How does it feel to know that I created it in my imagination first and got to see it coming together piece by piece? And have it all be mine?

How does it feel to love it and appreciate it?

How does it feel to be excited about what comes after that? And more good things after *that*?

How does it feel to be certain that I'm going to know what to do and how to do it when the time is right?

Why is it so easy for me to believe that all my plans are getting done?

And how great do I feel when all my words, thoughts, and actions are in keeping with the energy of the successful and joyful person I intend to be?

Action: Choose any one of your favorite "action" steps from Days 71 through 80 and try it again now. I suggest Days 76 or 77.

I Am Now Achieving All My Desires

I know that everything I say and think and do is creating my life. I'm a magnet for love, joy, and prosperity, and all that I wish to attract.

I feel empowered, as I am consistently in a state of wellbeing, joy, and abundance.
I'm feeling happy and free, and every day's a wonderful day because I choose it to be.
I'm getting better every day in every way.
I feel like celebrating every day just for being alive.
Nothing takes me out of my good-feeling place.
I make my own fun wherever I go.
I feel unstoppable in doing anything I wish to do.
I feel unstoppable in anything I want to be.
I feel unstoppable in anything I want to achieve.
And I'm never finished becoming who I am.
My desires change or expand as I evolve.
I have an ever-present knowing within me that keeps me moving forward.
I move forward in a state of belief and faith that my powerful ability to align with my desires and allow them to manifest is real. *So* very real.
I have the amazing ability to create anything I desire. Anything at all!
And it feels incredible.

If there are any qualities or talents that I don't yet possess, I just intend to practice being in the feeling of what that would be like and I easily create it for myself. The ideas and steps I'll take to get there come to me with ease. I am a very powerful creator.

How does it feel to know that I am now achieving anything I want? I love knowing that just the thought and intention of this is raising my vibration and leaving me wide open to the most magnificent life experiences.

Can I feel how close I am to aligning with amazing opportunities, new friendships, an easy fun relationship with my partner or meeting someone new, or anything that is meant to be for me? I say *yay* to this! Bring more of it to me. I'm ready!

Why is it so easy for me to believe that I can feel my way into *any* reality I desire; a desire I *wish* for, *dream* of, *plan* for, *believe* in, and expect? It's done! And I'm ready for it.

How good does it feel to acknowledge that I *want* what I want because I know it will bring me more joy? And as I anticipate its arrival, it will thrill and excite me to think of it and plan for it.

I am now achieving everything I desire. Isn't it great to know that every little thing I do is moving me closer to it? And everything I do, I do with heart. By nature, I don't know any other way.

And I love that my plan continues to evolve. It's becoming clearer and I feel really good when I think about it. All the details are being worked out. And I always keep an image of the best possible outcome impressed upon my mind. I love all of this. It's *so* exciting!

I love being me. I love being in this body. I love living this life. I wouldn't want to be anyone else. I believe in myself. I feel the value of getting to be who I am. I love the way I think and feel. I love knowing what I know. I love that I cherish my thoughts and ideas. I love when I let myself revel in the spirit of fun. And I love knowing that I can do anything.

I can choose how I want to feel. I can choose what I want to do. I get to choose what I believe and what I invite into my life. I can create any feeling and any reality I want to exist in. I am using my creative mind to be what I want to be. I can see it, feel it, taste it, and touch it and it's mine.

I am now achieving blissful wellbeing. I am now feeling happy and free. I am now achieving all that I wish for. I love that I gave myself permission to have as much fun as I can have. And to know that it's all I need to do to get to the point of taking inspired action and achieving my dreams!

My consistent thoughts are creating my reality.

So I am focused on the wellbeing, the joy and abundance, and all the spectacular things around me.

And I am attracting all that I desire.

Why is it so easy for me to believe this now?

Action: Choose any one of your favorite "action" steps from Days 81 through 90 and try it again now. I suggest Days 82 or 84.

Moving Forward & Upward on My Journey

The following is instilled in my mind and I feel it with *all* my heart.

By nature...I am in a state of blissful wellbeing.
By nature...I am happy and free.
By nature...I am abundant and unlimited.
By nature...I am pure love and light.
By nature...I am guided and supported.

And by nature, I have the ability to be, and have, and do *all* that I desire.

As I am *true* to my nature, I'm feeling the way I'm meant to feel. I am in *love* with life. I am *confident* and at ease. I am aligning with a state of *blissful* wellbeing. I am feeling *happy* and free. And I am *limitless*.

I am focused and unstoppable in my spirit of joy. I am *continually* attracting more good things into my life. And I'm having *way* more fun.

I smile my way through my day and see my desires coming to life *right* before my eyes. I intend to practice feeling this way and create the joyful and abundant life I was born to live.

And I'm getting good at deciding what I want. I follow my heart's desire and put my heart into everything I do.

What else am I good at?

I am a *magnificent* creator.
It's like being the architect of my life.
As I wake up every morning, I see my life as a blank canvas.
My new story is essentially *always* being told.
Some parts I'm keeping; others I'm redesigning.
But it *always* feels good when I think of creating my life as I wish it to be.
And I'm not concerned about having it all happen at once.
I'm loving where I am, and I'm really excited about what's to come.
I'm getting myself into alignment with anything I want to attract into my life.
And I'm doing so with childlike abandon.

I allow myself the freedom to follow my dreams.
I have zero limitations.

I have boundless energy to accomplish *all* of my goals.
And everything I do, I do with faith and purpose.
I decide what I want and hold on to that image.
I put all the bits and pieces together in my mind first.
If it feels good to think of them, I see all the little details,
and I'm always in the picture.
It stays in my thoughts and becomes a part of who I am.
And I love knowing that when it feels good to think of it I'm getting lined up with it.
There's a vibrational version of everything I've wished for.
And it's finding its way to me.
It's inevitably becoming mine.
And *oh* my, it feels so good. *So* very good!

I am holding a mental picture of myself in the highest level of joy, wellbeing, and abundant prosperity until it's *who I am.*

I am now in the qualities and energy and spirit of *all* that I wish for. And therefore, I am now achieving *everything* I desire. Everything I wish for is coming to me.

And I expect every day to bring me good news. I am always thinking that something wonderful is about to happen.

How does it feel when I wake up one day and it has happened? I got my wish!

Every last one!

Action: You are so good at being in charge of how you feel that you can use any anchor word or action to feel any way you wish, any time you want.

1-2-3, Mind, Body, and Spirit, it's time to be in harmony with one another. Show me how it feels.

On the count of three I'm going to breathe in and say **"Harmony,"** and when I say that it means that in that moment I decided that I will feel my mind, body, and spirit unite in a blissful feeling of wellbeing, freedom, and limitless abundance.

My body will feel relaxed and energized at the same time, completely free of resistance. My mind will feel clear and spacious with blissful clarity, and my head will feel lighter. My spirit will be completely free.

Slowly breathe in, **1-2-3 Harmony**. Actively breathing with the whole body, I'm calling light to myself, my eyelids, forehead, face, and body are softening...even softer.....twice as soft, slowing down my breath, my mind is transforming thoughts to blissful clarity. I feel the energy in and around my face becoming lighter and freer, clear and spacious mind...clearing right now, *breathing in* wellbeing, joy, freedom, limitless abundance. I am full of energy, feeling limitless, feeling lighter and brighter, feeling blissfully happy and free.

And very slowly, show me one last time...how does it feel when I *allow* myself to feel blissful? Breathe it in.

Show me how it feels when I *allow* myself to feel lighter and freer. Breathe in.

Show me how it feels when I *allow* myself to have a clear mind. Breathing in violet light.

And show me how it feels to have more energy than I did a moment ago. Breathe it in to every cell.

How does it feel when I *allow* myself to have twice as much energy than I do right now? *Deep* breath.

How does it feel to have twice as much *clarity* than I did a moment ago?

Lastly, show me how it feels when I *allow* myself to feel even happier than I was a moment ago.

The next time I breathe in and think of the word harmony, I will feel an immediate shift in my energy and feel lighter and freer.

Thank you, my Mind, Body, and Spirit for allowing this blissful wellbeing to stay with me today, and come back to me anytime I call upon it by thinking 1-2-3 **Harmony**. This is my powerful intention.

If you're ever having a low point on any given day, start from where you began with this: Breathing in, 1-2-3 **Ease**, I am at ease; Breathing in 1-2-3 **Free**, I feel free; Breathing in 1-2-3 **Wish**, my wishes come true; Breathing in 1-2-3 **Harmony**, I am in harmony with all that is. And then ask yourself how it feels when you allow blissful wellbeing to flow.

Additionally, you can practice seeing the word "Free" written over your head and heart and anywhere on your body to allow ease and replace any stress, physical discomfort, or a negative thought.

Just like pressing a button, the moment you put your attention somewhere and think of the word "Free," you're deciding right then to immediately release what's happening and allow yourself to feel good. If desired, you can also try using this to balance your energy centers.

How does it feel to be a vibrational match to blissful wellbeing?

How does it feel to be happy and free?

How does it feel to be aligned with all that you wish for?

How does it feel to be your magnificent self?

Why is it so easy for you to achieve anything you want now?

Congratulations! You made it all the way to Day 100!

This is what I wish for you now or when the time is right for you:

> You've set yourself free.
> You've become your own best friend.
> You're allowing yourself to feel the wellbeing and abundance flowing to you.
> You are now achieving vibrational alignment with all your desires.
> Your wishes for a blissful life are coming true, and the better you feel, the better it will be.
> It's yours. It's available to you.
> It's time. You're ready.
> You have a strong desire for it.
> You believe in it. You're feeling it.
> You're energetically aligned with it. It's done.
> There is no limit to what you can be, or have, or do.
> I wish you *more*. More of everything you wish for.

I hope this book has helped you on your life's journey to feel a little (or a lot) more happy and free, as you were born to be!

I wish for all your dreams to come true for you!

One Last Pep Talk

Every day I choose to be in the qualities of the person I was born to be.

Any time I feel off, I just ask myself: How does it feel to be happy and free? How does it feel to see all things through the eyes of love, including myself? How does my inner spirit feel right now?

My body will respond to my questions. I will feel the answers. I will feel a shift in my energy. With more practice I am feeling the pulsation of that energy.

To get a bigger response, I ask more questions, such as: How does it feel to be in the harmony of my mind, body and spirit? How does it feel to have all of my energies in balance? How does it feel to have tremendous inner strength and courage? How does that feel? How does it feel to be aligned with all my desires?

How does it feel to raise my vibration with these questions? What's it like to feel free to be at ease with myself and all that is? And to know that I was born to live in joy and abundance? How does it feel to be magnetic to all that I wish for? And to know that it's all coming?

How does it feel to be really good at being my authentic self?

What else am I good at?
I'm really good at practicing, practicing, practicing.
And being one with the energy of anything I want to bring into my reality.
I am great at supporting myself, loving myself, and being my own cheerleader.
I am great at doing everything I do in a great way.
The way that I choose to. The way that feels good to me.
I am the master of my mind and my thoughts. I am the master of my life.

I love being connected to my higher consciousness and using my ability to guide my thoughts to feel how I want to feel.
I love creating an amazing life that I love.
And I am a masterful creator.
This confidence shows in my body language.
Feeling blissful is a part of who I am now.
I feel like I've literally stepped into my most abundant life.

And I care so much about bringing my passions to life that I'm living and breathing it.
I've created it...perfectly. I can see it unfolding right before my eyes.
Just as I imagined, or even better.

I believe in it with childlike abandon.
And I can feel the energy of it with a certainty that it's coming.
And everything *always* works out for me.
And oh, it's truly meant to be.
All in perfect timing.
And when it comes, it all feels so natural to me, so incredibly good!

And I say thank you. Thank you for all the amazing experiences and emotions I've had before now that guide me to follow my most joyful path.

And thank you for all my wishes and dreams and plans falling into place and coming to life. I'm ready.

Blissful wellbeing and unlimited abundance is a part of me now and always. My alignment with all my desires is inevitable. I am now in the magnificent joy of who I am as I revel in the delicious anticipation of all the great things that are coming my way.

My Homework – Suggestions for Continued Success

The pages to follow are intended as a tool kit for success, in case you find it helpful. And the last couple pages will have some final intentions and recommended reading.

Continue doing your daily intentions in your appreciation journal to keep your positive momentum up. And keep adding to your wish list journal.

If you feel the need to continue with more actions and intentions, consider starting a new journal, where you can write down questions, affirmations, and intentions for anything that's on your mind. Inspire yourself to no end as you would for any dear friend.

As desired, you could also reread your favorite "days" of this book or pick a page and it will likely be just the one you needed to hear.

Create a life statement that tells the story of how you want to live. This will be telling the details of your desired end result for all your goals and dreams. It will include how you wish to feel, what qualities and energy you're in, and what you've achieved.

Consider it your lifelong pep talk that you will give yourself daily and instill it and recall it from memory as you wish. If it's longer, read it to yourself or aloud when you get in bed.

Begin with "I am now achieving _______" and write a couple paragraphs, or make it a page long if desired. It could be as simple as: I am now achieving all my desires. I have an abundance mindset and I'm open and receptive to the unlimited abundance that's available to me. I am focused on the joy in my life and feeling good.

Or it might look like this:

I've decided—I am spending every precious moment of my life in loving appreciation. I wake up EVERY day feeling this way and know that I AM A MAGNET for LOVE ♥ and JOY and PROSPERITY and SUCCESS. I only SPEAK of what I LOVE. I am forever RICH. I feel how I want to feel and see myself in this magnificent GREAT WAY. How does it feel to _______? To be me, to be pure positive energy, ❂ in charge of my actions✵, to feel complete wellbeing 🏃🦵🦿🚴, clear-minded, fun 🎻, total clarity, all knowing, 🗣♥ master creator, 🏠🪝🏰🎰🏭⚔️🏚🍷🌴 abundant, doing everything in a GREAT WAY. 🦴🐌⚫

Continue writing to your future self. Date it six months or so from the time you write it. Write it from your perspective after you've achieved your desires. Imagine you're sharing your good news with a supportive friend. Be very descriptive with all the details of what you've achieved. Include how you're feeling and how it's changed your life.

Allow yourself to feel excited as you write it. Intend for it to come true and place it in a special box. Feel free to write one of these every few months as your desires change. Pull them out and read them occasionally to see what's come true. Once you've achieved them, take them out of the box and place them in an envelope.

Minimally, take the time each day to follow a routine affirmation process like this one:

I love that I am ___________.
I love my ___________.
I love being ___________.
I love having ___________.
I love doing ___________.
I love creating more ___________.
I love how easy ___________.
I love ___________.

Here's an example:

I love that I am being the person I was born to be.
I love my life and all it brings.
I love being happy and healthy.
I love having time to do what I love.
I love doing what feels good to me.
I love creating more fun wherever I go.
I love how easy it is for me to attract more abundance in my life.
I love celebrating my life every day!

Now, your turn...

I LOVE that I am ___________.
I love my ___________.
I love being ___________.
I love having ___________.
I love doing ___________.
I love creating more ___________.
I love how easy ___________.
I love ___________.

Practice saying and believing this every day at the same time, and watch how you begin to attract more good things into your life. When will you say it? In the mirror in the morning or before you go to sleep? Or as soon as you get in the car?

Another suggestion for daily reminders to keep you aligned with your desires:

What is one question you can ask yourself daily that will inspire a feeling of blissful wellbeing?

What is one question you can ask yourself daily that will inspire a feeling of self-acceptance?

What is one question you can ask yourself daily that will inspire a feeling of love and appreciation for your life and all it brings?

What is one question you can ask yourself daily that will inspire a feeling of limitless abundance?

Come up with a question for each and write them down and stick it on your mirror, phone case, or another visible location.

Also, to practice finding the feeling state of anything you wish to achieve, ask yourself:

How do I want to feel?
What qualities and energy do I wish to be in to align with my desire?
What are the words that describe how I feel when I'm in those qualities?

What state of mind do I need to achieve blissful wellbeing?
What state of mind do I need to feel in love with life?
What state of mind do I need to be in to attract new friends?
What state of mind do I need to be in to have energy all day?
And be focused and unstoppable in my spirit of joy?
What state of mind do I need to be in to achieve all of my goals and desires?

Always remember that wellbeing is a choice. Love and appreciation is a choice. Living in joy and abundance is a choice. Being your authentic self is a choice. Feeling happy is a choice. Freedom is a choice. And you're now achieving alignment with every bit of it.

Remember if you believe it, it's true. It's true for you. You have a choice in everything you think and say and do. You have a choice in everything you believe and expect. You have a choice in how your life will turn out.

Think of it like a blank canvas and you're the artist. And begin to create a magnificent masterpiece. One that you will flourish in. It's all you. And you can do it! Always know your power. Own it and make it yours.

All your wishes and desires are finding their way to you. Just allow yourself to be at ease with all of it, and it will come easily. How would you finish this sentence? I am now achieving ___________.

How does it feel to be a vibrational match to all my desires? Why is it so easy for me to attract all that I wish for?

If not already, the realization of these intentions are coming about and becoming your reality. It may happen quickly or slowly, depending on the strength of your desire, belief and expectation of it, and consistency of your focus on joy and wellbeing. But it will come. All in perfect timing. Hold that thought, have faith it will come, believe in it, and let it be.

This is what I live by and wish for you to feel...

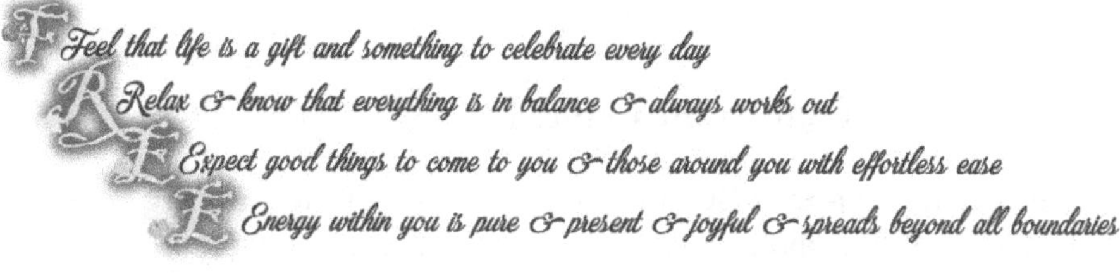

One last intention for you...

My mind, body, and spirit are in harmony and I allow myself to let this energy stay with me, now and always.

I have set myself free!

Thank you so much...

I hope you enjoyed the book and will continue to benefit from having read it. If you're interested in being notified about upcoming courses, journals or workbooks, as well as any giveaways, please visit our website https://wishmorewellness.com/ and subscribe to the mailing list or follow my Amazon author page.

I would also appreciate it so much if you would
please consider doing a review of this book on Amazon. It's very helpful to an author's success, and it would mean so much to me.

Thank you!

WHAT'S NEXT?

Don't forget to join the FREE Mini-Workshop (about 30-40 Minutes) where I share how I went from daily struggle to what feels like blissful wellbeing...

FREE MINI-WORKSHOP
3 Steps to Wellbeing & Achieving Your Dreams

Includes Guided Visualization Exercises
https://courses.wishmorewellness.com/courses/Mini-Workshop-3-Steps

More JOURNALS and a WORKBOOK SERIES...

Join my website mailing list at https://wishmorewellness.com/ or follow on Amazon amazon.com/author/susanbalogh **to receive updates on new releases!**

PLEASE also share your success stories with me!
Be sure to join the Wish*More Wellness Facebook Group
so you can share any milestones or achievements that manifest for you,
or feel free to email me at suebalogh@wishmorewellness.com.
I would love to hear your stories, truly!

Acknowledgements

I would like to express my heartfelt appreciation for anyone who truly made it possible for me to write this book. Through their teaching, mentoring, or encouragement, I feel they directly contributed to my ability to create a life I love.

To my Qi Gong teacher, Lee Holden, for being so wonderfully down to earth and making the training fun and easy.

To my Reiki teacher, Lisa Guyman, for sharing her expertise in such an easy, gentle manner, and for getting me started on the career path I was meant to take.

To a great mentor and meditation and metaphysics teacher from my earlier years, Richard D'Angelo, who teaches with so much heart. He provided my first successful experience in manifesting my desires through his detailed guided meditations. In just a few short weeks, I had a new house and a huge salary increase that was exactly what I envisioned.

I know that I need to recognize the many students and clients I've had over the years who continue to surprise and delight me with their achievements, and are teaching me and inspiring me to be a better coach!

Thank you to my *fantabulous* parents for being genuinely extraordinary in their ability to live life to the fullest. Talk about role models!

And most importantly, to my wonderful daughter and son-in-law and sweet little grand-boo for their unconditional love and putting up with my being late for nearly every occasion we had planned during this writing process. I also feel more inspired to be successful *because* of them!

And last but not least, this book would not be in the excellent shape it's in if not for my amazing editor, Beth Wojiski. She went above and beyond the call of duty, big time! She is not only an incredible editor and writer, but someone I can now call my friend. It's so nice to have someone who "gets me." I honestly felt as though she had a way of reading my mind. I've never thought of using the word "breezy" for anything because it always sounded so silly to me. But if anything can be called breezy, it was our working relationship throughout this process. Not to mention how she *always* enthusiastically responded to every one of the zillion emails and requests I sent her. You can check out her unique and refreshingly positive blog here: www.PositivelyBee.com

Recommended Reading

Creating Affluence: The A-to-Z Steps to a Richer Life by Deepak Chopra

Creating Money: Attracting Abundance by Sanaya Roman

Genie in Your Genes: Epigenetic Medicine and the New Biology of Intention by Dawson Church

The Great Little Book of Afformations by Noah St. John

The Hidden Messages in Water by Masaru Emoto

Ho'oponopono: The Hawaiian Forgiveness Ritual as the Key to Your Life's Fulfillment by Ulrich E. Duprée

The Law of Attraction: The Basics of the Teachings of Abraham by Esther Hicks

The Science of Being Well by Wallace D. Wattles

The Science of Getting Rich by Wallace D. Wattles

Secrets The Secret Never Told You by Linda West

The Seven Spiritual Laws of Success: A Practical Guide to the Fulfillment of Your Dreams by Deepak Chopra

The Wisdom of Your Cells: How Your Beliefs Control Your Biology by Bruce H. Lipton

You Can't Eat Love by Leslie Lindsey Davis

I also highly recommend guided meditations by Sanaya Roman and Alexander or Kenneth Soares.

If you'd like to learn more Qi Gong and experience the amazing health benefits it offers, I highly recommend Qi Gong for Self-Healing (DVD) by Lee Holden. I received my Qi Gong teacher certification through him and I find his teaching style easy, thorough, and uplifting. You will also find some downloadable videos that I offer on my website.

At 83, my skeptic mother felt better after just three of his Qi Gong sessions, and she was experiencing a pretty severe back injury pain at the time. I looked into teaching it soon after that and never looked back. I truly believe that practicing just ten minutes a day will keep the doctor away! Regular practice has brought many people back to good health after a serious illness, even those who were not expected to improve.

Share the Love & Gift a Friend!

Do you know someone who could use this book?

You can gift the kindle version directly into their email inbox. Just choose the Amazon purchase option "Buy for Others."

★★★ <u>The Wish*More Wellness Project</u> ★★★

Please help us grow a community of uplifters by sharing your milestones and success stories to encourage others to believe in their ability to create the life they wish for and go after their dreams. Use the hashtag #wishmorewellness on social media when posting about your achievements and share it with the Wishmore Wellness Facebook Group. Thank you for helping to create more wellbeing!

Set Yourself Free & Be Happy!

You're perfect and exactly where you're meant to be in your life right now and constantly becoming more of who you truly are, and will always be moving toward a better place.

All good things come your way with effortless ease. The possibilities are limitless.

This is only the beginning, and you're moving forward and upward on your journey of life.

Let each kind word, thought, and action begin with you and create a better life for you and those around you, one moment at a time.

Wishing you freedom, love & all that you wish for.

Susan

Wheresoever you go, go with all your heart – *Confucius*

www.ingramcontent.com/pod-product-compliance
Lightning Source LLC
Chambersburg PA
CBHW080344030726
47598CB00009B/2621